Risk Management for Security Professionals

Risk Management for Security Professionals

Carl A. Roper

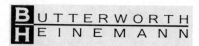

An Imprint of Elsevier

Boston Oxford Auckland Johannesburg Melbourne New Delhi

Butterworth Heinemann
An Imprint of Elsevier

This book is printed on acid-free paper.

Library of Congress Cataloging-in-Publication Data

Roper, C.A. (Carl A.)
  Risk management for security professionals/ C.A. Roper.
      p. cm.
    Includes index.
  ISBN-13: 978-0-7506-7113-2 ISBN-10: 0-7506-7113-0
    1.   Private security services. 2. Industries—Security measures.
    3. Risk management. I. Title.
HV8290.R66 1999
658.4'7—dc21

ISBN-13: 978-0-7506-7113-2
ISBN-10: 0-7506-7113-0

99-11119
CIP

The publisher offers special discounts on bulk orders of this book.
For information, please contact:
Manager of Special Sales
Elsevier
200 Wheeler Road
Burlington, MA 01803
Tel: 781-313-4700
Fax: 781-313-4802

For information on all security publications available, contact our World Wide
Web homepage at http://www.bhusa.com/security

10 9 8 7 6 5 4
Printed in the United States of America.

Dedicated to
The members of the Risk Management Training Working Group,
U.S. Security Policy Board, who created and presented the first true
Analytical Risk Management course.

The Risk Management Training Working Group team members who developed the course were awarded the National Intelligence Meritorious Unit Citation by the Director of Central Intelligence in May 1996 at the CIA headquarters, Langley, VA. The citation reads in part:

> In recognition of its superior performance in designing a course that trains security officers to help their customers realistically assess security risks and maximize the protection of Intelligence Community facilities for the least cost. The course demonstrates concrete ways to define security threats and vulnerabilities, and employs systems analysis techniques to bring consistency to our security decisions.

Contents

Introduction

Risk management has been proclaimed to be the guiding philosophy of our modern security programs. Gail Howell, Chief of the Security Division in the Office for Security and Counterintelligence, Defense Intelligence Agency, has referred to it as "our new way of doing business, and [it] will be with us for years to come."

In contrast with risk avoidance (doing everything possible to prevent loss or damage without reference to the degree of risk present), risk management offers a rational and defensible method for making decisions about the expenditure of scarce resources and the selection of cost-effective countermeasures to protect valued assets. Through risk management, we should be able to answer the question—one often left unanswered in the past—"how much security is enough?"

Risk management is a term we have heard over and over during the past several years. It is not a new term; in fact, it has been around for many years. What is new to all those within the security profession is the fact that risk management is a baseline process that we should have been using for many years—but were only using a portion of it without realizing it.

As seasoned security professionals, any one or all of us might argue, however, that this is really no radical revolution. In reality, we will still continue to make commonsense judgment calls when time and resources are limited. But the methodology of risk management calls for a more deliberate, systematic approach to our decision-making than just an educated guess. Risk management, then, dictates that we do only those things that can be justified as the result of a systematic assessment of the actual degree of risk in a given situation.

When we look back to the various security procedures and programs that have been developed and implemented for an organization or a program, you might say, "Sure, I've been doing risk management for years." Actually, you were probably doing risk avoidance. We threw money—lots of it—into solving a variety of security problems. We tried to protect everything, no matter what the costs involved. Sure, we protected everything, but in many cases, we overprotected, spending too much money and protecting those items that really didn't need protecting—those items that were being protected with associated costs that were two, three, or even four times that of what we wanted to protect. In essence, we wasted vast amounts of money.

In today's environment, with only a very, very few exceptions, we can no longer afford to protect in this manner. We must look first to the most critical assets and programs that require protection, then move downward, identifying and protecting the lesser critical items in a priority order.

We must also realize that not just everything can be protected as before. Technology is moving at a greater pace than ever before, and we must realize that what we invest in today will be overtaken by a newer technology tomorrow or next week. Also, as technology increases, so does our security overhead. We require more personnel, with the appropriate education, training, and background to run or monitor the various security protection systems. People cost money, and security resource funding is not what it used to be. We must learn to do more with less, be it people or money or specialized technology and other security related equipment. We can't just do something because it might have been done in the past. We must now justify—really justify—the need for more people, more money, and more equipment. Senior management must see a payback, a cost-benefit from security expenditures. Without such a benefit, expect your resources to dwindle.

Risk management, then, is that process methodology that will *provide a cost-benefit payback factor* to senior management.

In the following chapters, you will examine and "test" the risk management process in terms of how risk management decisions are made regarding how much and what king of security to put in place. You will see that it requires measurement, estimation, and careful judgment based on available data.

It requires that decisions be made—decisions that can put tremendous pressure on the security or risk management professional. The risk manager, whether within or outside the security department of an organization, must be able to present a convincing and clear analysis to sell the countermeasures approach to the asset owners—the senior decision-makers—within an organization. You, the reader of this book, are the newest candidate for embracing this more systematic approach to logical decision-making about the allocation of scarce security resources.

Historically, while budgets have been limited, security has had, to some extent, discretionary freedom to get the job done. Minimum standards are now becoming increasingly open to interpretation. And budgets are often negotiable with management (that is, when management is on our side). Thus, we have to make tough decisions and alert management to the placement of the resources where they are most needed. In a sense, then, the organization's risk management involves carefully educating management about the risk management strategy for carrying out an effective program, a program that includes:

- The value of what we are trying to protect, and the consequences of its loss;
- The magnitude of a foreign or other threat at a given physical location;
- The probability of inadvertent loss of sensitive information where employees lack sufficient knowledge of safeguarding rules and procedures;
- The human vulnerabilities of employees—their behaviors, attitudes, and current awareness; and
- Whether these people know how to use the countermeasures that have been selected and implemented.

The process as provided herein is one that was developed by the Risk Management Training Working Group (RMTWG) of the U.S. Security Policy Board several years ago. I was a member of the RMTWG and one of a dozen individuals initially authorized to provide training using this risk management course. I have taken the liberty of incorporating as much of this valuable information as possible within this book, thus assuring that you have the most complete and detailed information available to ensure your success as a risk manager.

Even though the initial development of this course was for the U.S. Government, the process can be applied anywhere. You have a home business; you own a small or large company; you want to protect your home; you have various assets that are on the move, such as in the transportation industry; or, you have a corporation that has far-flung subsidiaries located around the United States or the world. A realistic risk management program implementation for any or all of these is possible.

The risk management process that is presented here can vastly assist you in determining what must be protected; to what extent; where, who and what are your threats; what vulnerabilities are present; and then go on to assist you in determining appropriate countermeasures, as well as the costs and benefits of such countermeasures. The last item of concern addressed herein is selling your completed risk assessment to management, and then continuing to manage your program successfully.

Throughout this book we will look at these areas, and you will come to understand how the risk management process can help you. No matter what size your organization, no matter what program, process, or individual asset you need to protect, help is here.

Depending upon what portion of this book you are reading, I have also included various reference articles of interest in the Appendixes. These are provided for further reading, allowing you to understand various problems and concerns that arise within a given step of the risk management process.

To assist you further as you move through the various steps of the process, there will be review questions at the end of each chapter. In some instances, problems and thought-provoking challenges will be set forth for you to work on. Also, in Appendix A is a risk management case study with practical exercises for each step of the five-step process. You may use this as you move from one step to the other, or wait until you have completed the basic text before attempting the case study.

Who's Who in Risk Management

Player	Goals	Actions	Constraints	Payoff
Risk Manager	Minimize damage to organization by adversary	ID security vulnerabilities and indicators	Security budget Expected damage [risk]	Minimize gain by adversary
	Reduce, eliminate and/or control indicators			Minimize intelligence collection by adversary
		Manipulative indicators to deceive adversary; Add countermeasures	Needs of the organization	
	Apply security budget in most cost-effective manner	Remove countermeasures	The law; policies; requirements of contracts; etc.	Minimize cost of security
	Minimize intelligence collection by adversary			
Adversary	Maximize benefits derived from operations	ID targets for observation/ collection	Budget for intelligence	Maximize collection operations
	expected gain expected gain			Value of collected information
	ID security vulnerabilities	Carry out intelligence collection operations and, if appropriate, other actions	In-place countermeasures	
	Maximize the likelihood of detection, identification, and/or apprehension		Self-imposed rules	

1

Risk Management: A Short History and Its Importance

In the distant past, Og, one of our first risk managers, went out hunting. He left in his cave several animal skins, his hunting tools (some long, sharpened sticks and various types of stones for throwing), and two very valuable rocks: one that was very hard, and another that was a flaky type of rock from which he could make sparks and then fire. From this fire, he cooked his meat and other items to eat, and also obtained warmth at night and during the cold seasons of his years.

When he left, Og had several options: first, he could just leave everything and assume it would be there when he returned; second, he might hide the various items around the nooks and crannies of his cave, and perhaps secrete a few other items outside his cave dwelling in other hiding places; third, he might roll one or more stones over the entrance. And fourth, he could work with another, someone that he knew and trusted more than many others of his generation, and allow that person to provide a modicum of protection for his property. In return, this person would receive a share of the kill that Og would make.

It wasn't perfect, but then, Og lived in a very different time, where survival was important, and the technology of fire, which Og developed, made others desire it. This desire meant that others might spy upon Og to see how he used the rocks to make fire, follow him, and talk—in their way—of what type of rocks he had and where Og had obtained them, and why only they and not other rocks made fire.

Og had a new technology, a valued commodity, and an understanding of certain items (rocks in this case) that when properly selected from among many, could be used to create fire—something that was very valuable.

As Og went down the short list of his self-determined security protection options, he considered risk management in what he was to do. Og knew of the threats to his "fire rocks" and from whom those threats could come. He identified vulnerabilities, and looked at the various countermeasures options necessary. He would select one or a combination of countermeasures in order to protect his fire rocks from being stolen.

Og considered three countermeasures in this case. First, he would make it difficult for anyone to quickly find and make off with various items in his cave home—especially his "fire rocks"—by distributing them around the cave interior where they would not be easily found. Second, he decided to use a very large stone to cover the cave entrance. Third, and coupled with the second, he "hired" a neighbor to help protect his valuables. The neighbor was required because it would take two people to move the stone in front of or away from the cave entrance; the neighbor would also provide some visible measure of a security guard protecting the cave entrance.

Upon his return, Og and his neighbor rolled the stone away from the cave entrance, and then Og gave a reasonable a share of his hunt to the neighbor in payment for his services and invited him to share Og's fire in making dinner that evening.

Let's jump now to England in 1912. The White Star Line has just commissioned a new ship that is about to make its maiden voyage. It will carry over 2,000 passengers, in addition to the crew of hundreds. There will be valuable silver and crystal, as well as paintings; stocks, bonds, and cash in the purser's safe; and a wide variety of types of valuable cargo in the ship's hold.

The White Star Line is well aware of the dangers of ships upon the sea, like storms and, in this case, an occasional iceberg. But, this ship has been uniquely designed: it has the newest design and it was said that "not even God could sink this ship; it is unsinkable!"

Because of the design and construction of the Titanic, only a very minimal number of lifeboats will be included on board; even though they are not enough to carry all the ship's passengers in case of an emergency, these numbers meet the current requirements for life safety at sea. The ship also carries the newest electrical technology, a Marconi device—a wireless—for communicating with various other ships and distant shore stations. Further, there would be no reason to have massive amounts of insurance because *nothing can happen to the Titanic.*

We know what happened. In retrospect, as in everything else, we would have done many things differently. Unfortunately, where risk management and the protection of assets is concerned, we often don't get a second chance.

Lloyds of London, that great insurance firm, knew from over 300 years of experience, that no ship is unsinkable. They also knew that any reasonable person or organization would—or should—take out some insurance against the possibility of something happening, and would also take care to protect its employees and passengers. But it was not to be.

Here, then, we have an organization of shipping and transportation business executives who see a need, but do not follow up because they do not consider the consequence of their actions—or rather inaction—in the protection of varied assets. Their concern for security in terms of protection is probably limited to ensuring against unauthorized persons coming aboard for a "free ride" to America, and against theft and/or damage to the ship, its contents, and from the passengers. A very shortsighted view.

Had the White Star Line senior management concerned itself with the possibility of a major disaster happening to their new ship, they would have provided for a minimum amount of insurance to cover the ship, its various assets, and its cargo.

RISK MANAGEMENT OVERVIEW

Depending upon how you wish to view it, risk management is a process, a theory, a procedure, or a methodology for determining your assets, vulnerabilities, and threats, and then protecting them. Unfortunately, there are those individuals and organizations that talk about risk management but do something else. In some cases, risk management is viewed as the latest "buzz word," and it is really just physical security, or operations security, or acquisition protection. It is, to be sure, all these, but it is also more. And in the following pages and chapters, risk management as an accepted process will be laid out, discussed, and shown to be a proven methodology that can work for you and for your business or organization.

In essence, in these pages we will become to understand the basic concepts and principles of risk management; learn how the risk management concepts and methodology are being applied; and consider the challenges and issues related to the development and implementation of a risk management program.

Risk management, as presented here, has several goals:

- To provide the reader with a standardized, common approach to risk management through a framework that effectively links security strategies and related costs to realistic threat assessments and risk levels.
- To give an understanding of the basic concepts involved, and their principles.
- To provide you with a flexible, yet structured, analytical framework that can be applied to the risk assessment and decision support process in support of your business or organization.
- To develop and increase your personal awareness in terms of the potential loss impacts, threats, and vulnerabilities to your organizational assets.
- To ensure that various security recommendations are based on an integrated assessment of loss impacts, threats, vulnerabilities, and resource constraints.
- To develop and increase an awareness of security in terms of potential loss impacts, threats, and vulnerabilities.

- To ensure that security recommendations to the senior management decision-makers are based on an integrated assessment of loss impacts, threats, vulnerabilities, and customer resource constraints.

THE IMPORTANCE OF RISK MANAGEMENT

Risk management is important to each of us simply because it is the *best* method available that allows us to determine the protection required for varied assets at the most reasonable cost. This it is an investment in the present and the future, an investment that benefits everyone concerned. And security/loss prevention personnel play an integral part in this investment, for it is these personnel that typically will be the most closely involved in the risk management process.

The security of an organization is based upon many things, thus at this point a definition for the all-encompassing word "security" is necessary. This definition is somewhat lengthy, simply because it is intended to cover everything for the organization.

Security is an integrated system of activities, systems, programs, facilities, and policies for the protection of organizational information, government information (classified and sensitive unclassified) if appropriate, government and organizational facilities, personnel, property, and equipment.

This, then, covers the varied assets that security is designed to protect. Within the security realm we have five disciplines that will affect the risk management program: physical, personnel, information, communications, and technical (computer, technical security countermeasures, etc.).

In addition to the varied security disciplines, there are also costs that are incurred in support of the security program, and these costs are also relative to the risk management program of the organization.

The obvious costs include personnel, equipment, products, certain facilities, and training. There are also less obvious costs incurred, such as the unknown loss of emerging or currently critical technology, lost business or other opportunities, inept actions at various levels of the organizations, and the costs of over- (i.e., unnecessary) protection to organizational assets.

As we move through the risk management process, consider the five security disciplines and the various obvious and not-so-obvious costs that are associated with the process.

Many organizations have numerous security plans for the protection of assets. There should be only one security plan. Within that plan the programs to be protected are defined, and the critical elements of the programs are defined and prioritized. The various threats to the identified critical elements are identified. And finally, the vulnerabilities to the programs in terms of the various previously identified threats are determined.

The currently available or "in place" countermeasures are then identified and reviewed as to their adequacy, then other possible countermeasures necessary are identified. Each countermeasure (current or possible) has an associated cost, and that needs to be determined. Once the counter-measures and costs are determined, then and only then are the most cost-effective countermeasures selected and applied to counter the varied threats and reduce or eliminate vulnerabilities. From here on, then, it is only a matter of reviewing what is in place, identifying any new threats or countermeasures found, and monitoring and revising the program as needed.

The problem—or concern, if you will—is getting to this point. For a very small business or organization, it may take a few days or weeks; for others it may well extend into many months, a year, or more. Continual review and updating may be required also, due to the size of the organiza-tion or the number of programs involved for which risk management will be applied. All of the above are part of protection planning. Each touches upon another, and all are important and cannot be given only face value.

Documentation of the risk management process is also important. Documentation will take place in laying out the program, and as various policies and procedures are developed. Documentation includes the iden-tification of critical elements, threats, and vulnerabilities; reports developed in-house or received from other sources; and any security classification guides required for government projects, and then documentation for pro-gram specific plans and procedures necessary.

The methodology used in risk management is more than just the old "physical security survey" of the past, but a valuable tool to managers who are responsible for accepting risks, and for planning and funding security programs. With the supporting documentation for your decisions, the methodology provides the capability for accountability and consistency, is adaptable for integration with other existing risk management tools, and is flexibly structured to permit the use of the currently existing security doc-umentation that you already have. Thus, you are not reinventing the wheel, but giving that wheel a better tread on which to move down the road.

You will also find that the methodology can be used in the government classified and the corporate/business unclassified environments with equal ease. The methodology is useful in conducting both quantitative and quali-tative assessments, and is appropriate also for various types of organiza-tions, facilities, and customer bases.

In the future, one finds that the information used within the risk man-agement survey and the various outcome reports and determinations is a valued reference source for the security staff, senior management, and, in some cases, your customers (those people in your organization you are sup-porting with the risk management survey). The customers in this case, would be those who have contracted for you to develop or manufacture a unique product item for them. That customer will want to be assured that you have taken the most reasonable steps, methods, and procedures to

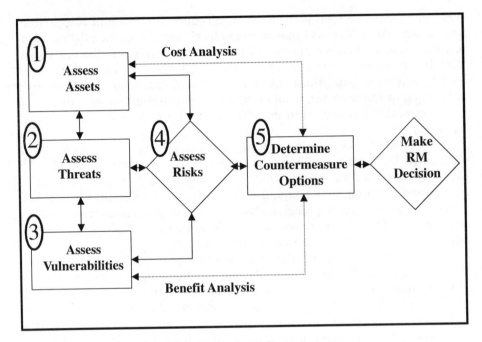

Figure 1.1   The Five-Step Risk Management Process.

ensure the protection of this item for anyone else who might be interested in it. This risk management process allows for such a determination to be made by the customer.

The importance of the process is one thing; but what is the risk management process? The process (shown in Figure 1.1) consists of five steps. Each step of the structure has several substeps that are detailed and consistent. The substeps ensure that all data is gathered and appropriate to the step. Record-keeping is important, as an audit trail will document the various judgments made during each of the steps. Objectivity is built into the process as well, since it takes on a team approach. And the process allows for flexibility. Whether your organization or project is small or complex, the process fills your need.

This process allows you, the security processional, to use a *validated* systems approach to risk management when performing facility security activities related to the protection of people, information, activities, and property. As such, as a benefit, it is specifically designed for security officers, analysts, and others that are or will be involved within the risk management process. A further benefit is that it presents analytical techniques that can be used to redesign your security processes and accelerate cultural change within the organization.

This process will allow you to:

- Identify critical assets *in need of protection.*
- Assess various types of threats to *critical assets.*
- Determine site-specific vulnerabilities related to *a particular type of threat.*
- Determine the consequences, or ramifications of *undesirable events upon continuing operations.*
- Estimate relative risk levels associated with *specific undesirable events.*
- Identify specific risk mitigation activities and countermeasures that could be *used to reduce the likelihood of an undesirable event.*
- Analyze the costs and benefits of various *risk mitigation strategies.*
- Develop a *communication strategy* to present risk analysis results and countermeasure options or recommendations to senior management and/or your customer.

THE SYSTEMS APPROACH

This risk management process uses the systems approach, that is, an analytic methodology used for managing information to develop your knowledge or to make reasoned judgments. This approach, then, usually starts with an expert opinion upon which an analytic framework is established.

The expert opinion may be one that has been determined by someone else, or perhaps by you if you are the knowledgeable security person within your organization who specializes in specific protection strategies. The process, as you will see, uses nonintuitive means to add a level of depth and rigor to the traditional analysis techniques.

The reader needs to be aware that there are many different approaches today and that they are highly creative. Some approaches can be as simple as monitoring and classifying events, where as others are more complex, using computer modeling to play out a political, military, or economic scenario to determine how one will proceed with a given operation or project.

Why Use a Systems Approach?

In today's society, the phrase "systems approach" usually means some form of computer modeling, design, assessment, or whatever. Well, yes, it does refer to these, but it is an approach that can be used in other ways as well. It is only a tool, be it one on a computer, or one that you do with paper and pencil.

The systems approach allows you to:

- Identify your focus. It brings a greater structure, discipline, and clarity to an analytic problem.

- Highlight new questions and issues. You will broaden your perspective. It stimulates new insights and ideas and allows you to rethink existing lines of analysis.
- Analyze trends and generate alternative scenarios, and recognize impending changes or threats to your interests.
- Come to terms with "unknowables," and make sense of a large volume of sometimes contradictory and often confusing evidence and information.
- Guard against locking into a particular track. Overcome a current mindset by enhancing your objectivity, identifying any bias, and relating unfolding events to developments in others places and times.
- Identify collection gaps and inconsistencies in logic.
- Facilitate information sharing among analysts and others involved, and also highlight areas and bases of analytic disagreement.
- Add credibility to new or unpopular judgments.

The question then arises, "when should you use a systems approach, especially in the risk management process?" There are four "answers," each important to your analytic process:

1. *When the facts or the importance of the information is unclear.* This is a great concern when the information leads one to wonder "what" or "so what" because the relevance of the information is not so obvious. In many cases, until a person is somewhat acquainted with the entire risk management process, the obtaining and/or reporting of items of information may seem to be fragmentary, sources of such information may seem to be biased or one-sided, or the particular issues in question are underreported. For example, sources (whether from people or various documentation) report some criminal activity in your area, but give no indication of the extent of such activity, their capabilities, or the type(s) of information being obtained.
2. *The reporting of information is particularly rich, and the issues and dynamics of such reporting become complex and/or confusing.* Here we have diverse issues and interests being noted. Such issues, then, may well shape your immediate and/or long-term future.
3. *Your mindset impedes recognizing change, especially where politicization is possible or the impact of such change would be high.* Various source reports, for example, suggest that a given country—one that would be generally viewed as incapable of producing a state-of-the-art technology item such as the one your company has recently designed and is now starting to produce—is currently pursuing a similar program, but there is no evidence that the country has obtained outside assistance.

4.   A situation suddenly presents new analytic directions, unknowns, or unknowables. For example, following the collapse of the Soviet Union, instability in the new Russian Republics has created a host of political, economic, military, and security uncertainties.

The methodology used in this process is valuable to senior management and to you as a manager. Senior management is responsible for accepting risk and for funding the security programs to protect the various assets, but you are responsible for planning and implementing the various security measures that will actually protect the assets.

Furthermore, this methodology allows you the capability of providing accountability and consistency within the entire program, and is adaptable for integration with other existing risk management tools that you may be currently employing.

The methodology's flexibility is structured to permit the use of currently existing security documentation within your files, and can be used in unclassified or even government-classified environments.

In the short-term future of your organization, the methodology becomes appropriate for various types of programs, projects, sites, and in-house customers, and is a wonderful information source of detailed asset, threat, vulnerability, and countermeasure data.

With the last several pages in mind, it is hoped that you have adopted the mindset that the analytic process will greatly benefit you within the risk management environment. How you think and evaluate information; how you relate the "bottom line" of each item to the overall risk management goal of providing maximum protection at a reasonable cost; and how such thinking will improve the issue of threat data handling are important. All these have to do with the process of carefully analyzing and sifting data obtained, but more importantly, thinking carefully through each item. It will take time, but it will be time well worth the effort.

SUMMARY

In summary, as you move into the various aspects of the risk management process, remember that security costs money; we can't protect everything, so let's protect the most essential assets first of all, and then work downward.

There should be one security plan, and the plan should be integrated into the program and the appropriate assets requiring protection, not just laid over it.

Countermeasures that are devised and implemented must be cost-effective and built to counter the identified threats and vulnerabilities to the program assets.

PROBLEMS TO GET YOUR MIND MOVING

Below is an experiment in analytical thinking. This is a two-part problem. Complete the first part on this page, before you turn to the second part of the problem on the following page. In part one below are the numbers 1 to 100 inside the square. Taking a pen or pencil, and using a watch (or a second person with a watch) to time yourself, find the number one and circle it; then move to the number two, circling it also. You must move to the next highest number; do not circle or skip any number that is not the next highest number. You will have 60 seconds to complete this task. At the end of one minute, count the numbers you have circled.

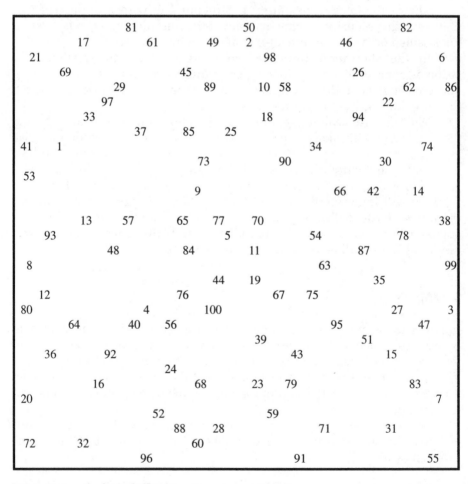

Figure 1.2   Analytical Thinking Experiment, Part I.

Part II is similar to Part I. The only difference is that one big square has been divided into four smaller squares. Again, you have 60 seconds to see how many numbers you can circle starting with the number one.

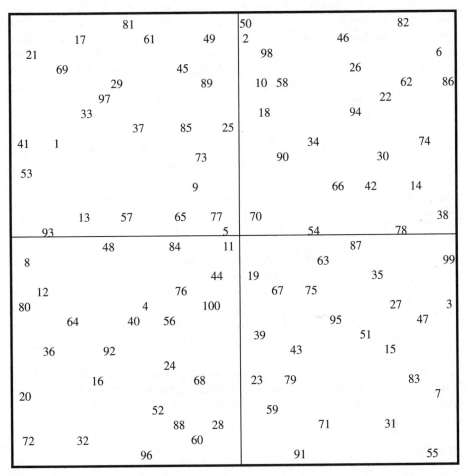

Figure 1.3   Analytical Thinking Experiment, Part II.

    Turn the page for a short discussion of your performance in these two problems.

Okay, how did you perform? Typically, between Parts I and II, you should have increased the amount of numbers circled by at least 40 percent. In very good cases, you might have been able to almost double the amount circled. Why is this possible?

There are several factors involved, and they rely upon your ability to think and *analyze* the problem in front of you.

Part I really was a "scatter-brain" approach, because there was no given logic to the location of the numbers within the larger square. Also, how a person located the next number in relation to the number before could not be easily ascertained. To this end, then, you could not determine quickly whether there was really any logic to the numerical layout. This caused a pause—a slight consternation—in your mind's process of locating a given number because there were too many in one big box.

In Part II, there was a very basic and major difference from the first part; Part I was just a big square with numbers "scattered" about, while Part II had four smaller squares with twenty-five numbers within each of the squares.

You then realized that the numbers were in a type of sequential order, although you might not have immediately seen this. In terms of the locations of the numbers, they were laid out in a unique fashion:

- Number one was in the upper right; two in the lower right; three in the lower left; and so on.
- Each next ascending number was in the following square in a clockwise rotation from the number before it.
- As you circled a number, you eliminated that number from being looked at the next time you came to that square. This reduced the amount of time required to locate the following number and, in turn, allowed you to move more rapidly in locating the next appropriate number.

Your then performed a series of analytic processes, thus increasing your skills in locating the next ascending number, and increasing the amount of numbers located and circled in Part II as opposed to Part I.

REVIEW

1. In your own words, what is risk management?
2. Risk management is said to be a systems approach. What are the advantages of using a systems approach in the risk management process?
3. State at least three goals of risk management.
4. What are some of the reasons to use a systems approach in risk management?

2

Key Terms and Definitions

Each profession or field of endeavor has its own unique terminology and definitions; risk management is no different. As I researched the subject matter, I found that different organizations (and sometimes, their subelements) might "revise" a given term to meet their own needs. Thus, in many places, the terms referred to the same thing, but were defined differently and thus were interpreted and used in a slightly different manner. Herein, the terms and their definitions are those used by risk managers and practitioners who have the ability to see beyond local organizational boundaries. The use of a set of terms that crosses organizational boundaries means that everyone is on the same wavelength when talking with another individual from a different organization, even in a different state or country, or business enterprise.

Risk Management. The process of selecting and implementing security countermeasures to achieve an acceptable level of risk at an acceptable cost.

Risk. The potential for damage or loss of an *asset.*

Asset. Any person, facility, material, information, or activity that has a positive value to its owner. The asset may also have a given level of value to an adversary, as well as its owner, although the nature and magnitude of those values may differ dramatically.

Impact. The amount of loss or damage that can be expected; it may be influenced by time or other factors.

Threat. Any indication, circumstance, or event with the potential to cause the loss of or damage to an asset. It can also be defined as the intention and capability of an *adversary* to undertake actions that would be detrimental to the interests of the asset owner.

Adversary. An individual, group, organization, or government that conducts activities, or has the *intention* and *capability* to conduct activities, that are detrimental to the owner and/or his assets. Adversaries may include the intelligence services of a host nation, third-party nations, political or terrorist groups (including home-grown militants, animal rights activists, and environmental organizations or fringe groups thereof), criminals, and also private interests.

Vulnerability.   Any weakness that can be exploited by an adversary to gain access to an asset. A vulnerability may result from building characteristics; equipment properties; locations of people, equipment, and buildings; operational and personnel practices; and personal behavior.

Risk Assessment.   The process of evaluating the *threats* and *vulnerabilities* to an asset so as to give an expert opinion on the probability of loss or damage, and its *impact*, as a guide to taking some positive action.

Countermeasure.   An action taken or a physical entity used to reduce or eliminate one or more vulnerabilities. The cost of a possible countermeasure may be monetary, but it may also include certain nonmonetary costs, such as reduced operational efficiency, adverse publicity, unfavorable working conditions, and political consequences.

Cost-Benefit Analysis.   Part of the management decision-making process in which the costs and benefits of each alternative are compared and the most appropriate alternative is selected.

In considering the above terms and their definitions, there are some thoughts and concerns you may have that need to be resolved.

When defining risk management, what is meant by "acceptable?" Really, what *is* considered "acceptable?" As a risk manager, you must come to terms with how much you are willing to spend to protect an asset. You would not normally spent $10,000 to protect a $3,000 piece of equipment or even a $10,000 piece of equipment; but would you be willing to spend that $10,000 to protect a piece of equipment that is worth, say, $100,000 or $500,000—half a million? Sure you would.

On the other hand, suppose your company has just designed and built a singular piece of equipment that is like no other known to mankind. It would be considered advanced state-of-the-art technology, because no other company or government is even close to its design and development. Its cost is immeasurable in terms of what it can do for the company, even though it has less than $100,000 in individual parts. The knowledge that put it together—the unique design configuration, the metal work and technology that went into it, the time that was spent in trial and error—all these are worth hundreds of thousands of dollars. And finally, the fact that it cannot be duplicated (were something unfortunate to happen to it) for at least five years, means that you are willing to spend in excess of perhaps a several hundred thousand or more dollars to protect it. It is that unique—and valuable—in terms of your return on investment once it is integrated into your manufacturing process.

So, then, what is "acceptable?" This is something you must determine. In some instances, senior management has already made that decision for you; in other cases, you must seek out subject matter experts—professionals—for their opinion, in order to determine its worth and then come up with what is acceptable. Every case is usually different. The bottom line is coming to terms with how much will be spent to protect an asset, given what the downside of its loss or damage would be to the company and the immediate future of the company.

When looking at risk, you must be acutely aware that the level of risk is based on a combination of two factors. First, the value placed on that asset by its owner, and the consequence, impact, or adverse effect of loss or damage to that asset. This loss or damage may be long- or short-term in nature. Second, a determination will have to be made as to what is the likelihood that a specific vulnerability to a given asset will be exploited by a particular threat.

Assets are typically broken down into five basic categories:

1. people
2. facilities
3. equipment and materials
4. information
5. activities and operations

There are lots of assets that are critical, and if they are critical to the company and its future well-being, how critical and valuable would they be to an adversary or a competitor?

An impact statement, clear and concise, is most beneficial in such cases. It assists you in gaining support for the risk management program by showing the relative importance of one or more assets and how the program can help protect them.

When considering the amount of loss or damage (the impact) that can be expected, it is always beneficial for the risk manager to have a clear and concise impact statement developed for each asset that requires some level of protection. Such a statement will help you to gain support for your overall risk management program within the organization.

In discussing threat, be aware that you are primarily looking at the intent, capability, and motivation of an adversary towards your assets. The initial categories of threat include insider, terrorist, intelligence service, environmental, criminal, and military. When focused, they can affect the economic, political, military, and national security of a nation, in addition to the well-being and survival of private enterprise, be they a small business or a large corporation.

The risk assessment is where everything will come together for the risk manager. You see, risk management is not a science, but rather an art, and expert opinion is the key to taking solid action to protect the critical assets of an organization.

Within the definition of the cost-benefit analysis, understand that costs include not only the cost of tangible materials, but also the ongoing operational costs associated with countermeasure implementation; and that benefits are expressed in terms of the amount of risk reduction, based on the overall effectiveness of the countermeasures with respect to the assessed vulnerabilities that have been previously identified.

REVIEW

In your own words, provide a definition of the following terms. Afterwards, check back through the chapter and see how close you came to the actual definition.

1. Asset
2. Vulnerability
3. Risk
4. Threat
5. Countermeasure

3

Risk Management Process Overview

BACKGROUND

The purpose of this book is to assist you in developing and implementing a risk management plan for your organization, whether you are a professional in security, Operations Security (OPSEC), or acquisitions systems, a project manager, or in the audit or another area that has a similar mindset for protection of assets.

Risk management is not just an empty buzzword—a restructuring of something from the past—that has been reworked to go with the current thought process of business, bur rather a process that is the *core business process of security protection.*

Risk management is the process of selecting and implementing security countermeasures to achieve an acceptable level of risk at an acceptable cost. You or management may have already determined what is acceptable, or this may be something that will have to be worked out between you. In either case, since risk is the potential for damage or loss to a given asset or assets, its level is based on the value the owner places on that asset, and the consequence or impact of the adverse effect of the loss or damage to that asset. Risk is also the likelihood that a specific vulnerability to the asset will be exploited by a particular threat. In this regard, not all threats are able to exploit an asset's vulnerability. Thus, consider the risk formula in Figure 3.1.

Using this as your background, consider the diagram shown in Figure 3.2. It depicts the effect that a reduced level in any one of the three areas will have on the overall risk level. The focus here is to determine the relative magnitude of each of the circles, given a variety of pieces of information. You will note in the diagram that the risk is greater when all of the factors are significant. The inclusion of appropriate countermeasures can reduce vulnerabilities, as seen when at least one of the three circles is shown as smaller due to appropriate countermeasures being implemented.

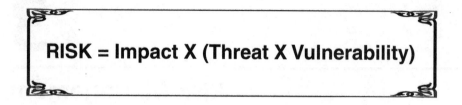

Threat X Vulnerability = Probability
Impact = Expected Impact (Asset Value)

Figure 3.1 The risk management formula.

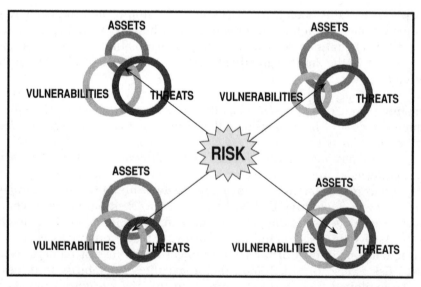

Figure 3.2 The reduction of any of the three categories reduces the overall risk.

Risk is the point of intersection of the three variables of assets, threats, and vulnerabilities. You cannot have risk without these variables. To adequately manage risk, all three variables must be reduced to whatever extent possible.

Your focus as a risk manager, then, is to determine through assessment the magnitude of each variable, given a variety of information, and then determine how to reduce the risk level.

In order to perform a valid risk analysis, three basic activities are necessary:

1. The collection and evaluation of accurate and detailed information regarding the nature and value of the assets; the degree of the specific type of threat(s) to the assets (in terms of undesirable events happening to them); and the extent of known, related vulnerabilities to each identified asset.
2. The identification and evaluation of risks.
3. A cost-benefit analysis of the various countermeasures (currently and planned) that will mitigate the various selected risks.

Our goal throughout the entire process is to stress the value of systematically going through these three basic analytical activities and documenting the findings *before* recommending or implementing a security strategy that will work to protect the varied assets requiring protection.

Be aware that many individuals will tend to focus very heavily on assessing the vulnerabilities and countermeasures. What is necessary is emphasizing the techniques for collecting the asset and threat data, and recognizing that these two factors are most significant in making the difference between risk avoidance and risk management.

These activities, then, are ongoing in that risk management is a dynamic process, involving continuous monitoring of changes to assets, threats, and vulnerabilities.

In considering the basic analytical activities, it becomes necessary to quickly walk through the various steps as illustrated in Figure 3.3. Each step contains from three to five substeps, with each of the substeps being performed in the appropriate order to ensure that the process is accomplished with maximum accuracy.

The chart illustrates the risk management process flow. The first three steps focus very heavily on data collection. Please note that the steps are numbered sequentially, and that information obtained in a following step will generally impact on the previous step.

For example, the value of an asset is assessed in Step 1 based upon its value to the owner. After Step 2, the value is reassessed based on its value to the adversary. After Step 3, which deals with vulnerabilities, the Step 1 assets would again be reevaluated in light of the latest information. At each stage, if necessary, data results may need to be adjusted because the new information dictates such an adjustment. (Note that in risk management, if nobody else really wants a given asset, it is probably not necessary to protect it.)

All the information is integrated during the assessment at Step 4, and the risks are prioritized in terms of their criticality. Countermeasures are assessed in terms of cost and benefit. Notice that cost reasonableness is based on the cost ratio between the asset value and the countermeasure cost. Benefit is assessed in terms of how effective the countermeasure is in reducing the vulnerability.

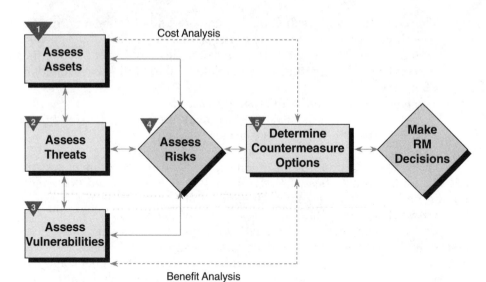

Figure 3.3   Risk management process flow.

STEP 1. Asset Assessment. Step 1 is where you identify the various assets and the loss impacts:

1.1: Determine critical assets requiring protection.

1.2: Identify undesirable events and expected impacts.

1.3: Value/prioritize assets based on the consequence of loss.

STEP 2. Threat Assessment. Here we identify and characterize the threats:

2.1: Identify the threat categories and adversaries.

2.2: Assess the intent and motivation of known or suspected adversaries.

2.3: Assess the capabilities of an adversary or threat.

2.4: Determine the frequency of threat-related incidents based on historical data.

2.5: Estimate the degree of threat relative to each critical asset.

STEP 3. Vulnerability Assessment. The identification and characterization of vulnerabilities:

3.1: Identify potential vulnerabilities related to specific assets or undesirable events.

3.2: Identify existing countermeasures in place and their level of effectiveness in reducing vulnerabilities.

3.3: Estimate the degree of vulnerability relative to each asset and threat.

STEP 4. Risk Assessment. To assess risk and determine your priorities for asset protection:

4.1: Estimate the degree of impact relative to each critical asset.

4.2: Estimate the likelihood of attack by a potential adversary/ threat.

4.3: Estimate the likelihood that a specific vulnerability will be exploited.

4.4: Aggregate the degree of impact (asset value) with the likelihood of a successful attack (threat X vulnerability) to determine your relative degree of risk.

4.5: Prioritize the risks based on an integrated assessment.

STEP 5. Countermeasure Assessment. Identify countermeasures, costs, and trade-offs, and select an appropriate protection strategy:

5.1: Identify potential countermeasures to reduce vulnerabilities.

5.2: Identify each countermeasure capability and effectiveness.

5.3: Identify countermeasure costs.

5.4: Conduct a countermeasure cost-benefit and trade-off analysis.

5.5: Prioritize your options and prepare appropriate recommendations for the senior level management decision-maker.

For each step there are several forms that are used. Why? To document what has happened. Documentation is important, for without it you can never be sure if you have the appropriate information, all the information, or whether or not the information is valid. Valid information is a key to each substep and also important when performing the overall risk assessment. You need to be able to go back and review what has transpired and, in the future, when changes to assets, vulnerabilities, or threats are identified, to plug them in where appropriate and determine how they affect the current countermeasures to see if other changes or additions to your protection strategy are necessary.

In Appendix B, "Forms Used in the Risk Management Process," are page-size blank copies of the various forms and aids used for each step. The forms are in the sequential order of the process, that is, broken down by each step. Also, at the end of Appendix B, there are two "overview" forms that may be used to highlight the various data obtained from the initial Step forms. By using this form as an overview of the process, you can quickly determine where you are in the process and what has been accomplished, and point out the highlights. These two forms are very practical when providing an overview to senior decision-makers that have neither the time nor the inclination to review the various detailed forms and backup data that you have previously collected and analyzed.

A SHORT WALK-THROUGH OF THE PROCESS

This walk-through is, essentially, a short case study that you can perform on your own, or just follow the data provided to observe and understand how it all relates. Box 3.1 provides information on the scenario.

Box 3.1   A simple case study.

- You are about to go on a two-week trip and will be leaving your home and valued possessions behind.
- Recently, there has been a rash of thefts in your neighborhood: car stereos, TVs, VCRs, jewelry, and even lawn furniture have been stolen.
- There have been several incidents of vandalism—at the park two blocks away, and at the neighborhood elementary school.
- There was an attempted break-in at the neighbor's house just three days ago.
- The possessions you will be leaving behind include the family silver set [80 years old]; two color TV sets [3 years old] and one wide-screen set [new]; 2 VCRs [new]; a coin collection [complete Lincoln penny set, 20 gold coins]; family heirloom pictures and misc. household items handed down through five generations; a family computer system; a 1997 car; and a 1998 4X4 truck.
- Home-based business [avg income of $350K/year], business records, 2 computer systems [one with CAD], many technical ref books and specialized software [most of which was created by you]. Replacement value of equipment/software is estimated at $120K. Without it, you are out of business for a minimum of one year.
- The house is 35 years old; it still has the original locks that came with it. You have one small floodlight for the back yard. There are two doors, front and back; the front door is solid wood, while the back has a 3 paned window. You have no alarm system, since there has never been a need for one.

In order to start the risk process, ask yourself some questions:

What assets are of value to you?

Which ones are most in need of protection?

What threats or dangers could cause harm to your assets?

How is your house vulnerable as a result of your absence?

What are the greatest risks to your home and/or home-based business and assets?

What countermeasures are currently in place to help mitigate these risks?

What additional countermeasures or actions will you take to protect your assets?

With these questions in mind, let's move through the process, remembering that at each step of the way, the answers to the questions become vitally important.

In Step 1, Asset Assessment, you are determining the critical assets that will require protection, identifying what undesirable events could happen and what the expected impact of such an undesirable event would be to each asset, and also prioritizing the various assets based upon the consequence of their loss.

Remember that an asset is any person, facility, material, or information that has a positive value to you. The asset may also have value to an adversary, although the nature and magnitude of such value may differ. Impact is the amount of loss or damage that can be expected, as may be influenced by time or other factors.

Not all assets and activities warrant the same level of protection. The cost of reducing risk to the asset must be reasonable in relation to its overall value. Such value need not be assessed strictly in dollars. A potential loss impact may be stated in terms of lives or interests.

What happens now is to succinctly identify each asset and the impact of a loss to it. The scenario identifies a number of assets, but you also have others, those being typical of any business person, such as furniture, dishes, tools, and so on.

First, identify the various assets that you possess. Note "possess" versus "own." You may have borrowed items from a neighbor, relative, friend, or coworker and have them in your home and/or home-based business. You don't "own" them, but you currently "possess" them. Put the assets in a listing form. You need to identify *all* possible assets. Figure 3.4 illustrates one method of breaking out the list; in this case, by various types of assets.

Understanding the nature and value of the assets you desire to protect allows you to make more rational decisions about related vulnerabilities, and about the allocation of protective countermeasures. It also helps ensure that you will protect your most critical assets first and allocate resources where they will have the greatest impact.

Up front, it is very important to recognize that the loss of people, information, and activities is difficult to quantify in terms of dollars. Therefore, it may be more appropriate to provide a qualitative statement expressing the consequence of that loss than it would be to quantify it in terms of dollars.

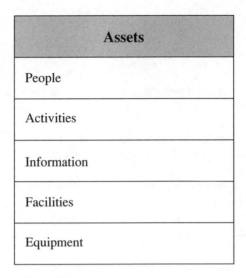

Figure 3.4   Identify *all* possible assets.

This initial assessment should be revisited after Step 2 is completed, where you will be assessing the specific threats and adversaries related to those assets. This assessment will become one of the key elements in the overall risk assessment.

Identify those undesirable events and expected impacts through analysis and creative thinking. Properly value and prioritize assets based on the consequence of their loss as depicted in Figure 3.5.

Moving on to Step 2, we must look at the threats and adversaries to the assets. Remember from Chapter 2, "Key Terms and Definitions," that threat is any indication, circumstance, or event with the potential to cause loss of, or damage to, an asset. An adversary in our sample problem here is an individual or group that conducts activities—or has the intention and capability to conduct activities—that would be detrimental to your assets.

The second step is to understand the specific threats to those assets previously identified. Understanding the threat requires an understanding of the adversaries' perspective, in terms of their intentions and motives, as well as their capabilities to get at and compromise the assets.

Review the scenario and gather the appropriate data on what the threats area, who are the adversaries, and what assets they "require to meet their objectives." In assessing the threat, it is important to investigate both the intentions and capabilities of your adversaries, because the overall threat may be reduced sharply when either one of these elements are missing.

To identify and characterize the threat, prepare a list of potential threats and, once identified, determine if there is a specific group or individual; assess their intent, capability, and history (if known); and then make a

Critical Assets	Potential Undesirable Events	Impact Level
People	Assault Accident/Injury/Medical/Emergency	High High
Activities		
Information		
Facilities		
Equipment		

Figure 3.5   Asset Impact Assessment Chart.

judgment based on your assessment of the threat level as it relates to each specific asset or undesirable event that could occur.

Box 3.2 illustrates those threats and/or adversaries that are related to the assets, as well as any potentially undesirable events that could occur. The threat levels indicated are based on the threat rating criteria shown in Box 3.3.

Box 3.2   Potential threats/adversaries to your assets while on vacation.

- **Insider**
  disgruntled neighbor
  disgruntled neighbor [who, specifically, is taking care of your home while you are away]
- **Outsider Criminal**
  professional burglars
  teen-age/young adult gangs
- **Environmental**
  fire/lightning
  tornado
  flooding
- **Other**
  graffiti artists
  druggies

Box 3.3 Threat Rating Criteria.

- **Critical**—a definite threat exists against the assets; and the adversary has both the *capability* and *intent* to launch an attack; and that the subject or similar assets are targeted on a frequently recurring basis.
- **High**—a credible threat exists against the assets based on our knowledge of the adversary's *capability* and *intent* to attack the assets and based on related incidents having taken place at similar type facilities.
- **Medium**—there is a possible threat to the assets based on the adversary's desire to compromise the assets and the possibility that the adversary could obtain the capability through a third party who has demonstrated the capability in related incidents.
- **Low**—little or no credible evidence of capability, intent, with no history of actual or planned threats against the assets.

Be aware that the overall likelihood that any of these threats will place your assets in jeopardy is dependent upon the vulnerability of your facility or your home. Thus, it is important to understand that when you are estimating threat ratings, you are looking specifically at the intent and capability of the adversary. These elements, then, will be factored together with your vulnerability rating (Step 3) to determine the actual probability or likelihood of a successful intrusion into your home and/or home-based business while on vacation.

Moving on to Step 3, the vulnerability assessment of your home and/or home-based business, you are looking at various weaknesses that can be exploited by someone to gain access to your assets. In identifying weaknesses of the home and/or home-based business, you also analyze the various activities that take place while you are away, as well as the actual physical structure itself. Look at your residence from the adversary's perspective, as it provides you with the basis for understanding the true, rather than any hypothetical, vulnerabilities. As you move through the vulnerabilities, look for those that are directly related to the assets in Step 1 and the threats in Step 2.

Don't assume that the existing countermeasures are adequate. This is an assumption commonly made by security professionals, because nothing has happened in the past, they must be working. Perhaps, however, it is because nobody tried to see if they were adequate. They may be out-of-date, obsolete, or faulty, or may fall into the "looks good but does nothing" category.

The chart in Figure 3.6 identifies the vulnerabilities to your home and/or home-based business. (Note that if you are doing this based on your actual home or home-based business and assets, the vulnerabilities, like the previous assets and threats, will be different.)

Critical Assets	Potential Undesirable Events	Threat Category/ Adversary	Threat Level
People			
Activities			
Information			
Facilities			
Equipment			

Figure 3.6   Threat Assessment Chart.

Potential Undesirable Events	Impact Rating	Threat Rating	Vuln. Rating	Overall Rating	Risk Acceptable?

Figure 3.7   The Risk Analysis Matrix identifies unacceptable risks and determines your protection priorities.

The risk assessment is the process of evaluating the threats and vulnerabilities to your previously identified assets. Here, you are determining the likelihood that a specific undesirable event—given current conditions, and based on an overall assessment of all the previously collected data—is likely to occur. First, you begin with a baseline review of the existing risk under current conditions, including any countermeasures already in place. Figure 3.7 is used to illustrate the risk assessment determinations made.

Critical Assets	Potential Undesirable Events	Vulnerablity Description	Threat Level
People			
Activities			
Information			
Facilities			
Equipment			

Figure 3.8   Vulnerability Assessment Chart.

Undesirable Events	Existing Risk Level	Related Vulnerabilities	Countermeasure Options	New Risk Level
1.				
2.				
3.				

Figure 3.9   Linking Countermeasure Options to High Priority Vulnerabilities.

During Step 5 you will identify countermeasures that are to be taken to reduce or eliminate one or more vulnerabilities, and then perform a cost-benefit analysis to determine which countermeasures are most effective given the cost of implementing them. Benefits are expressed in terms of the amount of risk reduction that is possible based on the overall effectiveness of the countermeasures.

Countermeasures should relate directly to the vulnerabilities associated with an unacceptable risk. Once the countermeasure is identified, what is its cost and how effective will it be? Figure 3.9 illustrates the countermeasures option chart.

Since this is your home and/or home-based business, you need not give a formal presentation to "management," because you are making the decisions on what security measures to implement, as well as how much funds are to be expended to protect the various assets.

REVIEW

Consider the diagram in Figure 3.2.

1. How would the risk level be affected if the asset circle were eliminated?
2. Which circle does security have the most control over? Why?
3. If you had no neighbors who could check your home daily, what alternative protective measures would you take? Why?
4. A day after leaving on vacation, you hear on the radio that there is the possibility of a tornado in your area. What will you do relative to the assets you want to protect? Are there one or more alternative courses of action that could be taken?

4

Asset Identification

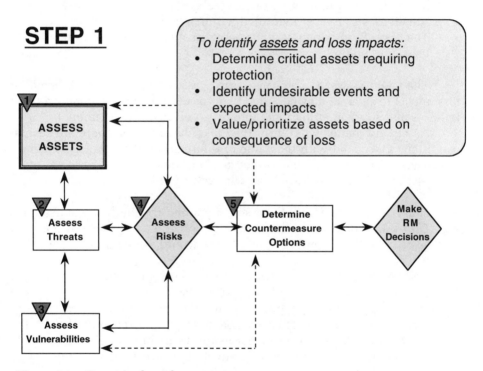

Figure 4.1 Step 1 in the risk management process.

There are many assets within an organization that have value. Risk managers, in order to perform their duties properly, need to identify those assets that are critical to the organization. The identification of various assets to an organization or person is the first step in the risk analysis process. Its purpose in identifying the various assets and loss impacts is three-fold:

- Determine critical assets requiring protection.
- Identify undesirable events and expected impacts.
- Value/prioritize assets based on the consequence of their loss.

There are several "givens" when determining assets:

- Not all assets and activities warrant the same level of protection.
- Not all assets are important over other items.
- Not all assets have the same value to different persons in the organization.
- Not all assets are absolutely essential to the organization, its well being, or to its profitability or survival.
- Not all assets are ever identified within a larger organization.
- The cost of reducing risk to an asset must be reasonable in relation to its overall value.

The value of assets is not necessarily assessed in dollars. A potential loss impact to an asset may be stated in terms of human lives, organizational interests and survival, or national interests (political and economic).

Assets, no matter what form they take, have value. There are several conditions associated with the value of information. Risk managers should keep these conditions in mind as they go about looking at the different types of assets. The conditions associated with value include:

- *Exclusive possession.* Is the asset only found within this organization?
- *Utility.* In order to complete a mission, program, or project, is the asset so critical, that completion or success would not be obtained without it?
- *Cost of creation or re-creation.* Was the cost so prohibitive to create, that re-creation of it could not possibly be done? (Value here refers to any research and development, or R&D; personnel salary costs; equipment used, purchased, or created towards the development of the asset; computer software or hardware, to include CAD design work; and security protection and administrative overhead associated with the asset at any time.)
- *Operational impact.* Is the asset absolutely necessary to the completion of the operation, program, or project? In essence, successful completion demands that the asset be available at all times.

Assets come in many forms, but they can be categorized into five general areas: people, activities and operations, information, facilities, and equipment and materials. Subareas of these areas are as follows.

Box 4.1 People

American Citizens:	Foreign Nationals:
Government personnel	Government personnel
Government contractors	Government contractors
Commercial contractors/vendors	Commercial contractors/vendors
Military personnel	Military personnel
Dependents	Dependents
Visitors	Visitors

Box 4.2 Activities and Operations

Personnel protective service
Conduct of sensitive training
Communications/networking
Conduct of sensitive negotiations
Interception of adversary operation/activities against organization
Intelligence collection/analysis (defensive posture of organization)
Sensitive movement of operations/personnel/property
Research, Development, Testing, and Evaluation (RDT&E) and sensitive technology
Production of sensitive technology
Protection of nuclear/biological/chemical materials
Protection of weapons, explosives, and equipment
Other

Box 4.3 Information

Government Classified:	Unclassified:
Sensitive Compartmentalized Information	System design
	Intellectual property
Top Secret	Patents and copyrighted information
Secret	
Confidential	System capabilities and vulnerabilities
Sensitive methods, techniques, and Procedures	Sensitive financial data
Other	Sensitive Unclassified

Box 4.4 Facilities

Domestic:
Organizational headquarters
Field offices/administrative buildings
Training facilities
Contractor facilities
Storage facilities
Production facilities
R&D laboratories
Power plants
Parking facilities
Aircraft hangers
Residences
Military bases
Communications facilities

Foreign/Overseas:
Embassies, legations, and consulates
Military bases
Other government sites
Organizational headquarters
Direct support facilities
Industry/manufacturing sites
Residences

Box 4.5 Equipment and Materials

Transportation equipment/vehicles
Maintenance equipment
Operational equipment (office/field)
Communications equipment
Security equipment
Weapons
Automated information systems equipment

The listings with their numerous subelements is somewhat generic; developing a more specific list is necessary for each type of organization, business, or activity with which you are currently or may become involved with in the future. An oil field refinery would have different assets than a hospital, but the various assets would fall within the five broad categories.

SOURCES OF ASSET INFORMATION

Any individual within an organization can list assets, but such a list of the critical assets of the organization would probably fall considerably short of what is really critical. Individuals view assets based on their particular knowledge of the organization, their role or position in the organization, and what activities fall under their prescribed duties. Nevertheless, the asset owners are generally the most important source of information about the assets in need of protection.

The "owners" are those individuals of a particular department, project, or piece of specific information and/or equipment that work with it on an everyday basis. Such owners generally have the best idea of what assets they have that are sensitive and valuable. As such, you must plan to conduct in-depth interviews with the owners and guide them through the process of identifying the most critical assets. These owners are your customers in that you are supporting them with your risk management expertise in order to better protect their varied assets. You should be somewhat familiar with your customer's mission and activities before conducting any interviews.

Asset information sources come from:

- Site personnel: asset owner, customer; facility manager, chief of operations; chief of security, others.
- Existing security plans.
- Rosters of documents, equipment, and personnel located at a particular site.
- Open sources.

I have found that a survey of equipment begins with the "paper trail" of the organization. What was spent to purchase items, and where did such items end up? Who signed for them? Where are they located? Why are they located in this particular location? Thus, the supply/equipment manager for the organization has a bountiful amount of information on file.

General records, such as those of the facility manager, are also of value in locating assets. Ground plans identify specific buildings, support areas, and their uses. From these you can identify where important assets are likely to be maintained.

From the security office you can learn where the most sensitive areas are; which require the most physical protection; which require controlled access even by employees; which require continual security guard personnel versus occasional security checks; and where security containers and security vaults are located.

From the mail room/document control coordinator you can learn which offices maintain sensitive documents. In many instances, document titles can also refer you to an area or areas where subject-related equipment (those items that could be either identified or directly tied to a document via the subject matter of the document) might be located.

Other sources, such as the company public relations office, professional organizations, professional magazines, and newspapers can supply information that you may not be aware of. Where you are now, where you are going, and what type of equipment and other assets are common to your type of organization can be gleaned from such areas.

You see, the adversary who may look over your organization uses open sources, so you should be doing the same. You may find out things you wished you knew a long time ago—and possibly a few things you didn't want to know.

There is a need to develop a structured survey questionnaire; it allows the interviewer to prompt the people that will be interviewed, and requires some crafting if you are to identify all the critical assets and the expected impacts if such assets were damaged, compromised, or destroyed. Questions can be open-ended, but should be backed up by more specific questions to ensure that complete and accurate information is elicited during the interview.

To objectively gather asset information:

- Develop a structured interview guide.
- Familiarize yourself with the mission and activities of the organization.
- Conduct in-depth interviews with the asset owners/users.
- Ask open-ended questions whenever possible.
- Prompt the interviewee to identify their assets and the expected impacts if compromised.

A structured asset survey questionnaire is shown in Box 4.6 and 4.7. Box 4.6 contains six basic open-ended questions. Box 4.7 contains six follow-up questions. During an interview using these two sets of questions, the interviewer would ask question 1 from the first list, then follow with questions 1 through 6 from the second list. Then the interviewer would question 2 from the first list, followed again by questions 1 to 6 from the second list, and so on. By going through the questions in this manner, all possible areas are covered.

Box 4.6   Structured Asset Survey, Part 1

1. What critical mission activities take place at this site?
2. Describe facility personnel, tenants, customers, and visitors.
3. What critical/sensitive information (both classified and unclassified) resides at the site?
4. Identify the critical/valuable equipment at the site.
5. Describe the specific location of the assets identified.
6. Describe expected impacts if assets were compromised.

Box 4.7   Structured Asset Survey, Part 2

1.   How does obtaining this asset help an adversary attain his/her goals?
2.   What would we lose? What would they gain?
3.   Is this asset still valuable to us once they have it?
4.   What did it cost us to develop this asset?
5.   If asset is compromised, what will be the impact on people's lives and on national security?
6.   How does the need for protecting this asset compare with other assets also judged to be of value?

Of the two listings, the first assists in identifying specific assets, while the latter is of great assistance in determining the assets' value and the potential short- and long-term loss impact. The answers to these questions will enable you to identify specific assets and undesirable events, as well as the potential impacts to the organization, program, or project if those undesirable events were to occur.

The one great concern that every interviewer has is that the interviewee will hold back information. Why? Because the information is "so sensitive," or should not be revealed to someone outside a particular office, and so forth. Basically, this withholding of information can become cause for concern. You may sense that information is being withheld, but are not in a position to challenge the person being interviewed. In such cases, you may have to go to more senior authority to obtain the answers. The concern arising from such a situation is that you may be put in an awkward position relative to the individual who was interviewed.

While the possibility of information being withheld is real, the greater concern is that the "right" questions were not asked in order to elicit the necessary responses. Appendix D, "Obtaining Asset Information—Conducting Interviews," discusses sources of asset information in terms of the methodology for the development of questions, as well as interview conduct techniques.

Once all interviews have been completed and the asset information obtained, you will need to assess the value of the information in order to properly prioritize the assets based on the consequence of their loss. You thus make an impact assessment, describing the consequence of loss if an undesirable event occurs.

Assimilating the value of the information in relationship to its true critical asset value is necessary in order to ensure that the "critical" asset is just that, not one that some individual felt should be critical because without it, he or she would be out of a job. It should be critical as an element of the success of the organization, its mission, an ongoing program, project, or operation. As such, think of the value determination based upon one or more of the following:

- The degree to which the asset is essential to the successful accomplishment of the mission, project, program, or operation.
- The development or replacement cost of the asset.
- The cost of other impacts (delays, missed opportunities for further success, lost advantage).
- The recoverability of the asset if it were lost, damaged, tampered with, stolen, or destroyed.
- The accrued advantage to the organization when associated with the asset.
- The competitive edge in having the asset when competitors do not possess it.
- The asset's strategic value in economic, political, or any other national level terms.
- The technical superiority provided by the asset.
- The amount of significant lead-time advantage (over other competitors, other nations, etc.) of the asset.

Prioritizing the assets based upon the consequence of loss is not terribly difficult. The consequences have been determined for each potential undesirable asset relating to a given asset. The asset criticality relative to the organization or project can now be established—and is established relative to all of the other critical assets.

In order to rank them you need a consistent rating scale. Figure 4.2 shows one such scale, and Box 4.8 contains the rating criteria applied to it.

First, across the top of the impact level decision matrix, it is necessary to identify the various loss factors that would occur if an undesirable event were to occur. Before the Yes/No for each loss column is determined, you need to come up with the rating criteria. Here, the example illustrates four levels: critical, high, medium, and low. It is not necessary to have four levels; you might have fewer levels, such as low, medium, and high; or more, such as critical, high-critical, high, medium-high, medium, low-medium, and low.

The more criteria levels you have, the more difficult the rating becomes. Why? Because, the criteria for each rating level must relate only to that level, and should not be written in such a way that would confuse another person who would review the criteria. Where confusion exists, the possibility of error and its impact expands rapidly, thus nullifying the results. In essence, keep each criteria simple and to the point.

Figure 4.3 is a completed asset/event impact assessment chart. Column 1 lists the various critical assets within the various categories. Column 2 states one or more potential undesirable events that could occur for each of the assets. Column 3, Consequence of Event, is obtained from the chart in

1	2	3	4	5	6	
Loss of Injury to Human Life	Loss of Top Secret or Secret Data	Loss of Confidential Data	Loss of Sensitive, Unclassified Data	Impaired or Halted Operations, Program or Project	Damage to or Loss of Costly Property	OVERALL IMPACT LEVEL
Yes	Yes/No	Yes/No	Yes/No	Yes/No	Yes/No	Critical/High
No	Yes	Yes/No	Yes/No	Yes/No	Yes/No	High
No	Yes/No	Yes	Yes/No	Yes	Yes/No	High
No	Yes/No	Yes/No	Yes	Yes	Yes/No	High
No	No	No	No	Yes/N	Yes	Medium
No	No	No	No	Yes	Yes/No	Medium
No	No	No	No	No	No	Low

Figure 4.2   Impact level decision matrix.

Box 4.8   Impact-level decision-matrix rating criteria.

- **Critical**—Indicates that compromise to the assets targeted would have grave consequences leading to loss of life or serious injury to people.
- **High**—Indicates that a compromise to assets would have serious consequences resulting in loss of classified or highly sensitive data that could impair operations affecting national interests for a limited period of time.
- **Medium**—Indicates that a compromise to the assets would have moderate consequences resulting in loss of confidential, sensitive data or costly equipment/property that would impair operations affecting national interests for a limited period of time.
- **Low**—Indicates little or no impact on human life or the continuation of operations affecting national security or national interests.

Figure 4.2. The impact level in Column 4 is also obtained from Figure 4.2. Columns 3 and 4 should match. Where several different numbers are indicated in Column 3, only the highest impact level is indicated in Column 4.

Understanding the nature and value of the assets you are protecting allows you to make more rational decisions about related vulnerabilities in Step 2, and also about the allocation of protection countermeasures in the future. It also helps ensure that you will protect the most critical items first, allocating resources where they will have the greatest impact.

Critical Assets	Potential Undesirable Events	Consequence of Event	Impact Level
People	Death	1	Critical
	Assault	1	Critical
	Accident/Injury/Medical Emergency	1	High
Activities	Disruption to Project/Operations	5,6	Medium
	Disruption to Communications	5,6	Medium
Information	Theft/Compromise of Classified Info.	2	High
	AIS Damage/Loss of Design Data	2,3,4	High
Facilities	Destruction of Unpopulated Building	6	High
	Theft/Damage to Computer Equipment	6	Medium
Equipment	Theft/Damage to Comm. Equipment	5,6	High

Figure 4.3   The completed asset/event impact asset assessment chart.

The completed chart is used by the risk analyst to assess the information now, and again when the threat and vulnerabilities in Steps 2 and 3 have been completed.

It is most important to recognize that the loss of people, information, and activities is sometimes difficult to quantify in terms of dollars. Therefore, it may be more appropriate to provide a statement expressing the consequence of loss than it would be to quantify the dollars.

Note: This initial assessment is revisited after Step 2 (threat assessment) is completed. Based upon the specific threats and adversaries to the identified assets, you may be able to reduce the potential undesirable events, the consequence of such an event happening, and the impact level to a given asset. For example, if there is no known adversary that wants or is known to do bodily harm, such as assault or deliberate injury, those undesirable events can be eliminated. But if it is determined there is a possibility for the destruction of an unpopulated versus a populated building (e.g., through arson by a disgruntled or recently fired employee with a grudge), and since you have a night watchman in the building, injury is possible, so the impact level for the first line within the facilities area of assets could be reduced from critical to high.

Do not set this assessment aside and forget about it. It will become one of the key elements in the overall risk assessment in Step 4.

REVIEW

1. Asset value is not always measured in dollars. How else can the value of an asset be stated?
2. What are the five categories of assets? State at least four items within each category.
3. Asset information sources can come from . . . ? State five or more.
4. What is a structured asset survey question? What types of questions are included? (Hint: if you haven't done so already, read Appendix D, "Obtaining Asset Information: Conducting Interviews.")

5

Threat Identification and Assessment

Threat: Any indication, circumstance, or event with the potential to cause the loss of or damage to an asset.

Note: It can also be defined as the intention and capability of an adversary to undertake actions that would be detrimental to U.S. interests.

Adversary: Any individual, group, organization, or government that conducts activities, or has the intention and capability to conduct activities detrimental to the U.S. Government or its assets.

STEP 2

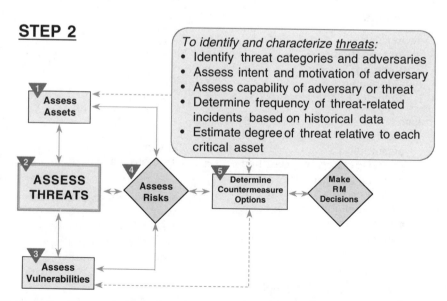

To identify and characterize _threats_:
- Identify threat categories and adversaries
- Assess intent and motivation of adversary
- Assess capability of adversary or threat
- Determine frequency of threat-related incidents based on historical data
- Estimate degree of threat relative to each critical asset

Figure 5.1 Step 2 is the identification and assessment of potential or known threats to your assets.

The second step in the risk management process (Figure 5.1) is to understand the specific threats to the assets identified in Step 1 of the analytical risk management process. Understanding threats requires an understanding of the adversaries' perspective, in terms of their intentions and motives, as well as their capabilities to compromise the assets.

This step is often the most difficult to attain because it requires making assumptions and speculations based on bits and pieces of information that may not be complete.

Gathering data to determine what the threats are, who your adversaries are, and what assets they want to meet their collection objectives is essential to the risk assessment process. When assessing threat, it is important to investigate both the intentions and capabilities of your adversaries, since the overall threat becomes sharply reduced when either one of these two elements is missing.

Begin by preparing a list of potential threat categories, then reviewing the list with a team of experts. There are only eight threat categories—foreign intelligence service, terrorist, insider, outsider criminal, environmental, foreign military, political, and other—but within these groups, various types of specific threats can be identified. Box 5.1 breaks down the subelements of

---

Box 5.1 Various types of threats within the eight general categories.

Foreign Intelligence Service
- HUMINT
- Technical

Terrorist
- Assassination
- Bombing
- Kidnapping
- Biological/chemical attacks

Insider
- Malicious acts by disgruntled personnel
- Espionage/theft of classified material for adversary
- Unauthorized disclosure of classified material
- Theft of property
- Inadvertent loss of classified material

Outsider Criminal
- Violent acts against people
- Theft/destruction of property

Environmental
- Fire
- Storms
- Pollution

Foreign Military
- Nuclear
- Biological
- Conventional
- Low-intensity conflict

Political
- Violence
- decisions made or not made

Other
- Private interests or agendas
- Media
- Economic environment [immediate, regional, national, international]

these categories. Keep in mind that while these are not the only possibilities, they have proven the most useful when analyzing threats related to personnel, facility, project, or program security.

Identified with the threats are a variety of adversaries that may well be targeting you and/or your facility and its projects and programs for one or more reasons. Box 5.2 lists the adversarial types.

Box 5.2 Adversaries can be distinguished in terms of their motivation or intentions.

Types of Adversaries

Terrorist	Political activist	Foreign agent
Criminal	Disgruntled employee	
Psychotic	White collar criminal	

- **Terrorist**: Motivated by cause. Wants attention; the more public the attempt or attack, the better the results.
- **Criminal**: Motivated by greed. Money is the primary goal.
- **Psychotic**: Motivation is unclear. Some sort of personal or job pressure has made them snap.
- **Disgruntled Employee**: Motivated by the desire to get even with the organization/company that wronged them.
- **White Collar Criminal**: Motivated same as any criminal, but the adversary is an insider.
- **Foreign Agent**: Motivated by greed and cause. The adversary is generally a foreign national.
- **Political Activist**: Includes environmental, animal rights, and other groups. Motivated by a cause, either theirs or others. Usually has direct ties to group. Following own agenda or personal 'view' of right and wrong.

GATHERING THREAT DATA

Up front, you need to determine who are your adversaries, and then perform some preliminary investigation of their intentions, capabilities, and any history they (as individuals or an organization) may have. Sometimes, brainstorming by yourself or with your risk assessment team can generate a variety of threat questions relative to threat identification. A sampling of questions raised is shown in Box 5.3.

- On-site discussion groups with your peers, and middle and senior management within the organization. Middle and senior management personnel attend meetings and receive or learn information that is

Box 5.3 Determining adversaries is more than just creating a list of names; thoroughness requires the answers to many questions.

Who is [are] the adversary[ies]?

What are each adversary's goals and objectives? How do they relate to our plan?

How does each adversary probably assess our intentions and capabilities?

What does the adversary probably know about our plan(s)?

- Based on previously observed operations and activities?
- Based on open source information?
- Based on his current intelligence operations?

What intelligence collection capabilities will the adversary have during each phase of our operation?

What HUMINT capability does he have?

- How many?
- What kind [diplomats, employees, illegals, etc]?
- Where are they? Where can they go?
- Who are they?
- When will they be collecting?
- What type[s] of information can they collect?
- What methods will they use [observation, open source, elicitation, penetration, theft]?

What SIGINT capability does he have?

- How many?
- What kind [embassy, satellite, local listening post, etc]
- Where are they located?
- When will they be operating?
- What are their specific capabilities [frequency, area of coverage, modulation, etc]?
- What kind of information can they collect?

What imaging capability does he have?

- How many?
- What kind [infrared, photo, radar, etc]?
- Where?
- When will it cover the area?
- What type of platform is used [surface, aircraft, satellite, etc]? Resolution?

Will other nations or groups cooperate in providing the adversary will intelligence information?

How rapidly will the adversary be able to provide their decision makers with assessments of collected information?

What factors can be expected to affect the adversary's ability to collect, analyze, and reaction or use the information collected?

What key questions will the adversary's decision makers likely requires answers to?

What possible adversary actions/reactions could interfere with, degrade, or exploit our program, project, or operation?

normally unavailable to you. They meet with their peers in other organizations and businesses and, informally, develop numerous contacts where information is rapidly passed back and forth. They are an excellent source of general information, and from such information, you can usually determine areas for specific follow-up.

- Interviewing on-site personnel. Here, consider subject matter specialists in fields related to your organization's mission and functions, a program or project, and so on. These specialists talk with others in their field, go to official and unofficial meetings and clubs with their peers. They hear a lot that tends to remain within the field. From such individuals you may learn of other organizations that are, perhaps, working on a similar project or program, and that have identified some threats and adversaries. Also, where and how were such threats identified? Answers to these kinds of questions can provide fruitful leads to more specific information on potential threats.
- Talking to threat specialists. Both within and outside the government, there are threat specialists and organizations that specialize in researching historic and current threat information in relation to products, organizations, and research that is on-going. From threat specialists, one can learn a great deal about who may or is targeting your organization, or like organizations, for products, R&D, new technologies, and so on. $\tau \tau \mathcal{I}$ C

  Threat specialists within government are contacted via your intelligence, counterintelligence (CI), or security office. The individual responding to the request will assist you in the development of your request for service. Military services have their own servicing CI office, but there are also national level offices that provide information. Depending on who you are, where you are located, and how you are connected to the national defense structure, the appropriate office will be notified.
- Reviewing National Counterintelligence Center (NACIC) literature. The NACIC, located in Washington, D.C., provides news, trends, and analysis on counterintelligence and security issues, both within and outside the government. It was organized to help protect organizations from technology theft, and also to be a conduit for a variety of information. Various agencies assist and support the NACIC to perform their mission. In this regard, through inquiry, you may obtain background and specific information relative to technology collection trends, discussion on the Internet as the fastest growing modus operandi for the unsolicited collection of information, current examples from the news of economic and business espionage, and more.

  The NACIC has a variety of services available, including operational program coordination with regional conferences and targeting seminars. Within the private sector support arena, regional awareness seminars, industry awareness videos, the awareness working group, special industry briefings, and the Counterintelligence News and Developments [CIND] newsletter; community training; threat products and common (across the board) services; policy and resource issues; information systems; and other products and services are also available.

The NACIC quarterly CIND is well developed in its scope, and provides a large amount of information. A variety of information and news related to economic security and espionage that can affect an organization is found in Appendix I, "Economic and Espionage News for the Risk Manager." The risk manager should review this and update such information on at least a quarterly basis. The NACIC currently maintains a Web address (http://www.nacic.gov). It is recommended that the reader connect to this site, since a lot of information is available for your perusal and use, in addition to NACIC contact information.

- Reviewing documents. You would be surprised what documentation there is within your own organization: previous security studies, investigative reports and studies, personnel contact rosters, project development projects, short- and long-term project and mission planning items, and so forth. Additionally, sensitive documents (government classified, corporate sensitive, R&D, purchasing, financial, marketing, etc.) provide information that can indicate and specify threats in one manner or another.
- Reviewing collected/finished intelligence. Within an intelligence or security office, a certain amount of collected (raw data) and finished intelligence reports reside. If such records are available and accessible, a review of specific subject area items can lend confidence to or otherwise highlight specific threats, now and in the near future.
- Reviewing existing threat assessments and incident reports. Has a threat assessment or analysis been performed on your facility? Have there been any incidents in the past that might or do indicate some form of espionage or undesirable activity? Such reports should be reviewed. Although the incident may have been closed, or the assessment/analysis is several years old, there is always information to be gleaned from them. Just because one incident happened and was closed, there is the possibility that another may be taking place; complacency is our own worst enemy!

To determine intent of the adversary, you must look to their goals and objectives, as well as what events might trigger the adversary to act. If "goals and objectives" sounds lofty, replace it with "goals and motivation." In this regard, there are a number of questions that should be asked. First, a short list of assessment questions that you should think about:

- Does the adversary have knowledge of the asset?
- How much does the adversary need the asset?
- Has the adversary demonstrated interest in the asset?
- How aggressive is the adversary in pursuit of the asset?

You may have been able to provide a simple, but nondetailed answer based upon past experience. But, whether or not you answered these questions, keep them in mind as you go through the more detailed list that follows:

- Who is the adversary? Are you sure? Any others?
- What are the specific goals and objectives of the adversary?
- What does the adversary gain by achieving these goals?
- How will (or can) the adversary obtains its goals through exploiting our assets?
- What motivates the adversary to pursue its objectives?
- How will the adversary obtain its goals through exploiting our asset(s)?
- Is there more than one path the adversary might take to obtain our asset(s)?
- If so, what is the probability that the adversary will choose one alternative means over another?
- Is the adversary aware that the asset exists?
- Does the adversary know where the asset is located?
- Is the adversary's intent to obtain, damage, or destroy the asset?
- Are there other means for the adversary to obtain his goals? Are those means easier, in terms of time, money, risk, and so on?
- What is the probability that the adversary will chose one alternative means over another?
- What specific events might provoke the adversary to act?
- What might the adversary lose in attempting to exploit our assets?
- Would that loss be a rational tradeoff, from the adversary's perspective?
- To what degree is the adversary motivated?
- Might the adversary use a surrogate (third party) to obtain the asset for them?
- Might a third party attempt to gain the asset—even though it is of no real value to them—and give, sell, or trade it to the primary adversary?

The risk manager wants to estimate the potential threats and adversaries identified in terms of intent, capability, and history. First, to determine intent, you must look at your adversary's goals and objectives, as well as what events might trigger the adversary to act. As you review the above questions and answers, keep in the back of your mind that not all of the assets that you might want to protect will require or warrant the same level of protection. Also, the assets value may not be able to be translated into dollars. The loss impact of an asset may be stated in terms of human lives,

ADVERSARY	INTENT		
	Needs	Wants	Indicators
Terrorist			
Criminal			
Country A			
Disgruntled employee			
Political activists			
White collar criminal			
Foreign agent			

Figure 5.2   Chart used for determining the intent of the adversary.

national interest (militarily, political, or economic), or in terms of public confidence in an organization. Keep these in mind when considering the intent of the adversary.

Threat is the most difficult and nebulous to assess. Because of this, it is very important to document both the assumptions and facts related to the threat. In Figure 5.2 is the first of several charts used to document threat data; this one deals with the intent of the adversary.

When considering the Intent (Yes/No) columns, keep in mind the initial four questions. Remember, too, that the lack of credible information may also be a significant factor or indicator. If the adversary is really good—topnotch and well experienced—you may not realize that an asset is being targeted by a specific adversary, much to your regret further down the road.

By this point, you will have filled in the intent chart with a yes or no and will also have the appropriate supporting data filed away for later referral if necessary.

Next, there are two distinct types of capability, which must be considered with respect to the adversary. The first is the capability to obtain, damage, or destroy the asset. The second is the adversary's capability to use the asset to achieve his objectives, once the asset is obtained.

Thus, you will need to consider these questions:

- What is known about the adversary's technical capabilities?
- What is known about the adversary's human capabilities?
- What is known about the adversary's modes of operation?

The diagram in Figure 5.3 illustrates a format to document the information collection capabilities of the various adversaries.

The array of capabilities depends upon the adversary. As an example, if you were looking at a terrorist group, you would have an array of capabilities such as sniping, explosives, kidnapping, and so on. If you had a new

ADVERSARY	CAPABILITIES					
	HUMINT	SIGINT	IMINT	MASINT	OSINT	DATAINT
1.						
2.						
3.						
4.						

Figure 5.3 Chart illustrates a format for capturing data relative to adversary collection techniques.

product that will be on the market in three to six months, and the production and marketing phases are about to begin, an adversary (read competitor) might be very interested. Such adversary capabilities might include items such as human sources of information (a corporate spy, an insider, a disgruntled employee), imagery (photography), open source (public records, overhearing employees talking), data intelligence (computer use to obtain insider information), and trash intelligence (going through your trash for information).

In assessing adversary capabilities, you can use high, medium, and low criteria (with appropriate data to back the ratings).

It is important also to recognize that a history of incidents does increase the threat level of an adversary. However, the absence of previous incidents may not have much significance, especially if capability and intent are high. Information pertaining to the questions above should be obtained and documented.

Review the threat data that you have available: check local newspapers and magazines, industry information, police statistics, and crime statistics in general for data. You need to determine what threat-related incidents there are in terms of frequency.

If a specific adversary is known, then use that as the starting point. What is their track record in the past for any type of incidents? Are they suspected, attempted, or successful?

Note: If you determine that there is intent, but no capability or history on the part of the adversary, another consideration that must be addressed is the relation of your adversary to others who may have the capability. The key question here is, "Is the adversary allied with other entities, and what are their capabilities?" If a third party is identified, you will need to analyze the threat level using the same set of questions described above.

The importance of history as an information factor can be drawn from the following example, which took place several years ago.

Jewelry has a particular fascination for people, especially if it is easy to come by. Over a period of weeks, on Thursdays, the local police department recorded the rear door alarm going off at a local jewelry store. Upon investigation, it was determined: (a) there was nobody around, and (b) no attempt had been made to force and/or enter the jewelry store. The police report indicated a false alarm, and the jeweler was billed accordingly for the police response to a false alarm.

After several weeks of this, the jeweler become frustrated, because the alarm installation company had checked out the alarm and it was working perfectly; no problems. But the jeweler had to pay increasing costs for false alarms (the city had a policy of increasing fines for continued false alarms).

One night, one of the officers reviewed the previous incidents over several weeks and noticed that besides each false alarm happening on a Thursday, it also happened within a twenty-minute time span. On a hunch, he parked his personal (not patrol) car in an out of the way place where he could observe the alley and back entrance to the jewelry shop. Sure enough, shortly after 10:00 P.M., a person came down the alley, banged on the door a couple of times real hard, and then ran away to another block to observe what happened.

The police officer picked up the suspect and, after some checking of his past, learned that he worked only late afternoon to evening jobs, moving around the city a couple of times a year. Further checking showed that wherever he was employed was within a dozen blocks of where he would be living, and also within a corridor to and from work that took him near a jewelry store on the way home. It didn't take much to figure out that he moved shortly after several attempted or successful jewelry store burglaries. His reasoning was that after a while, the police would give up, and when they didn't respond any more, that was the time to burglarize the place.

So, from a risk manager viewpoint, consider past incidents: are they real, false, accidental, or what? Even "false alarms" may be an indicator of suspected or attempted incidents.

Figure 5.4 is used to illustrate the history of the adversary. All supporting data, of course, would be maintained in your local backup threat/adversary reference files.

Now, all the threat data must be assimilated into an easy format for identification and tracking purposes, remembering, of course, that the detailed supporting data has been collated and filed away for future use, if necessary. Figure 5.5 depicts the threat information tracking sheet. Data is indicated as shown: the adversaries are listed in column 1, and columns 2, 3, and 4 indicate a yes or no.

Based upon the outcome of each row, you would refer to the threat-level decision matrix shown in Figure 5.6 to determine the threat level. Immediately following is the threat level rating criteria for each level possible (see Box 5.4).

ADVERSARY	HISTORY		
	Suspected Incidents	Attempted Incidents	Successful Incidents
1.			
2.			
3.			
4.			

Figure 5.4   This chart is a simple way to determine the frequency of threat-related incidents.

Adversary	Intent (Interest/Need)	Capability (Methods)	History (Incidents)
1.			
2.			
3.			
4.			

Figure 5.5   The threat information tracking sheet allows you to collate the information from the past three threat information sheets.

Intent	Capability	History	THREAT LEVEL
Yes	Yes	Yes	Critical
Yes	Yes	No	High
Yes	No	Yes or No	Medium
No	Yes or No	No	Low

Figure 5.6   Threat-level decision matrix.

Box 5.4 Threat-level decision matrix.

Rating Criteria:

Critical—Indicates that a definite threat exists against the assets and that the adversary has both the capability and intent to launch an attack, and that the subject or similar assets are targeted on a frequently recurring basis.

High—Indicates that a credible threat against the assets exists, based on our knowledge of the adversary's capability and intent to attack the assets and based on related incidents having taken place at similar facilities.

Medium—Indicates that there is a potential threat to the assets based on the adversary's desire to compromise the assets and the possibility that the adversary could obtain the capability through a third party who has demonstrated the capability in related incidents.

Low—Indicates little or no credible evidence of capability or intent, with no history of actual or planned threats against the assets.

Note: For a threat level of critical or high, BOTH intent and capability on the part of the adversary *must* be present.

The chart is but another tool used to document the various threat levels relative to the assets and their related undesirable events. The threat levels identified on the chart are based on the threat information documented in various threat assessments and other reports. The threat-rating criteria are derived from the chart on the previous page.

Critical Assets	Potential Undesirable Events	Threat Category/ Adversary	Threat Level
People	Assault/Serious Injury Accident/Injury/Medical Emergency		
Activities	Malicious Acts by Insider Disruption to Communications		
Information	Theft/Compromise of Classified Info. Exposure/Disclosure of System Data		
Facilities	Destruction of Unpopulated Building		
Equipment	Theft/Damage to AIS Equipment		

Figure 5.7 Threat Assessment Chart.

Note: The overall likelihood that any of these threats will place your organization's assets at risk is also dependent on the vulnerability of the facility. It is important to understand that when you are estimating threat ratings, you are looking specifically at the intent and capability of the adversary. These elements must be factored together with your vulnerability rating (Step 3) to determine the probability or likelihood of a successful attack.

Upon completion of the collection and assessment of the initial threat and adversarial data, the results are transferred to the threat assessment chart (see Figure 5.7), which provides the risk management with a short but valuable summary of all the threats against the critical assets and potential undesirable events.

REVIEW

1. Threat identification and assessment is difficult to attain. Why?
2. State at least five of the eight threat categories.
3. For each of the five stated categories, provide two to five examples.
4. There are seven types of adversaries. Give a general description of the motivation for least three that relate to your organization, facility, program, or project.

6

Conducting Site-Specific Threat Assessments

The threat assessment is probably the most important part of the entire risk assessment process. Every security feature—every countermeasure—is built around the identified and potential threats and vulnerabilities, with the threat being the most important. We can live with various vulnerabilities within the security structure, but we must protect against a known or potential threat. The concern, and a somewhat worrisome one at times, is determining who or what the threat actually is, where it comes from, and what damage it can do.

Within this chapter, we will be addressing where the threat fits into the overall risk assessment process; what are the "INTs" (explained below) that we should know about; what information and/or history on the threat do we possess; where does a person go to obtain threat-related data; how we ask for threat data; and the goal of threat assessment.

WHERE THREAT FITS INTO THE OVERALL RISK MANAGEMENT PROCESS

Quite simply, the United States is the single biggest intelligence target in the world. The Central Intelligence Agency/Department of Defense (CIA/DoD) Joint Security Commission Report on Redefining Security stated that "intelligence data defining the threat is critical to smart security decisions." The intelligence world has an apt phrase: "Hard intelligence is good to find; and Good intelligence is hard to find." Very apt and very true! It is necessary to obtain the best, most current, and most reliable information available about a potential or known threat and how the threat relates to your organization, facility, program, or project.

The threat comes in many forms, and the data the threat/adversary obtains is viewed in a cycle. This is the same cycle that we must use to obtain it in order to understand the threat or adversary that is against us. Figure 6.1 illustrates the intelligence cycle. When thinking of collecting data on the threat, we are using this cycle. Our planning is determining

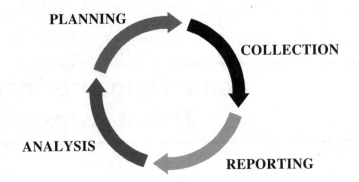

Intelligence Cycle

Figure 6.1   The intelligence collection cycle for the collection and evaluation of information.

what we must do (identify the threat); collection is obtaining any and all relevant threat data available; reporting is collating the data at a central point; and analysis is determining which threat data is applicable, how much of a threat it really is, and does the threat actually apply in this risk assessment.

WHAT ARE THOSE "INTS?"

Below are four informal definitions. Basically, all intelligence collection by a threat or adversary falls within one of these areas. But many times we need to be more specific about the type of collection activity that is being performed within these four areas. Box 6.1 identifies the numerous intelligence "INTs" that are used.

- HUMINT (Human Intelligence). The use of humans to collect information using a variety of techniques and methods.
- SIGINT (Signals Intelligence). The collection of information in the nonvisible portion of the electromagnetic spectrum.
- IMINT (Imagery intelligence). Those visual images, such as those obtained from film or video cameras, with the images being obtained from a hand-held device, airplane, or satellite imaging system.
- MASINT (Measurement and Signature Intelligence). The collection of data on system operations.

Box 6.1   There are lots of ways to get intelligence. Here are the acronyms that relate to the various methods used.

What Are Those "INTs"?

Some other "INTs" . . .

SIGINT	ELINT	RADINT
IMINT	TECHINT	LASINT
HUMINT	TRASHINT	IRINT
MASINT	RUMINT	FISINT
COMINT	TELINT	MEDINT
PHOTINT	OPINT	NUCINT
ACOUSTINT	ELECTRO-OPINT	COMPINT

The "INTs" in Box 6.1 are given in the acronym form for ease of speaking and quick conversation within the intelligence, security, and counterintelligence world. Below are the acronyms spelled out.

Signals Intelligence

Imagery Intelligence

Human Intelligence

Measurement and Signature Intelligence

Communications Intelligence

Medical Intelligence

Photographic Intelligence

Computer Intelligence

Electronics Intelligence

Technical Intelligence

Rumor Intelligence

Laser Intelligence

Telephone Intelligence

Operations Intelligence

Electro-Optical Intelligence

Radar Intelligence

Infra-Red Intelligence

Foreign Intelligence Service Intelligence

Nuclear Intelligence

Acoustic Intelligence

Biological Intelligence

WHERE DOES ONE GO TO GET DATA?

Good data is hard to find. It takes digging, a lot of research, and analysis to put together good threat information. In order to obtain data, there are several variables to include:

- Where you are,
- What you need, and
- Who you are.

Where are you in the hierarchy of importance? Within government, the higher (read more powerful and contact-wise) you are, the more likely and faster you will get the information desired. In the private sector, if you are tied to a government contract, go through the contract security office for assistance and support. For the wholly private sector with no government contracts (or contacts), some federal agencies and organizations can provide assistance, while others would be limited by law and security classification of information that would not be available or provided to you.

Organizations that are out there to provide advice, specific threat data, and other related information include:

Federal Bureau of Investigations (FBI)

Central Intelligence Agency (CIA)

Center for Security Evaluation (CIA/CSE)

Defense Intelligence Agency (DIA)

Defense Security Service (DSS) (formerly the Defense Investigative Service)

National Security Agency (NSA)

Other agencies and organizations that can, at time, provide assistance are available, but you have to ask the correct questions:

National Counterintelligence Center (NACIC)

CIA Counterintelligence Center (CIA/CIC)

Army Counterintelligence Center (ACIC)

On-Site Inspection Center (OSIA)

NRO Counterintelligence Staff (NRO-CI)

Joint Military Intelligence College (JMIC)

Department of Energy, Analysis Division (DOE/AD)

Department of the Navy's Criminal Investigative Service (NCIS)

National Photographic Interpretation Center (PIC)

Department of State's Security Awareness Staff—Bureau of Diplomatic Security

Department of State, Security Advisory Council

DoD Personnel Security Research Center (PERSEREC)

Department of the Air Force Special Investigations (AFOSI)

Within the private sector, there are a wide number of organizations available. To list them all here would be extremely lengthy. The easiest method to locate potential organizations is to use the World Wide Web. Search terms such as "threat data," "security threats," and so on, will give hundreds of computer hits. While many are in the United States, you can also track regionally around the world, or to specific countries. Also, depending upon the country, there are those that can support you in obtaining and passing on threat data for the private sector.

The great advantage of government organizations is the fact that they are easy to contact. Many have Websites and point of contact or telephone numbers you can use. Of course, for certain agencies and organizations, it is necessary that your organization be governmental or government affiliated—such as a contractor working on a government project or program. For the private sector, where threat and vulnerability information for a particular program or project is a concern, the best places to start are with the FBI or the NACIC. Contact can be most easily and best made through their Websites.

ASKING FOR THREAT DATA

You've contacted an organization, government or private sector, and a threat analyst has been assigned to assist you. What does the threat analyst require from you before he/she can start to perform the analysis? Essentially, a threat analyst needs information concerning:

- the asset requiring protection—you need to give an overall description that the analyst can understand;
- the identification of the critical information associated with the asset that requires protection;
- the players (i.e., who is involved);
- the schedule, if there is one, on mission or project completion.

What else does the threat analyst require?

- The types/locations of activity—plants, individual testing areas, production, travel and transportation plans, dates, etc.
- Sight sensitivities—if something is seen, is critical information revealed? (For example: new car designs/models for next year.)

- Electronic or emission sensitivities—between players, from the site.
- Testing/deployment scenarios, if any exist.

THE GOAL OF THREAT ASSESSMENT

Essentially, the threat assessment goal is quite simple: to understand the adversary from both a capability standpoint as well as their intent to collect critical information. In order to do that, you must have the perspective from the adversary's point of view.

REVIEW

1. What is RUMINT? COMPINT? PHOTINT? Can you think of an example of each?
2. From your organization, where would you go or who would you contact to start the initial inquiry about obtaining threat data? Why? Why not another organization?
3. State at least three types of initial information a threat analyst would require to assist your organization on a current project or program.
4. What is the initial goal of a threat assessment?

7

Vulnerability Identification and Assessment

Vulnerability: Any weakness that can be exploited by an adversary to gain access to an asset.

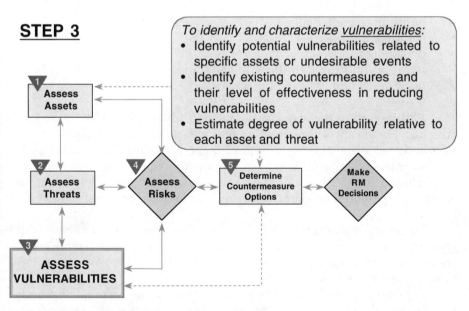

Figure 7.1 Step 3 of the risk analysis process.

The vulnerability assessment helps to identify those weaknesses that could be exploited by an adversary to gain access to one or more assets. Determining a facility's physical, technical, and operational vulnerabilities involves not only an analysis of the facility's unique characteristics, but also of how the tenants function in and around the facility. You must analyze the activities, as well as the facility's physical structure, from the adversary's perspective, thereby providing the basis for understanding the true rather than the hypothetical vulnerabilities.

For the identification of vulnerabilities, you must determine the possible paths an adversary might take. In doing so, you are identifying significant facility weaknesses that could be exploited—much to your disadvantage. Next, you will have to consider the relative importance of each weakness, one against the other, and each against the asset or assets to which an adversary desires to gain access. What are the current countermeasures the security department has put in place, and how effectively do the existing countermeasures address the assessed threats? Finally, you will need to identify and characterize the specific vulnerabilities that still exist, given the current countermeasures and their effectiveness.

You have probably already identified some vulnerabilities during the periods of time you viewed the assets and threats. It would be wrong not to have taken them into consideration when they were initially identified. Now we need to look at the vulnerabilities by groups. Vulnerabilities fall within five general areas:

• building characteristics;
• equipment properties;
• personnel behavior;
• locations of people, equipment, and buildings; and
• operational and personnel practices.

Within each of the above areas, we will identify and characterize specific and significant vulnerabilities that are related to the assets and the known or perceived threats to each of them. In conducting a vulnerability assessment, all significant facility and/or operational weaknesses that could be exploited to gain access to the assets should be separately identified, along with potential weaknesses of any countermeasures that may already be in place.

While the vulnerabilities fall within five areas, an awareness of the types of specific vulnerabilities are necessary to tie them to the more generic areas of physical, technical, and operational. Box 7.1 breaks down these three vulnerability types.

For example, in conducting an assessment of the corporate headquarters and its related vulnerabilities, the areas of vulnerability to consider are outlined above. Based on the protection of a specific asset, you would determine which of these areas might be included in the path of your

---

Box 7.1   Vulnerabilities typically fall within three areas.

Physical Vulnerabilities

- Compound perimeter security (gates, walls, fences, landscape, sewers, tunnels, parking area, alarms)
- Compound area (CCTV, motion detectors, lighting)
- Building perimeter (windows, doors, shipping docks, shielded enclosures, access control, alarms)
- Building interior (safes, locks, vents, building history—technical implants?)

Technical Vulnerabilities

- Acoustic equipment
- Secure phones
- Tempest/TSCM
- RF equipment

Operational Vulnerabilities

- Guard force
- Personnel procedures
- OPSEC issues (cover/deception)

---

adversary and could then be exploited. Within each of the areas above, you would list the countermeasures in place and determine where the weaknesses really are.

IDENTIFYING THE EFFECTIVENESS OF EXISTING COUNTERMEASURES

One of the most important aspects of this assessment is your understanding not only of the facility vulnerabilities, but also of the limitations of the existing countermeasures. Do they really perform the job as they are intended to, or are we making assumptions about the capabilities of security devices with no hard evidence of their overall effectiveness?

If you are a generalist, it may be necessary to consult with security specialists who are subject experts in various areas during this step of the process.

Use a structured format—this will help you track and document this information for use in the risk assessment and countermeasure selection steps (Steps 4 and 5).

As the existing countermeasures are identified and tied to one or more of your assets, you should be able to answer seven questions about the countermeasure. Understanding the answers leads you to a valid conclusion of its true effectiveness.

1. What type of protection does the countermeasure provide?
    - Deterrent?
    - Detection?

- • Delay?
- • Destruction?
2. What type of undesirable event does it guard against?
   - • Surreptitious?
   - • Forced entry?
   - • Technical implant?
   - • Theft of classified material?
3. When is it effective—during which hours of the day and under what conditions?
4. Where is it effective? What area does it cover?
5. What is the history of reported countermeasure malfunctions?
6. What is the correlation of countermeasure effectiveness to security incident reports that may indicate that the countermeasure was defeated?
7. What is the history of countermeasure maintenance/upgrades?

The answers to these questions are important. You may have felt, initially, that you knew them because you worked with the assets and the countermeasures every day as part of the security protection for your facility. But, one of the most important aspects of this assessment—and it is learned from the above questions—is your understanding not only of the facility's vulnerabilities, but also of the varying limitations of the existing countermeasures. Do they really perform the job as they were intended to, or have assumptions been made about the capabilities if various security devices with no hard evidence of their true overall effectiveness?

Figure 7.2 illustrates a method to determine the effectiveness of your current, existing countermeasures. The items in column 1 list the various countermeasures that you currently have in place. Column 2 and beyond are undesirable events that could happen if the countermeasure is ineffective. A number of possible untoward events that could happen are indicated, but I leave these column headings to you, as each facility's undesirable events will not necessarily be the same.

How effective is a current countermeasure? This is a judgment call on your part. In determining effectiveness ratings, use a 1–10 scale, or, if you use an L-M-H-C (low, medium, high, critical) scale, then you have to identify within each level of the scale what numbers apply.

As an example, let's use a numerical scale and take the first countermeasure, which refers to doors, locks, and bars. These could be separate items or grouped all together. For purposes of illustration, let's look at just the locks. How effective are your locks? The front door lock is relatively new, being a six-pin cylinder lock. It is also master-keyed, with the locking system having four keying levels (that's a lot of locks in the system). But you also know that over the past two years during which the lock retrofit program has been going on, several keys have already been lost (stolen, mis-

Current Countermeasures	Surreptitious Entry/Tech. Implant	Kidnapping/ Serious Injury	Documents Stolen/ Mishandled	Terrorist Attack/Bomb
Doors, locks, bars	4			
Alarms/sensors	5			
Contractor guards	7			
SPOs	9			
Military Guards	9			
Vary travel route		5		
Relocate Official		8		
Residence locks, bars		4		
Residence alarms/sensors		5		
Bullet-proof car		5		
Residence CCTV		4		
Security awareness		7	7	
Strict media controls			6	
System audit trail			6	
Passwords			6	
Defensive driving training				4
Vehicle checks				7
Emerg. procedures				4
Metal detectors				5
Fences/barriers				5

Figure 7.2   Identifying current countermeasures in place allows the risk manager to determine their effectiveness and their limitations.

placed, or just not turned in by departing employees), and it will be another six to twelve months before the entire system is completed. One other item of note is that you have a common keyway, which means it is not unique, and any key-cutting or locksmith shop probably has numerous key blanks that could fit into your lock keyways. Finally, since the retrofit started in the executive offices and the main building, you know there are numerous other locks that have yet to be replaced—such as those within the engineering and electrical departments, some of which are on the first floor exteriors of some buildings, and also those doors going into the basements and seldom-used storage areas.

The effectiveness of the locks depends on how you want to rate them. If the locks are separated into the old system and new system, you have two different ratings that can be assigned. If there is only to be one rating, go with the lower one. Why? Because someone that wants to get in will select the easiest way, and that is by using the poorer locks to attack and defeat. If the older locks are, say, fifteen to twenty-five years old—and this is not uncommon—their use over time will reduce their effectiveness. First, the pins have become slightly worn, the spring tension is not the greatest, and many are weak. Also, there has probably been lock repair and replacement over time, not by an authorized locksmiths but by someone from the engineer or carpenter shop. There may have been corners cut so that there are only four or five pins in the lock, or more master pins put in so that it is easier for numerous other unauthorized keys to be used. Lastly, the chances of a large number of unauthorized keys (duplicated by individual employees, not the organization) are floating around.

The effectiveness of the locks under these circumstances may well be 4–6 on a 10-point scale.

If, however, you broke the rating into two lines, you could have 9–10 for the new system, and 4–6 for the old system.

Using a two-tier rating level for locks gives you a better idea of the real level of protection against surreptitious or unauthorized entry.

More than likely, when the new locking system was put in place, the executive offices, the security offices, the finance, R&D, manufacturing and production data, computer room, terminal areas, and so on received the new locks first. The last to be installed will be the more remote areas, to include miscellaneous storage, janitorial spaces, some engineering and electrical, and the like.

This process is gone through for each countermeasure that has been identified. The resulting rating gives you a pretty good idea as to the true level of effectiveness of all your countermeasures.

DETERMINING VULNERABILITY LEVEL

The vulnerability of an asset is determined by a number of criteria, including the (a) number of different weaknesses in the security protective system that make the asset vulnerable; (b) difficulty of exploiting the vulnerability; and (c) effectiveness of existing countermeasure(s).

The exact criteria used to determine vulnerability would vary depending upon the type of asset, its value and its location. There are three questions to identify vulnerability level:

1. Is the asset made vulnerable by a single weakness (as opposed to multiple weaknesses) in the security protective system?
2. Does the nature of the vulnerability make it difficult to exploit?
3. Is the vulnerability of the asset lessened by multiple, effective layers of security countermeasures?

To answer the three questions above, you must collect data from a variety of sources. After you determine simple yes/no answers to the three questions above, use a chart similar to the one in Figure 7.3 to determine the vulnerability level.

Note. These questions are illustrative only. Although useful in determining vulnerability with a great number of assets, they may need to be tailored to determine vulnerability for the specific assets you are protecting.

Vulnerable through One Weakness?	Difficult to Exploit?	Multiple Layers of Countermeasures?	VULNER-ABILITY LEVEL
Yes (Single)	Yes	Yes	Low
Yes	Yes	No	Low
No (Multiple)	Yes	Yes	Low
Yes	No	Yes	Medium
Yes	No	No	Medium
No	No	Yes	High
No	Yes	No	High
No	No	No	Critical

Figure 7.3   The vulnerability-level decision matrix allows the risk manager to quickly ascertain the current vulnerability level.

UNDESIRABLE EVENTS AND VULNERABILITIES

Undesirable events are less likely if there are few vulnerabilities and the nature of the vulnerabilities makes them difficult to exploit. But, such events are more likely if the vulnerabilities have not been identified or protected against and are easy to exploit.

The likelihood that a targeted vulnerability will be successfully exploited is a function of the number and effectiveness of the security countermeasures put into place:

- If few, ineffective, or no countermeasures are put in place, the likelihood that the exploitation will be successful is very high.
- As redundant layers of effective security countermeasures are applied, the likelihood of successful exploitation drops, since the vulnerabilities, and consequently the risk, are reduced or eliminated.

To determine the relative level of vulnerability of each of the assets requiring protection, you need to have an in-depth knowledge of the capabilities of the existing countermeasures. You also need to know the physical and technical characteristics of the environment surrounding the assets you are protecting.

To estimate the degree or level of vulnerability, you must devise a scale or rating system that is appropriate to the overall scope of your tasking.

Critical Assets	Potential Undesirable Events	Vulnerability Identification	Vuln. Level
People	Assault/Serious Injury/Death Accident/Injury/Medical Emergency	Identify type and location of vulnerability in this column.	
Activities	Malicious Acts by Insider Disruption to Communications		
Information	Exposure/Disclosure of System Data Tech. Implant in Conf./R&D Areas		
Facilities	Destruction of Unpopulated Building		
Equipment	Theft/Damage to AIS Equipment Sabotage		

Figure 7.4   The vulnerability assessment chart allows the risk manager to state each vulnerability and tie it to the specific asset and potential undesirable event, then assign the proper vulnerability level.

Box 7.2   Vulnerability rating criteria.

Rating Criteria:

Critical—Indicates that there are no effective countermeasures currently in place and it would be extremely easy for adversaries to exploit weaknesses.

High—Indicates that although there are some countermeasures in place, there are still multiple weaknesses through which adversaries would be capable of exploiting the asset.

Medium—Indicates that there are effective countermeasures in place. However, one weakness does exist which adversaries would be capable of exploiting.

Low—Indicates that multiple layers of effective countermeasures exist, and adversaries would have considerable difficulty exploiting the asset.

THE VULNERABILITY CHART

Figure 7.4 illustrates a sample format for documenting the various judgments that have been made throughout this step regarding vulnerability in relationship to the potential assets and various undesirable events. A brief description of the specific vulnerabilities associated with each event can also be identified on this chart. More detailed information on the vulnerabilities would be maintained in your backup materials.

REVIEW

1. Vulnerabilities are weaknesses and may result from . . . ?
2. What are the three general types of vulnerabilities? Give at least two examples of each.
3. What types of protection will effective countermeasures provide protection against?
4. Undesirable events are less likely to occur if . . . ?
5. Undesirable events are more likely to occur if vulnerabilities . . . ?

8

The Risk Assessment

> The process of evaluating threats to and the vulnerabilities of an asset to give an expert opinion on the probability of loss or damage, and its impact, as a guide to taking action.

The fourth step in the analytical risk management process is to assess risks and determine your priorities for the protection of previously identified critical assets for your organization.

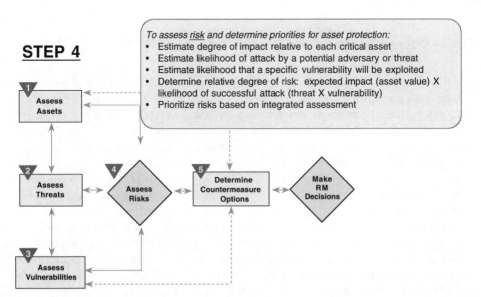

Figure 8.1   Step 4, the risk assessment, is where the overall asset risk is determined.

PUTTING IT ALL TOGETHER

During this step you will determine the likelihood that a specific undesirable event will occur, given the current conditions and based on an integrated assessment of the data you have collected on assets, threats, and vulnerabilities. Risk assessments generally begin with a baseline review of the existing risk under present conditions, to include the countermeasures already in place.

When the threat and vulnerability levels are combined, you can estimate the probability or likelihood of occurrence of the undesirable event. Probability and expected impact together are considered in the estimate of the risk level. To properly assess the risk and determine the priorities of asset protection, it is necessary to do the following.

Estimate the Degree of Impact of Undesirable Events Relative to Each Critical Asset

This initial procedure involves reviewing the impact ratings from Step 1, *taking into consideration* the information obtained in Steps 2 and 3. Solicit other expert judgments and make necessary revisions. In essence, where the threat is reduced, or where the vulnerabilities are minimal, the opportunity exists to "downgrade" the level of impact rating to the assets. Essentially, the lower the threat or vulnerabilities to assets, the lower the rating should be. Thus, what was a "high" can become a "medium" or "low" because of a reduced threat or vulnerability.

Estimate the Likelihood of an Attack from Potential Threats

Estimate the likelihood of an attack from potential threats or adversaries, based on capability, intent, and history. Review the threat rating from Step 2, taking into consideration the information obtained in Steps 1 and 3. Solicit other expert judgments and make necessary revisions. The information in Step 1 was reconsidered based upon information in Steps 2 and 3, and the same procedure is used at this point. With the new level(s) of Step 1, and the known vulnerabilities in Step 3, compare and analyze the information and relate it to the known threats of Step 2. The possibility of one or more of the threats being reduced because of the current level of countermeasures within the vulnerabilities category, or the various assets being at levels where they would be difficult (though not totally impossible) to obtain or destroy by a threat or adversary, the potential for the reduction of one or more threat levels may not always be possible. Consider each carefully and, where appropriate, reduce the threat levels. Don't expect to reduce all of them at least one level, but on the whole, one-third or more are usually able to be reduced one level.

Critical Assets	Potential Undesirable Events	Impact Rating	Threat Rating	Vuln. Rating
People	Assault Accident/Injury/Medical Emerg.	High High		
Activities	Disruption To Program/Project Disruption To Communications	Medium Medium		
Info.	Theft/Comp. Of Classified Info. Exposure/Disclosure of Project	High High		
Facilities	Destruction Of Unpop. Building	High		
Equip.	Theft/Damage To AIS Equip. Theft/Damage To Comm. Equip.	Medium High		

Figure 8.2   Estimating the degree of impact of undesirable events relative to each critical asset.

Critical Assets	Potential Undesirable Events	Impact Rating	Threat Rating	Vuln. Rating
People	Assault Accident/Injury/Medical Emerg.	High High	Low Medium	
Activities	Disruption To Program/Project Disruption To Communications	Medium Medium	Low Low	
Info.	Theft/Comp. Of Classified Info. Exposure/ Disclosure of Project	High High	Medium High	
Facilities	Destruction Of Unpop. Building	High	Low	
Equip.	Theft/Damage To AIS Equip. Theft/Damage To Comm. Equip.	Medium High	Low Low	

Figure 8.3   Estimating the likelihood of an attack from potential threats or adversaries based upon their capability, intent, and history.

Critical Assets	Potential Undesirable Events	Impact Rating	Threat Rating	Vuln. Rating
People	Assault Accident/Injury/Medical Emerg.	High High	Low Medium	Low Medium
Activities	Disruption To Program/Project Disruption To Communications	Medium Medium	Low Low	Low Medium
Info.	Theft/Comp. Of Classified Info. Exposure/Disclosure of Project	High High	Medium High	Low Low
Facilities	Destruction Of Unpop. Building	High	Low	Medium
Equip.	Theft/Damage To AIS Equip. Theft/Damage To Comm. Equip.	Medium High	Low Low	Low Medium

Figure 8.4   Estimating the likelihood that a specific vulnerability will be exploited by a particular threat/adversary.

Estimate the Likelihood that a Specific Vulnerability Will Be Exploited by a Particular Threat/Adversary

Review the Vulnerability Rating from Step 3, taking into consideration the information obtained in Steps 1 and 2. Solicit other expert judgments and make necessary revisions. Again, we follow the same procedures, except considerations are now focused on the new asset and threat levels in terms of the potential vulnerabilities that have been identified—and the current countermeasures in effect. Again, expect up to one-third of the vulnerability levels to be reduced at least one level.

At this juncture, the various ratings should have been revised, as appropriate, and it is now necessary to determine the overall risk level for each of your critical assets. The chart in Figure 8.5 provides a means of rapidly determining the overall risk level for each asset.

Note: Be aware that when the threat and vulnerability levels are combined, you can estimate the likelihood that the undesirable event will occur. Likelihood and expected impact are considered together in our estimate of the risk level.

Where the vulnerabilities are great and the threat is evident, the risk of exploitation is greater. Therefore, a higher priority for protection will need to be considered. Where the vulnerability is slight and/or the adversary has

Critical Assets	Potential Undesirable Events	Impact Rating	Threat Rating	Vuln. Rating	Overall Risk
People	Assault	High	Low	Low	Low
	Accident/Injury/Medical Emerg.	High	Medium	Medium	Medium
Activities	Disruption To Program/Project	Medium	Low	Low	Low
	Disruption To Communications	Medium	Low	Medium	Low
Info.	Theft/Comp. Of Classified Info.	High	Medium	Low	Low
	Exposure/Disclosure of Project	High	High	Low	Medium
Facilities	Destruction Of Unpop. Building	High	Low	Medium	Low
Equip.	Theft/Damage To AIS Equip.	Medium	Low	Low	Low
	Theft/Damage To Comm. Equip.	High	Low	Medium	Low

Figure 8.5   Identifying the individual judgments made to determine the overall risk level.

Potential Undesirable Events	Impact Rating	Threat Rating	Vuln. Rating	Overall Risk	Risk Acceptable?
Assault	High	Low	Low	Low	**Yes/No**
Accident/Injury/Medical Emerg.	High	Medium	Medium	Medium	
Disruption To Program/Project	Medium	Low	Low	Low	
Disruption To Communications	Medium	Low	Medium	Low	
Theft/Comp. Of Classified Info.	High	Medium	Low	Low	
Exposure/Disclosure of Project	High	High	Low	Medium	
Destruction Of Unpop. Building	High	Low	Medium	Low	
Theft/Damage To AIS Equip.	Medium	Low	Low	Low	
Theft/Damage To Comm. Equip.	High	Low	Medium	Low	

Figure 8.6   Identifying your unacceptable risks and determining your security priorities to begin managing the residual risk based on the analytical approach.

little capability to exploit vulnerabilities (now or in the future), the risk is lower and the priority for new countermeasures should therefore be lower.

The areas of greatest risk that you identify here will serve as the basis for deciding where to focus your countermeasures and what countermeasures to apply.

Figure 8.6 has the revised ratings. The risk manager is now ready to determine the security priorities. Without determining the priorities (acceptance or nonacceptance) of risk, the risk manager is not actually managing risk based on an analytical approach. All of the previous steps have been done in order to help you make a rational assessment of your risks and identify which are most critical.

In the last column, then, the risk manager should indicate if the overall risk level is acceptable (Yes). In this regard, is the organization willing to accept the risk and do nothing? Or, if the risk is unacceptable (No), then additional security countermeasures will have to be implemented to further protect the asset from its current protection posture.

REVIEW

1. Is it possible to estimate the degree of impact of an undesirable event if the risk manager were to review the results of each step individually, never referring to other step results? Why?
2. When reviewing step results and comparing them to others, is it expected that based on the results of other steps (and the associated background information for those decisions) the risk manager could be able to reduce any of the individual ratings within any of the rating columns? Why?
3. If the organization is willing to accept risk, what does this indicate?
4. What is indicated when an organization is not willing to accept the risk?

9

Cost-Benefit Analysis

Countermeasure: An action taken or a physical entity used to reduce or eliminate one or more vulnerabilities.

Cost-Benefit Analysis: Part of the management decision-making process in
which the costs and benefits of each alternative are compared, and the most
appropriate alternative is selected.

Based on the information obtained and analyzed in the previous steps, you
can now begin to identify the various countermeasures that are linked to
your greatest risks. Follow the sub-steps as indicated in Figure 9-1. Remember that countermeasures can reduce the vulnerability, as well as the threat
level to an acceptable level.

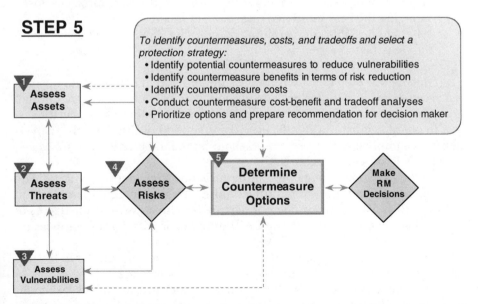

Figure 9.1 Step 5 is the selection of new countermeasures and the preparation of
the cost-benefit analysis.

PROCEDURES	EQUIPMENT (Physical/Technical)	MANPOWER
• Security policies • Security procedures • Training • Awareness programs • Legal prosecution • Security investigations • Polygraph • Disclosure statements • Personnel transfer • Contingency/emergency response planning • OPSEC procedures • Cover procedures	• Locking mechanism • Window bars • Doors • Fences • Alarms/sensors • Hardware/software • Badges • Lighting • TEMPEST device • Paper shredder • Weapons • Closed-circuit TV • Safe haven • Vault	• Contractor guard force • SPOs • Local guards • Military guards

Figure 9.2   Typical countermeasures that could be identified within the three distinct areas of countermeasures.

IDENTIFY POTENTIAL COUNTERMEASURES TO REDUCE VULNERABILITIES

- What are the possible protection solutions for this specific scenario?
- What are the best solutions, regardless of financial constraints?
- What are possible compensating countermeasures where the best solution may be too expensive?

During this step consider the possible protection solutions for specific risk scenarios. A countermeasure option can be defined as an optimal grouping of security countermeasures that work together as a security system to guard against the significant risks identified during the risk analysis phase. A sample countermeasure breakout by the three general countermeasure types is shown at Figure 9.2.

In determining acceptable countermeasures, consider if it will mitigate the risk; reduce the level from critical to high, high to medium, or medium to low; will it detect, delay, deter or destroy the threat; what is the degree of risk mitigation the countermeasure will provide; or will the countermeasure help or not.

When determining countermeasure options, a format similar to the one presented in Figure 9.3 should be used by the risk manager.

You could choose to employ a single countermeasure or several countermeasures in combination to lower risk for each event. Two or more countermeasures may work together in a compensating fashion to guard against a

Undesirable Events	Existing Risk Level	Related Vulnerabilities	Countermeasure Options	New Risk Level
1.				
2.				
3.				
4.				

Figure 9.3 Linking countermeasures options to high priority vulnerabilities allows you to determine a new (and lower) risk level.

vulnerability for which neither would provide adequate protection individually. Notice that certain countermeasures will appear several times in the matrix. If one of these countermeasures is selected, it could mitigate the risk of several undesirable events.

It is necessary to determine the effect that each countermeasure option will have on the existing risk level. Answer the questions (see Figure 9.1) for identifying potential countermeasures that can be implemented to reduce your identified vulnerabilities, and then determine the new level of risk using the matrix in Figure 9.4 to accomplish this.

IDENTIFYING COUNTERMEASURE OPTIONS

Identify the Benefit of Each Option

- How does this option mitigate risk?
- Does this option detect, deter, or destroy the threat?
- To what degree does this option mitigate risk?

Countermeasure benefits can be defined in terms of the level of risk reduction they can provide. Consider each of the questions above. Figure 9.4 will assist you in tracking judgments related to the relative level of risk reduction and benefit gained with each countermeasure.

Countermeasures	Surreptitious Entry/Tech. Implant	Kidnapping Official	Documents Stolen/ Mishandled	Terrorist/ Bomb Attack
Doors, locks, bars	•			•
Alarms/sensors	•			•
Contractor guards	•	•		•
SPOs	•	•		•
Military Guards				•
Vary travel route		•		
Relocate Personnel		•		
Residence locks, bars		•		
Residence alarms/sensors		•		
Bullet-proof car		•		
Residence CCTV		•		
Security awareness			•	
Strict media controls			•	
System audit trail			•	
Passwords			•	
Defensive driving training		•		•
Vehicle checks				•
Emerg. procedures				•
Metal detectors				•
Fences/barriers				•

Figure 9.4 Tracking judgments using this type of a matrix allows the risk manager to select those countermeasures that actually reduce the asset risk levels, and backs up his or her decisions for senior management.

You have the option of using either quantitative ratings as shown, or a qualitative rating such as high, medium, or low. During this step, you should be considering not only the cost of tangible materials, but also the on-going operational costs associated with countermeasure implementation.

MEASURING COSTS OF COUNTERMEASURES

Costs associated with countermeasures may be measured in terms of dollars, inconvenience, or personnel, as illustrated in Figure 9.5.

Every countermeasure has a cost associated with it that can be measured in terms of dollars, inconvenience, time, or personnel. In order to select the most appropriate countermeasure option, the cost associated with each countermeasure must be determined.

Consideration is given not only to the cost of tangible materials, but also to the on-going operational costs associated with a countermeasure and its implementation. Written procedures are usually the least expensive type of security countermeasure. Hardware is generally more expensive than written procedures, and manpower costs are typically the most expensive form of countermeasures.

Identify Cost Differences

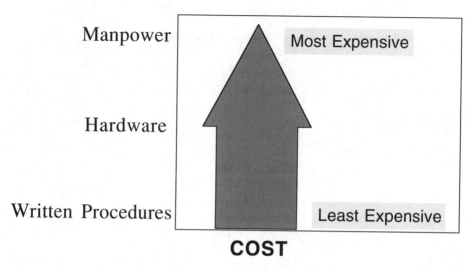

Manpower

Hardware

Written Procedures

Most Expensive

Least Expensive

COST

Figure 9.5 Costs can spiral rapidly when the risk manager moves from written procedures to the selection of costly hardware, or to use more manpower for security countermeasures.

Determining the Dollar Cost of a Countermeasure

- Purchase price
- Life-cycle maintenance costs
  - Installation
  - Preventive maintenance
  - Repair
  - Warranty
  - Replacement
- Life expectancy
- Salaries for staff/contractors to implement, maintain, monitor, or train others to use countermeasure.

When determining the dollar cost of a countermeasure, include the purchase price as well as the life-cycle maintenance costs. This may include installation, preventative maintenance, repair, warranty, and replacement costs. Countermeasure life expectancy should also be considered when determining costs, since the countermeasure will eventually need to be replaced. Dollar costs may also include the salaries of staff or contractors to implement, maintain, monitor, or train others to utilize the countermeasure.

Undesirable Events	Procedures	Equipment	Manpower
Surreptitious entry/ technical implant	• Procedures to secure facility after hours Cost: moderately inconvenient	• Doors, locks, bars Cost: $5,000 • Alarm/sensor system Cost: $20,000	• Contractor guards Cost: $100,000 • SPOs Cost: $200,000 • Military Guards Cost: $250,000
Kidnapping Official	• Vary travel route to work Cost: Minimal inconvenience • Relocate Official Cost: $10,000	• Doors, locks, bars Cost: $5,000 • Alarm/sensor system Cost: $30,000 • Bullet-proof car Cost: $40,000 • Residential CCTV Cost: $170,000	• Contractor guards Cost: $100,000 • SPOs Cost: $250,000
Documents stolen/mishandled	• Security Awareness Briefing Cost: negligible • Strict magnetic media control procedures Cost: moderately inconvenient	• System audit trail Cost: $125,000 • Passwords Cost: $50,000	N/A
Terrorist attack	• Defensive driving training Cost: $80,000 • Vehicle checks Cost: $200,000 • Emergency procedures Cost: $15,000	• Doors, locks, bars Cost: $5,000 • Alarm/sensor system Cost: $30,000 • Metal detectors Cost: $20,000 • Fences/barriers Cost: $90,000	• Contractor guards Cost: $100,000 • SPOs Cost: $200,000 • Military Guards Cost: $250,000

Figure 9.6   When identifying the cost of each option, all costs must be firmly linked to each of the previously determined specific undesirable event.

Determining Costs in Other Terms

Inconvenience.

- Is inconvenience *offset* by measure of risk reduction gained?
- Is it possible that, through procedure redesign, the same or a greater level of risk reduction can be achieved, but with far less inconvenience?

Time.   Must include the time to implement or oversee the countermeasure to be put into use, *and* the time to prepare for its implementation, as well as all time required for oversight and follow-up or evaluation.

Personnel.   Determine the number of staff needed to use (monitor, activate/deactivate, etc.) the countermeasure, as well as the staff knowledge, skills, and abilities of the personnel required. Additionally, there will be the staff training needs and costs that should be considered.

To select the most appropriate countermeasure option, the cost associated with each selected countermeasure must be determined. Shown in Figure 9.6 is the format used for identifying selected countermeasures and their individual costs.

At this juncture, the process includes identifying the countermeasure, but also its costs as the countermeasure applies to a specific undesirable event. "What are the material and operational costs of each option, in terms of dollars?" is the question to be asked in each instance.

To select the most appropriate countermeasure option, the cost associated with each countermeasure must be determined. The figure provides such a format for identifying the associated costs. The general principle to follow when analyzing countermeasures is to select the least expensive countermeasure that will satisfy the customer and also reduce the risk to an acceptable level.

Analyze the Cost and Benefits of Each Option

* How does asset value compare to proposed cost of protection?
* Which option provides best protection at lowest cost?

Based upon the results of your risk assessment, determine the various countermeasure options available to mitigate the risk, reducing it to an acceptable or conditionally acceptable level.

Prioritize Countermeasure Options that Address Risks

* Identify countermeasures that address more than one undesirable event.
* Select three or four countermeasure options that *collectively* lower the risk for all of the events identified. Determine how each option affects the overall risk level.
* Calculate the cost of each option so that the costs and benefits of each option can be compared.
* Ensure that a maximum number of undesirable events have been addressed by the various options recommended.

The cost information will be used to help you decide which countermeasure option to recommend to the customer. One of the options you identify should represent a risk avoidance/elimination approach, providing maximum protection (most likely at the greatest cost), one should represent the least expensive approach, and the other option(s) should be between these two extremes.

You can determine the optimum security countermeasures for each event separately, and then combine them to select a countermeasure. Alternately, you might note that certain countermeasures would lower the risk of several events at the same time, and select one or more of these countermeasures to

Undesirable Events	Countermeasures	Risk Level Reduced From/To	Cost
Surreptitious entry	Doors, locks, bars Alarms/sensor system	HIGH to VERY LOW	$ 5,000 $20,000
Injury to Sr. Scientist	Vary travel route to work Bullet-proof car/driver	LOW to VERY LOW	minimal $20,000
Documents stolen/mishandled	System audit trail Passwords Security Education	MEDIUM to VERY LOW	$125,000 $50,000 minimal
Terrorist bombing attack	Military Guards Defensive driving training Vehicle checks Emergency procedures Metal detectors Fences/barriers	MEDIUM to LOW	$250,000 $80,000 $200,000 $15,000 $20,000 $90,000
OVERALL RISK/TOTAL COST		**MED. to VERY LOW**	**$875,000**

Figure 9.7   Countermeasure Option Package 1, the most expensive.

determine a countermeasure option. You must ensure that all of the unwanted events have been addressed by the various options you create.

Based upon the results of the risk assessment, the risk manager must determine the various countermeasure options available to mitigate the risk, reducing it to an acceptable or conditionally acceptable level. Questions such as "How does asset value compare to proposed cost of protection?" and "Which options provide the best protection at the lowest cost?" are most appropriate for building countermeasure option packages.

Figure 9.7 is the first of several option packages that would be used in a presentation to senior management and the ultimate decision-maker. Here, Countermeasure Option 1 (Maximum Protection) reduces the overall average risk level for these five undesirable events from *medium* to *very low* at a cost of $875,000.

Figure 9.8, Countermeasure Option 2 (Least Expensive), only costs $25,000 but does not reduce the overall average risk level.

Figure 9.9, Countermeasure Option 3 (Recommended) reduces the overall average risk level for these five events from *medium* to *low* at a cost of $120,000.

Once several options are identified, their advantages and disadvantages are presented to the customer. One of the options should be recommended and the rationale clearly spelled out. The customer makes the final decision about countermeasures employed and assumes the risks present in that option.

Undesirable Events	Countermeasures	Risk Level From/To	Cost
Surreptitious entry	Doors, locks, bars	HIGH to MEDIUM	$5,000
Injury to Sr. Scientist	Vary travel route to work	LOW to LOWER	None (inconvenience)
Documents stolen/mishandled	Security Awareness Briefing	MEDIUM to LOW	Minimal
Terrorist bombing attack	Emergency procedures Metal detectors	HIGH to HIGH/MEDIUM	$15,000 $ 5,000
OVERALL RISK/ TOTAL COST		MEDIUM to MEDIUM	$25,000

Figure 9.8   Countermeasure Option Package 2 is the least expensive.

Undesirable Events	Countermeasures	Risk Level Reduced From/To	Cost
Surreptitious entry/ technical implant	Doors, locks, bars	HIGH to MEDIUM	$5,000
Injury to Sr. scientist	Vary travel route	LOW to VERY LOW	None [inconvenience]
Documents stolen/mishandled	Security awareness briefing	MEDIUM to LOW	minimal
Terrorist bombing attack	SPOs Emergency procedures	HIGH/MED to MEDIUM	$100,00 $15,000
OVERALL RISK/ TOTAL COST		MEDIUM to LOW	$120,000

Figure 9.9   Countermeasure Option Package 3 is the one recommended for the overall lowering of the risk level and the costs involved.

THERE ARE NO SIMPLE ANSWERS

How does the value of a given critical asset compare to the proposed costs of protection, and which options from among the option packages will provide the best protection at the lowest possible cost? There are not simple answers to these questions.

The cost of protective measures should not typically exceed a reasonable percentage of the total value of the assets requiring protection. However, there is no one "reasonable" percentage across the board for all assets, or even for all assets within a given group.

The managers responsible for the assets must balance the benefits of risk reduction against the cost of reducing risk. In some cases, even the individual asset managers may have to go to a higher level of authority for approval to implement countermeasures; this is most certainly true in organizations where micromanagement—especially of funds—is concerned. Consider the various influencing factors that management must weigh before expending personnel, materials, or funds for a countermeasure. Influencing factors include (a) the value of the asset; (b) the current exposure to loss/harm; (c) the availability of the identified protective measures; (d) availability of funds; and (e) any mandatory security requirements that must be included in the protection scheme.

So, when the questions arise as to how does asset value compare to the proposed cost of protection, or, which options provide the best protection at the lowest cost, there are no simple answers.

ANALYZING MARGINAL BENEFITS

There is a general principle used in risk management: Select the least expensive countermeasure that will satisfy the customer and reduce risk to an acceptable level.

However, countermeasure may protect against more than one vulnerability, and thus, compensating countermeasures are used in a complementary manner to form a security system. Therefore, it is important to determine the cost of the various optional countermeasure groupings. A particular grouping may be less expensive than the sum of the costs for the least expensive countermeasure for each undesirable event, yet still provide adequate protection.

In the end, the questions that must be answered are, does the countermeasure:

- reduce risk to an acceptable level?
- protects against more than one vulnerability?
- prove less expensive than other countermeasures that could provide the same level of protection?
- satisfy the customer's requirement for protection of the asset?

After the cost of each optional countermeasure grouping is determined, then cost differences and the marginal benefits of each option can be compared.

APPLYING THE PROCESS TO MEET CUSTOMER
REQUIREMENTS AND RECOMMEND OPTIONS

The risk assessment started when a tasking order was given to the risk manager to perform a risk assessment of a program or project. The assessment ends when the customer requirements are satisfied. Thus, the need now arises to readdress the tasking. As the risk manager, you determined what you thought the customer wanted; was it achieved? Maybe yes, maybe no. It's time to go back and redefine the risk management task.

Let's take a look at a typical tasking statement developed for a risk assessment of an organization (see Box 9.1). What is interesting, first of all, is that the tasking is actually written by the risk manager. The tasking is based on the requirements, either verbal or written, that initially directed that some form of risk assessment be performed for the organization. It provides the decision-maker with exactly what will be provided as the end product. This is important. What management wants, what they say they want, what the risk manager thinks management wants, and the final product, may all be different. The formal tasking statement is a series of specific statements of what will transpire in the risk assessment process. Further, it sets out what will be provided to senior decision-making personnel as the end product.

The tasking statement really clarifies the purpose for which the risk assessment was performed. Upon completion, it is forwarded to the tasking office for their agreement. In essence, approval of the tasking statement tells the risk manager exactly what is expected in terms of the final product. At the same time, the risk manager should be talking to the senior management staff to find out:

- What decisions will be made based on the analysis?
- What is the purpose of the decision(s) to be made?
- What is the ultimate goal, or result to be achieved from the decision?
- Exactly who asked the question? Is this person in the position to actually make the final decision, or is there someone else who will make the decision?
- Who are your customers? Is it the senior manager, the CEO, another manager related to a program or project? Or someone else?
- Who are the decision-makers? What do they want to know? Why do they need your support?

You might look at the above questions in a different order, or even think "what does it matter? I've got a good assessment here, so let them worry about what to do with it." This is an important step, however—to you and to them—since many major management decisions will be made based upon the information provided, and the wrong decision could stop the lifeblood flow of the organization.

Box 9.1   Sample tasking statement.

The Risk Management Office will conduct a series of interviews with a cross-section of personnel within the organization to obtain a balanced perspective on information pertaining to the critical assets, threats, and vulnerabilities of the subject site. The interviewees will be carefully chosen so that the information obtained will include the concerns and opinions of employees of various positions and grade levels. Throughout these interviews, a consistent series of topics and questions will b e covered with each interviewee in order to determine site-specific information on critical assets, threats, and vulnerabilities.

Specific individuals to be interviewed include: The Chief Executive Officer; Chief of Administrative Services; Chief of Project Operations; Chief, Security Division; Captain of the Security Guard Force at the project location; Director of Special Projects; and the site Project Director. Additionally, specialists and professionals in various fields associated with the project relating to the subject area of this risk assessment will be interviewed to obtain information of a more specialized nature. Information related to the site's current security posture and the specific countermeasures in place there will be derived primarily through interviews with site security personnel and the recent zero-based review for this facility.

In addition to the information provided by site personnel, threat data will be obtained from a variety of outside sources. Since the project of concern is tied closely to the Department of Defense, sources will also include the National Counter-Intelligence Center [NACIC]; FBI; the Component senior intelligence and security office; and, through the Defense Security Service representative, other senior level national intelligence organizations. Also, the local police department, sheriffs' office, and regional state police barracks for this area will be contacted for information of a more regional and local nature.

This assessment will also be based on information contained in recent threat assessments conducted for other facilities within the geographic areas that have applicability.

A survey of open source data will be conducted using various databases and the world-wide-web [WWW] to determine any degree of exposure and public knowledge of the site and the project that may be known by the general public. Additionally, various professional organizations that have a general subject area interest in portions of the project will be contacted and any information obtained will be considered in the context of the project.

The Risk Management Office will provide senior decision-making personnel with a macro-level Risk Assessment report outlining the findings, conclusions, and general recommendations covering the major security issues warranting further investigation. The assessment will be delivered 30 days after task initiation.

Consider next the scope of the task or problem what has been presented to you as a risk manager. In performing the risk analysis, was it thorough enough? It should have covered all major assets, with the most critical ones being specifically identified. Consider also what was not included in your analysis, and why you did not include it. Perhaps, something was not included because there was nothing specific in the tasking. Think back; could it have been implied that a particular area should have been included?

Was there a specific level of detail necessary to support your findings? I have found that with different organizations, or even components of the same organization, the various ways of doing something are different, and the results are also different. Completeness is necessary, especially in risk management. Detail is important.

Consider also that the information to be presented to management must be current and valid. How long will the information on which you have based your analysis be valid? If you spent a good portion of the analysis on assets, of which 30 percent were to be replaced in the next twelve to eighteen months, *and you knew about the replacement before you started the analysis*, what good is the overall analysis if future projections and costing is now being determined by senior management? The bottom line would be a massive waste of dollars to protect assets that will be replaced, and no consideration given to protecting the new assets, which will soon be on-site.

Lastly, do you know of other information that may be supplied to the senior management decision-maker that will come from different sources? If so, you need to be aware of the sources, what types of information they are providing (based on the same or different taskings), and whether or not this other information will be used to support, provide an opposite view, or undermine your analytical efforts.

The risk manager must present the analysis to senior management, either as a report or, more typically, as a management summary or report, along with a formal presentation in which the report and its recommendations are "sold" to the decision-maker and the immediate staff.

In presenting information, you must consider the constraints encountered in the risk assessment. The answers to the following questions become important in justifying to management any limitations to the assessment.

- Did the risk management team have access to the best information sources?
- Were there problems in getting the needed information? Were they anticipated or unexpected? Did time play a major factor? To what extent? Was the information just unavailable, or are there other reasons it could not be obtained?
- What was the customer's span of influence? Does the decision-maker actually have the influence (and power) to make the hard and fast decisions, and ensure that they are carried out? If not, why not? Who does?

- Were there conflicting interests? Sometimes, a tasking for a risk assessment is given, and it is to back up someone else in the chain of command who has other reasons for wanting it, that is, to make their program look better, or to eliminate a competing program by showing that costs, materials, and so on, are too expensive.
- Were there politically correct or politically incorrect answers? There are instances where a certain "answer" is required and you are to provide it—without really knowing what is desired. This can be a very dangerous position for the risk manager. Loyalty to the organization is one thing; providing the facts without shading the truth is another. Anticipate such types of taskings; be firm and loyal to the facts, no matter what the outcome answer of the assessment may be.
- Were there any resource constraints? Identify them.
- Does the customer's authority include the resources to implement change? Is the money available to implement the recommendations?
- Is this risk analysis worthwhile at this time? What is coming down the road that may change the impact of the tasking (e.g., a move to another facility, a change in the program or project, a new project taking over, etc.).

At this point, identify and list any constraints encountered related to conducting the risk analysis. In addition to the above questions, others that may have relevance include

- Are there multiple customers with conflicting interests?
- What are the driving political, economic, or legal constraints that had an impact on the risk assessment team's ability to successfully complete the task?

Some managers want to see "numbers," others to see the results, while still others want detailed information. In almost all cases, however, the managers want to be able to access the background data if necessary. Thus, what customer products will be necessary can impact on what level of detail is put into the assessment and what materials will be maintained for the foreseeable future. Customer products include the asset assessment, impact assessment, threat assessment, vulnerability assessment, risk assessment or analysis, the cost/benefit analysis, and the final risk management report.

Knowing what management wants is a big part of "selling" the assessment. Go back to the tasking statement to identify the approach and end product desired.

- What type of assessment and product do they actually need to answer their questions?
- What specific information do you need to conduct the assessment?
- What sources will you use?

Customer products that are used to document the risk management process include those listed above. What you are doing is validating the assessment of customer requirements with the customer via the tasking document. This validation ensures that you produce the appropriate type of product document, and that its internal contents are accurate and desired. Knowing how the product will be used by the decision-maker is important. You can provide all the required data, but if it isn't known how it will be used, you probably will not have answered the tasking properly. Furthermore, you may have generated a product that has only a slight value, one that will have to be reworked, costing time and personnel hours (weeks or months, even), and that also puts you in a somewhat precarious position relative to the "value" of your work.

To ensure its completeness, ask yourself:

- What will you provide as a product?
- What will that product include?
- How will the product be used?
- What is the schedule for completing the product?

KEY CONSIDERATIONS IN RECOMMENDING COUNTERMEASURE OPTIONS

When you present your recommendations to senior management, you can use the outline in Box 9.2 to structure your report or briefing.

Box 9.2   This outline allows the risk manager to properly formulate a presentation for senior management in an orderly manner to match the risk analysis process.

- Review the purpose and scope of the RM task with the customer
- Present your findings
  - Assets
  - Threats
  - Vulnerabilities
- Present the conclusions of your analysis
  - Overall risks and priorities
- Present your recommendations
  - Countermeasures
  - Customer responsibilities

The statements below break out what is included within each area:

- Review assets: Which assets are critical and why? Explain loss impacts.
- Review specific threats: What are they? Who are the adversaries? Explain their capability, intent, and the history related to undesirable events.
- Review vulnerabilities: What are they? How do vulnerabilities relate to threats?
- Review overall risks and priorities: What are the risks? Which risks are of the greatest concern? Why? What might happen if they are not reduced?
- Identify countermeasures: How much do countermeasures reduce vulnerabilities or risks? What are direct and indirect costs? How will they impact end-users? What risks will remain after various countermeasure options are implemented?
- What do you consider the customer's responsibilities to be in selecting and implementing countermeasures? Why should the customer invest in recommended countermeasures? Why should the customer discontinue using existing countermeasures that you consider to be unwarranted?

The risk management team will, of course, have all the background documentation and other information that was developed during the course of the risk analysis survey. The documentation would be in specific files, or broken down, by risk assessment step and then by asset, into various binders, and each would also have a summary of the information therein. All decisions made, especially relative to the impact or other levels for each step of the analysis, would be tied to the justifications for those decisions. In essence, a large organization, or a major project or program, could then well have a file cabinet or even a large number of binders full of backup supporting documentation that would be maintained for an indefinite period of time. This backup must be available for further reassessments that may be required, and also to support further actions that have been made in the past. Another great thing about these files is that, in the future, you may not have to perform all the steps from scratch for another analysis, since much of the information is already at your fingertips.

SUMMARY

As you finish up this section, you complete the risk assessment process. As you have proceeded through this book, you have moved from asset assessment, through threat and vulnerability, to the integration of all information into the risk assessment, then on to make hard choices about countermeasures, and finally, to ensure that the information developed is what the senior management decision-maker(s) actually desired.

Unless you have had risk management assistance in the past, you are now just past the beginner stage, and movement onward as the organizational risk manager holds great potential for you.

Take advantage of Appendix A, "Risk Management Case Study and Practical Exercises," and work through the case study and its practical exercises to get a feel for how the process works and comes to fruition.

You are about to become very important to the organization; although you may not see it at this time, your knowledge of the process and how it is used to the greater benefit of your organization is important. Use the information well and succeed beyond your current expectations. Take advantage of the various appendixes for further information. Reread as necessary to maintain your educational knowledge level in risk management. Look to other books, magazines, professional societies, and other risk managers, and use the Internet to learn more about risk management. You can also contact me at roperc@erols.com with your thoughts, ideas, or questions. A true risk manager is always available to provide advice and/or assistance.

10

Risk Management and Your Organization

The material in this chapter has been included to provide you with some of the background and various considerations to take into account within your organization. It is meant to provide you with a better "starting point" for the development and initial implementation—then the continuance—of your local risk management program. All of the thoughts, ideas, and areas included are "generic" in how they may be applied by your organization, thus they become food for thought and become valuable only if you desire to have and maintain a successful risk management program.

Management of any function involves planning, organizing, and control. In risk management, the risk administrator must consider problems such as policy formulation, handling risk, how the work will be organized within the organization, staffing (generalists or specialists), at what level decisions involving pure risk will be made, definition of goals and objectives, and setting up controls to assure adequate discharge of the risk management functions and their evaluation.

YOUR ROLE AS THE DAY-TO-DAY RISK MANAGER

Senior management within your organization is typically not concerned about the day-to-day functional operations, but views your work in terms of mission accomplishment based upon various programs and goals that are to be completed at some point in the future. Your responsibilities definitely overlap all the decisions you make in these areas.

What you should be doing, what you would like to be doing, and what you actually do are typically different. Look at them, making a list for each, and determine which ones are really applicable. Others may apply down the road, but not now. Stick to the ones that really apply.

THE RISK MANAGER

You have either been "selected," "appointed," or "volunteered" as the organizational risk manager. A full-time risk manager is highly recommended if a project, program, or organization is large enough to afford one and funding is available. In many instances, though, the risk manager will be a "part-time" position, an additional function of your current position. The role you assume in this position will be to identify, capture, and then formalize the various risk management activities within the organization.

What you do is somewhat up to you. Fair, good, great, or exceptional work output and the ability to design and implement a risk management program is your primary goal. The problem is that you are not a "shaker and mover" within the organization, but more of a small office or branch within the organization whose power and authority lay within the risk management policy that has been approved by senior management. As the risk manager, you do not really have any direct responsibility to assume the risks that are identified through the risk assessment process. More likely, your position is that of a mid-level manager who is responsible for program planning and control.

Who Is Responsible for Risk Management?

If you answer "me," you are taking a simplistic view. The division of responsibility, you might think, is where the line is drawn between the survey team and the upper echelons of the organization. Essentially, everyone in the organization has some responsibility, albeit not in their job description. But you, as the "designated" risk manager, need to consider and reinforce—at every opportunity—the objective of risk control to ensure that the program works. Thus, remember that the objective is the elimination and/or reduction of both risk itself and loss. Imagination and initiative in this area can go a long way!

A risk management program never "just happens," it is created and directed by an individual assigned such duties. Day-to-day oversight is performed, specifically, by that individual to ensure that the program meets its goals and objectives, and also to ensure that it is working properly. In general, top level management reviews the program results and makes the major decisions relative to the selection and implementation of countermeasure options.

Risk Program Manager Responsibilities

As the risk program manager for your organization, it is essential early on to establish a centralized risk management element within the organization. The element should have all responsibilities defined, the limits of authority determined, and the appropriate resources should be available. Reporting should be to senior management, not to an intermediary. The team of personnel that make up the risk management element needs to be practical, flexible, consistent, and dynamic in their approach and understanding of what must be accomplished.

The breadth of general responsibilities of the designated risk manager will, obviously, vary with the capabilities of each individual. In general, though, possible responsibilities include:

- exposure identification
- risk evaluation
- risk control:
    - protection of personnel safety, vehicle fleet safety, and property conservation
    - environmental
    - protection of product safety and emergency preparedness (crisis situations)
- review of all major contracts
- review of financing/budget coordination with any internal audit departments
- liaison with Automated Information Systems (AIS) for loss control
- control of risk retention program and loss reserves connected therewith
- input to strategic planning with respect to exposures to accidental loss
- administration of all losses
- coordination with legal counsel
- maintenance of vital records

Within these areas you may be deeply or only peripherally involved. These are all parts of risk management that you probably never thought of, were never concerned about, and have no interest in. Nevertheless, they are closely aligned and related to the program. You see, planning for the management of risk in all these areas makes sense in order to eliminate risk wherever possible, to isolate and minimize risk, to allow for the development of alternate courses of action, and to establish time and financial reserves to cover risks that cannot be avoided.

An effective risk management process accurately considers (1) what information is being exposed; and (2) where, when, and to whom. It is essential for the implementation of threat-appropriate, rational, and cost-effective security countermeasures to balance the security requirements with the future operations and marketing potential of the organization.

An essential function of the risk manager is policy formulation. Policies must be made up with the assistance and cooperation of top management. The risk-taking characteristics of both the risk manager and top management should be considered in formulating appropriate risk management policies. Note also, that risk management efficiency is judged by both economic and noneconomic measures. Again, senior management support *and* involvement is not only important, it is essential to the success of the overall program. You will be using an integrated approach that is dynamic in its nature, but for true success senior management involvement is necessary. Without it, the program may not fail, but it will never reach its full potential.

What Is Involved and at What Levels?

As a risk manager, you may be involved in the development of the program, provide oversight to the program, be in charge of the program, or be a "worker bee" within the program. No matter at what level within the organization you perform, remember that there is always someone above you who will probably have the final say in what you do, and how you do it.

In general, you will at least have an understanding of, if not be personally involved in:

- program and policy formulation and its implementation;
- risk identification through decision flowcharts, loss exposure surveys and checklists, use of financial statements, and appraisals and valuation;
- record keeping; and
- risk management objectives and evaluation.

Program development and policy formulation will include, but not necessarily be limited to:

- what do you, as the risk manager, plan to accomplish;
- the development of the organizational risk management plan and internal policies;
- loss control concepts and how they are affected by the risk analysis process; and
- the training and education of employees of the organization at all levels, whether or not they are directly involved in the program or project.

An essential function of the risk manager is policy formulation. Risk management policies must be made up with the assistance and cooperation of top management. The risk-taking characteristics of both the risk manager and top management should be considered in formulating appropriate risk management policies.

The first and most important step in program creation is the preparation and approval of written policy statements on risk.

CONSIDERATIONS FOR THE DEVELOPMENT OF RISK MANAGEMENT POLICY

Since the purpose of risk management is to identify risks as early as possible, adjust the security strategy to mitigate those risks, and develop and implement a process as an integral part of the security policy for the organization, it is imperative the risk manger consider, evaluate, and implement appropriate measures to reduce the risk where possible. Thus, the risk manager needs to take an approach plan based upon those identified risks, employing the analytical risk process to mange the risks. The following considerations should be seriously considered in policy development.

1. Plan risk management activities.
2. Ensure that risk management is an integral part of the defined process.
3. Identify and deal with risk in a positive manner, such that identification is recognized and rewarded, and results in positive mitigation actions.
4. Have a group/team that is responsible for coordinating risk management activities. Provide adequate resources for risk management activities.
5. Require training for individuals performing risk management activities.
6. Integrate risk identification, analysis, and mitigation activities into the development and/or planning process for all programs or projects, or for organizational security and safety.
7. Develop the risk management plan according to the program or project's defined process.
8. Perform the project's risk management activities in accordance with your local risk management plan.
9. Identify, analyze, and take appropriate risk mitigation actions during the planning phase of a program or project.
10. Track risk mitigation actions to completion.
11. Make and use measurements to determine the status of the risk management activities.
12. Record and track resources expended for risk management activities.
13. Review the activities for risk management with senior management on a periodic basis.
14. Review the activities for risk management with the project/program manager, operations personnel, and so on, on both a periodic and event-driven basis.

The role of leadership

One of the responsibilities of the risk manager is that of leadership in the area of loss prevention and control. Loss control itself is an activity that must be carried on throughout the organization and on many different levels.

Because loss control is so important in its effect on the success of risk management, generally the risk manager must take a leading role in the planning, organizing, and controlling of activities that are directed at preventing or reducing losses.

Decision-making involves making three basic decisions:

1. What will be the cost of reduction of the threat in terms of protection of assets?
2. What must be accomplished in terms of the preservation of the organization's financial stability?
3. What must be accomplished in terms of the protection of the organization's personnel, physical assets, and key processes?

Note that none of the three questions stands alone; they are all interrelated. Thus you will need to continually examine the nature and scope of any decisions you make.

To make a decision is to select a course of action from a variety of alternatives. It is very important to identify those situations in which valid alternative courses of action are present. This will save time and limits the amount of frustration encountered in exploring impossible strategies and analyzing their potential impact. There is a qualifying need to conduct a thorough search for satisfactory alternatives.

The risk manager needs to have a decision flow-chart, if only in his or her mind. The flow chart is an important tool in the administration of your risk management functions. Major elements in the decision process are: (a) recognition of the possibility of loss; (b) measurement of the possible size of loss; and (c) dealing with the risk of remaining severe losses that cannot be handled by the traditional methods of avoidance, abatement, diversification, and transfer.

Another significant tool for risk management is the loss exposure survey and various loss prevention or other types of checklists. They must be tailored to the particular needs of the organization and should be divided in accordance with the major classes of risks faced.

Avoid a Haphazard Approach

A haphazard approach to decision-making results in inconsistent and usually suboptimal decisions. When exposures are not recognized, loss potentials inaccurately quantified, and risk control and financial opportunities overlooked, the organization's attainment of its objectives is hindered and the rewards are reduced.

Thus, risk managers at any level should attempt to take a consistent, comprehensive approach to decision-making and to make use of some type of quantified, structured approach. Note that by introducing structure, we do not signal the exit of intuitive, imaginative, and experienced judgment; rather, we create a framework for applying these judgments as effectively as possible.

The risk manager first recognizes the need for a decision when he compares actual with expected results.

The Identification of Alternatives

The identification of alternatives and the selection of a "game plan" or set of actions focusing on the gap between what is expected and what actually occurs are important, characterized by a series of steps in the decision process:

* discovering the gap; determining what is wrong
* searching for alternatives; brainstorming solutions
* analyzing and evaluating alternatives; projecting results
* making the right choice; selecting the plan; following up to make sure the plan works

Record-Keeping

Record-keeping is another important function of the risk manager. It is necessary to keep track of the existence and status of all major/critical records, thus being able to furnish information on exposures to loss, to furnish information on losses incurred in the past, and to assist in any recovery of claims that may be related to past or on-going contracts and insurers.

In the evaluation of risk management, the extent to which the risk manager reduces the costs of risk as well as the cost of performing risk management functions must be calculated. It is the function of general/upper management to make regular evaluations of the performance of the risk manager. Without appropriate oversight, many unnecessary errors in the conduct of the risk management program can regularly occur.

MANAGING YOUR MANAGEMENT

The following collection of hints and tips was developed by Joe Grau, a security trainer and instructor for the Department of Defense Security Institute. This information is for getting your organization's managers to play active, constructive roles in your—actually, their—security risk management program. Some of these suggestions deal with style, general approach, and specific tactics. Others focus on positioning yourself to be able to influence their performance, rather than on the influencing process itself. Not all of them will work for everyone, and not all of them will work in every situation. But they are all worth considering.

In presenting this list of ideas, there are two shortcuts taken. First, the top manager will be referred to as "the boss." The "boss" might be a military officer, a senior civilian executive, or a corporate chief executive officer or chief operating officer. The boss will also be referred to as "he"—with the understanding that this is a time-saving convention only, and that this role applies equally to women in senior management positions.

1. *Be positive.* Approaching managers with the built-in assumption that they don't care or won't respond positively to security is disastrous. There's a lot of truth in the idea that people rise and fall to meet our expectations. If we communicate an expectation that the boss will react negatively, we set him up to do just that.
   - Never apologize for your own program. If you believe that the security program is an important part of the organization's life, act like it.
   - Don't over-sell. You approach the boss with a request for support, and immediately give him 4,216 reasons to grant it. The boss may have quickly seen the logic of the request and was predisposed to grant it. But your obvious anxiety makes him do a mental double-take. He begins to doubt his immediate reaction.
   - Don't under-request. Our pessimism about what we will be able to wring out of management sometimes leads us to minimize what we ask for. That ensures that we'll never get more than the minimum. Say you need an hour of a manager's time for a presentation. But you know that the manager is a very busy person and you cut down your request to a half-hour. This is not enough to do the job right, but it's better than nothing, you figure. Your chances of getting an hour with the big boss are now zero because you limited the maximum amount of desired presentation time. Would your chances have been better if you had asked for an entire hour? I don't know, but I do know they would have been better than zero!

2. *Talk opportunities.* Providing support to the risk management program isn't a favor management does for its staff. It's an opportunity for the manager to promote quality in a function for which he is responsible.

3. *Emphasize payoffs, not requirements.* Managers tend to be even more resentful than most people of things we do because "the book" requires them. Downplay compliance and highlight benefits.

4. *Internalize the risk management program.* In order to promote ownership of the program by managers, present it as a necessity for doing business rather than as a set of externally-imposed requirements. Position it as something we need, rather than something they say we must do.

5. *Focus on the organization rather than the program.* Most managers (with the exception of technical folks thrust in management roles)

focus their attention on the organization itself, with various programs seen as pieces of the whole. They are usually more responsible to discussions based on the organization rather than a specific program.

6. *Explain collateral benefits.* Many things we do for security's sake also have other beneficial effects for the organization. If we make sure managers know about these, it facilitates acceptance of and investment in the measure. For example, many of the same measures that help keep information confidential on a computer are important contributors to virus protection. Visit controls required by a program help provide a more crime-free and orderly workplace. Classified document accountability systems can contribute to easy retrievability of information. In a more general sense, establishing a climate of risk management security that protects classified information will also heighten protection for other information that must be protected if the organization is to stay healthy—like corporate proprietary information and trade secrets.

7. *Don't assume knowledge or understanding.* Just because a top manager is a top manager doesn't tell you beans about his knowledge or understanding of the risk management or security programs. This is especially true when it comes to knowledge of basic program concepts. If they were ever taught these concepts, how long ago was it, and how often have they been reminded of them? What are your chances that they will recall them? If understanding the concept is necessary for understanding your request or learning what you're teaching, better make sure the basic understanding is there.

8. *Be specific.* Don't just ask your management to "care" or "show support" or "put command emphasis" on risk management. Ask the boss to do specific things. Providing management support to a program is a role, and we should identify specific tasks to be performed.

9. *Adapt to the manager's style.* By the time they reach senior positions, many people have adopted a "style" of learning and management that they heavily favor. Sometimes, they get so attached to this style that we mere mortals would call it a "hang-up." For instance, some managers see themselves as "strategic thinkers" only concernrd with "broad issues," while others want every detail laid out for them. Some favor learning from print, others want live discussion of issues, some are into charts and graphs. Learning about and accommodating the manager's style smoothes communication. Bucking the tide can cause credibility problems and build resistance to your ideas. Failing to learn can leave you ineffectual and frustrated. Members of the manger's staff can often be valuable sources of information and guidance.

10. *Be time-conscious.* Many managers operate under heavy pressures and demands for their time. And those who don't often act like they do. Being busy is something of a status symbol for many managers. Accommodate this by being careful to use your time with the manager profitably. Never allow the manager to suspect his time has been

wasted. That translates too easily into the perception that security itself is a waste of time.

11. *Speak "managementese."* A basic principle of teaching is the benefit of establishing a close connection between what you're teaching and the student's work setting. Using the language (or "buzz words") of management sends a signal that what you have to say has relevance to their duties and concerns. It also helps you establish credibility.

12. *Be part of the management team.* Like birds of a feather, managers tend to flock together. Managers tend to have a higher comfort level when dealing with other managers who are on the same team. This facilitates communication and learning. Also, the more managers view you as part of the organization management team, the more readily they will accept your recommendations as being in the organization's best interests. Some specifics include:

    • Know the organization. The more you know the organization, the better you can talk to managers in terms of their specific situations and concerns.

    • Be aware of current issues. Keep current on the various influences that are impacting your organization—things like downsizing, employee empowerment, privatization, market trends, fiscal uncertainties, etc.

    • Participate in management. Invest some of your effort in management activities, even if they don't directly impact the risk management program. Get involved (or, at least, show interest) in management initiatives like TQM (Total Quality Management), employee wellness, and so forth. One manager became a regular instructor in his organization's TQM training, which was presented by line managers. His staff reported a noticeable change in the ease with which they could deal with managers in other elements.

13. *Establish a visible presence.* You want your top management to perceive the risk management program as an integral part of the organization's operation and of their management responsibilities. Keeping yourself visible to management can contribute to this, besides raising the perception of you as part of the management team. For example, attend and have something to contribute to staff meetings. Don't be one of those people who sit along the wall of the conference room and fervently hope nobody asks them anything. Send signals that risk management is something management needs to hear about.

14. *Talk tradeoffs and least-cost solutions.* Managers tend to be very conscious of and concerned about resources. When presenting new or changed requirements and your plans for meeting them, be sure you're ready to discuss what alternatives you've considered and why you selected the one you're presenting.

15. *Don't be a habitual bearer of bad news.* People tend to generalize their perceptions of us to our programs. If the only time a manager sees the risk manager is when things go wrong, risk management becomes perceived as a program where bad news is the norm. The result? Avoidance. Yet, there are others who hesitate to "bother" the boss unless it's urgent—which usually means just after the dam has burst.

16. Learn to deal with the staff. Almost every manager is surrounded by staff, be it a single secretary or administrative assistant, or a whole battalion of aides, executive officers, administrative officers, and the like. Staffs exist to enhance the effectiveness of managers by providing effective communications, minimizing distractions, and organizing the flow of information to and decisions from the mangers. In many organizations, staffs also perform other, well-intentioned but less legitimate functions, like protecting the manager or advancing their own views and objectives.

- Distinguish the manager from the staff. As you form your perceptions of the manager's attitudes and behavior, do your best to sort out the influence of the manager himself from that of the staff. We've all run across cases where our perceptions of a manager's wishes or instructions were clouded, colored, or even twisted by the "spin" put on them by the staff. Be alert for this; recognizing it can save a lot of trouble.

- Get to know the staff. The more you know about the perceptions, attitudes, opinions, and styles of staff members, the better you can understand how they might filter communications with the boss. This will enable you to eliminate the filtering or compensate for it.

- Learn how the staff operates. Watch the staff carefully. Figure out who has the power to control what. Who actually controls access to the manager? Who has the greatest influence on how the manager spends his time? How does the flow of information to the manager work, and who's involved? Which staff members have the greatest influence on the manager's perceptions and opinions? Are there issues in which the manager tends to defer to a staff member's judgment? Whose?

- Cooperate. Staff members often work in a very high-pressure environment, and sometimes feel defensive if a "we-they" atmosphere has developed between them and the line managers. They tend to be quick to recognize and appreciate someone's willingness to cooperate. They'll often be most willing to pay back that cooperation, making it possible to turn them into very influential allies for your risk management program.

- Build alliances. Let the staff members know that you value their ability to help you deal effectively with the manager. Ask for their help. Say "thanks" when you get it. Don't just ask them to do things for you; ask for their advice about how best to get things done.

Risk exists only in the future tense.

There are no past risks—only actual occurrences.

QUESTIONS FOR THE RISK MANAGER

There are lots of questions the risk manager will ask, and the answers will provide a great deal of information. Some will relate directly to each of the various steps within the risk management process; other answers will become background for the risk manager and his team of personnel who conduct the risk assessment. All of the information developed from the various questions becomes part of the office files, to be used in the immediate and distant future when conducting future risk assessments, or for the administration of the organization's risk management program.

- Where can the risk manager obtain a Table of Organization for the program, project, or the organization?
- What is the product or service being provided? (For each identified, obtain appropriate information.)
- When will the program/project end?
- What is classified, if this is a government program or project? Documents, equipment, processes, technology, hardware, and so on?
- What is unclassified sensitive or proprietary? Government or that owned by the organization?
- If there is a contract, obtain a copy of DD Form 254 (Contract Security Specification Guidance) and classification guidance (if government). Is the classification guide or contract classified or controlled in any manner, disallowing unauthorized personnel access to it? The DD Form 254 is performance and security requirement details and specifications under a DoD program or project.
- Is there proper and adequate guidance for classified or sensitive proprietary information?
- Is there a dissemination of guidance to personnel on the program or project, and how is the dissemination accomplished?
- How many people are on the program or project?
- How many have a clearance?
- How many generate classified or sensitive proprietary material?
- How many work with classified or sensitive proprietary material?
- Can justification be given for the number of personnel on the program or project?

- Does everyone require access to everything, or is access controlled? If so, how and to what extent?
- What are the procedures for the generation of classified or sensitive proprietary material?
- Who may classify such material when generated?
- What are the accountability procedures for such material?
- Are special markings, reproduction, and dissemination rules in effect? Are they followed?
- How is transmission into or out of the facility handled?
- What procedures are in effect for the mailroom, shipping, and receiving areas?
- How is such material disposed of? How is it retained and controlled long-term?

For visitors to the facility project or program:

- How are incoming visitors handled?
- How are visits to other facilities handled?
- What are the procedures when there are foreign visitors?
- Are tour groups of the facility authorized? To what extent? What controls?
- What are the procedures for access to closed or restricted areas?
- Are there long-term visitors? If so, what procedures are in effect for the handling and protection of classified or sensitive proprietary information and materials?
- What are the procedures for contractors and subcontractors? Are they built into the contracts?
- Are there contractors or consultants on the program or project? If so, is there any conflict of interest?

What are the procedures for:

- Reporting of foreign travel?
- Public release of information relating to the program or project? How is it handled? Is the security department and/or risk manager involved in ensuring that sensitive information is not lost?
- The reporting of adverse information? How is it handled?
- How are employees (and contractors) handled, and if termination is for cause, what procedures are in place to ensure that valuable information is not lost?
- Is there a badge identification system in effect?
- Is the badge coded for access to various sensitive or restricted areas?
- Is there accounting for the badge?
- What are the procedures for badge safeguarding?

- Does the organization, program, or project have appropriate support from the Security Office, including the provision for providing recurring and specialized security education, training, and motivation programs to all affected employees?

How is information (classified, sensitive unclassified, proprietary) protected:

- In security containers? How were they obtained, and where from?
- When are lock combinations changed?
- What are the procedures when containers are moved?
- Who has access to the containers?
- Who changes the combinations?
- How is need-to-know determined for employees and visitors?

Does the program or project involve foreign contracts, foreign contacts, overseas work, foreign military, or other aspects of international programs? Is the Department of Defense, Department of Commerce, or the Department of State involved in identifying critical information, technology, processes, procedures, and materials that may have export restrictions placed upon them?

- Is there any unauthorized material (i.e., bootleg)?
- How was it received? Was it hand-carried into the facility?
- What was the reason for obtaining it?
- Are there other copies? Who has them? Do other facilities of the project have copies?
- Has such material been placed into some accountability process, and is it being properly safeguarded?
- Was it reproduced? How many copies? What happened to them?

You have now read through and considered the many aspects of the risk management program. Appendix A, which follows immediately, will allow you, through a case study composed of several practical exercises, the use of this gained knowledge in a practice situation. You have the abilities—otherwise, you would not have obtained this book for the knowledge it contains—and now can put them into effect. You don't have to recall everything from memory; that is what the book is for—to refresh your memory and ensure you follow through the various steps. Also, you have the author's e-mail address where you can post questions, comments, concerns; and your own thoughts, experiences, and—if desired—summaries of your own risk analyses for comment. I wish you well in the wonderful and challenging world of risk management.

Risk Management Case Study and Practical Exercises

INTRODUCTION TO THE CASE STUDY

Please take some time to carefully read the case study introductory materials. The materials provide you with some background resources necessary to successfully complete the various practical exercises within the case study.

The case study has been divided into the areas relating to the various book chapters containing the steps of the risk management process. The practical exercises allow you the opportunity to understand *and apply* the appropriate principles and practices. As such, the case study is designed to provide you with a working understanding of the practicalities necessary for applying the analytical risk management methodology. The goal of the case study is to help you to properly apply the risk process when performing risk management activities back at your organization.

Each part of the practical exercise contains the objectives for that exercise, the directions you will need to follow, and all of the materials necessary for completion. Thus, the practical exercises allow you the opportunity to apply the knowledge gained to accomplish the skill objectives listed below.

Objectives

When given a scenario involving risk, the reader will be able to:

1. Identify assets requiring protection and related undesirable events in each of the following categories:
   a. Information
   b. Equipment
   c. Facilities

      d. Personnel
      e. Activities

2. Determine the impact, threat, vulnerability, and risk levels related to undesirable events.
3. Identify countermeasure options that could be used to protect these assets.
4. Develop a presentation—structured around the case study, emphasizing the process methodology used, data determination, analysis criterion and sensitivity levels, countermeasure options, recommendations, and your rationale—for delivery to the organizational decision-makers.

The case study you will be using has been constructed around a contractor facility that has received a Government contract for research and development of a DoD project. Various items of information have been included to assist in the successful completion of the various portions of the case study.

To further simulate the case study, "pretend" that government classified information has been included. Were this a real government project, a certain amount of classified information would be made available to the government contractor. For readers who do not anticipate (now or in the future) ever having to deal with government classified, view the materials as "sensitive proprietary information of a private company." These materials have been created to give you a "flavor" as to areas of concern and the analytical processes and research required for any risk management endeavor you may undertake in the future.

The case study materials will include:

- Case Study background
- Contracted System General Description
- Simulated classified information
- Simulated security classification guide for the case study project
- E. F. Electronics, Inc. (the contractor): organizational, personnel, and facility background
- Practical Exercises 1–5
- Various forms for each Practical Exercise (PE)
- Physical security countermeasures listing
- Security costs breakdown sheets
- The framework for estimating security costs

In this case study, you should be able to stimulate your thinking, bring out your analytical abilities, and allow yourself to demonstrate your skills in developing a proper risk analysis leading to a successful conclusion, resulting in the selection and presentation of several viable risk options that would be presented to senior management.

CASE STUDY SCENARIO

Background

The executive leadership of your company, E. F. Electronics, Inc., recently obtained a new Government contract to design, develop, and manufacture a number of highly sophisticated communication satellites for the U.S. Government. Within this contract there will also be a series of specialized studies conducted. The contractor, E. F. Electronics, Inc., has selected their Anytown plant and the development and manufacturing site for the contract.

After the decision was made to use this plant, and considerable resources were invested in the revitalization of the plant, it was learned through some business magazines, newspapers, and also various reports (none over five years old) that from recent economic conditions, criminal activities, and political activists in the area, the plant may be at risk of becoming a potential target.

The Director for Planning and Operations has formed a Risk Management (RM) Group and tasked *your* RM team to determine the risk factors at this site, providing the results to the senior management decision-makers. You have a short time-frame to accomplish this most important task, but have the advantage of knowing there are other individuals and organizations collecting information in support of the project.

About E. F. Electronics, Inc.

E. F. Electronics, Inc. is a long-time Government contractor in a variety of areas, having worked with the Department of Defense, the Intelligence Community, and the Department of Commerce in the past. It is a minority-owned business, formerly specializing in petrochemical production, with various subelement fluids being generated also for commercial and military applications. E. F. Electronics is also deeply involved in advanced state-of-the-art R&D within the electronics and optics fields. It is currently a world recognized leader in photo-optic design and development.

E. F. Electronics maintains a small Government contracts office in Washington, D.C., and has sent a letter to the facility management directing the plant to prepare for full R&D and production of the satellites under the new contract. A note in the letter indicated that the potential for a long-term follow-on contract is very possible.

E. F. Electronics has a dedicated security office at Anytown. Personnel are familiar with and closely follow the U.S. Government requirements. Additionally, the project security classification guide (SCG) and DD Form 254 have been carefully studied. The facility meets all DoD and U.S. Government requirements. The facility is approved for classified storage, holding a Secret level facility clearance. All project personnel will have access up to the Secret level.

Anytown R&D/Manufacturing Site

The Anytown site was selected for the contract because it is very accessible to the major highway system for transport of the satellite to the launch site. Also, it is reasonably close (in terms of travel time) to Washington, D.C. In this regard, it is far enough away to be removed from the hectic and stressful conditions surrounding a major industrial area, but still provides reasonable access to local cities, as well as the regional airport that has direct flights to Washington, D.C., to Southern Florida, and the Yuma, Arizona Proving Grounds.

Anytown was initially a large petrochemical site, but, over the years, the company had downsized, selling off portions of its property to other entities. While a full one-third of the site has been converted by the Kasko Oil Company, a small chemical plant is still owned and operated by E. F. Electronics, Inc. Currently, the site is shared with three other organizations:

1. The Kasko Oil Company regional distribution center purchased and occupies slightly over one-third of the original site.
2. J-Soft computer design recently leased the second floor of the former plans building. A part of the third floor was also leased to be used for storage and testing of their equipment. J-Soft is a subsidiary of the Kazimara Electronics Company of Japan. This is but one of several J-Soft locations throughout the United States, others being located in Albuquerque, NM, and the Silicon Valley area of southern California. The third floor has recently received a lot of specialized electronic equipment over the past two weeks. Because of the sensitivity of J-Soft design efforts, they have installed their own interior and perimeter alarm system, and brought in their own company security guard force from Japan.
3. The Wanker County Environmental Coalition (WEC) leases a small part of the third floor overlooking the exterior fence. The rest of the floor belongs to J-Soft.
4. The first floor houses an E. F. Electronics-owned restaurant, which is open to all E. F. Electronics, Kasko, J-Soft, and WEC personnel. It also is available to people from off-site. Having excellent food fare and very reasonable prices, it is heavily frequented by employees of all the companies on the site, in addition to the public.

E. F. Electronics Project Activities

E. F. Electronics intends to store its project working papers and Government furnished information in GSA approved security containers and will be using personal computer (PC) systems. Offices have been set up in part of the R&D building for storage. E. F. Electronics will be storing sensitive classified Government documents on the second floor of the building. It is vital that this information remain in a securely protected area and not be stolen or leaked. These official Government documents would also be considered very valuable to international businesses and possibly foreign governments, not to mention other U.S. businesses, for making decisions and considering potential products that have an extremely high market value.

The facility personnel will generally work an eight-hour day from Monday to Friday, but could be called in on weekends if significant events occurred or when project deadlines are fast approaching. The R&D, computer, and electronics teams tend to work a couple of hours overtime most days. Computer personnel, in particular, work at all hours, taking breaks when necessary, in the development of various programs. Typically, on evenings and weekends, there are only computer personnel present, and then only four to seven of them.

Each day (less on weekends) between 4:00 P.M. and 10:00 P.M., a locally contracted cleaning crew reports to building 4 and receives a cleaning crew badge and cleans buildings 4 and 4A. The crew chief vouches for all personnel each day. Trash is taken to a contractor-furnished recycling truck where it is then transported to a recycling center each evening by one of the cleaning crew. All other E. F. Electronics buildings are cleaned after buildings 4 and 4A are completed (less the J-Soft area).

Anytown Community and Surrounding Area

The socioeconomic status of the residents in the greater Anytown community has been declining for several years because newer business parks have been constructed closer to the larger cities that are more convenient for big businesses. Many of the more successful businesses in the area have relocated there, forcing numerous residents of Anytown into unemployment.

The current unemployment rate is 10 percent. Crime is on the increase. Many of the younger residents are unemployed, frustrated, and angry and have become involved in illegal activities. The community is generally not considered a highly desirable place to live anymore, although some of the better sections of the area are still in good condition. During daylight hours numerous small businesses still operate on slim margins. Many workers consider themselves safe, but know better than to venture into some parts of Anytown at night. The local businesses only employ 60 percent of the residents of working age. Wages are low and most jobs are for unskilled workers, with skilled workers obtained through professional organizations, personal contacts, and major city newspaper advertising for specific skills required.

Local politicians have promised to fight crime and increase employment opportunities for local residents, however the trends have been moving in the opposite direction in both these areas for some time.

E. F. ELECTRONICS PROJECT STAFF

E. F. Electronics has assigned 300-350 employees to work at the Anytown facility. There is a diverse mix of people, as follows.

There is a ten-member project management team led by Jerry Kazalinski. Kazalinski and this team will direct the project through its various phases. These are the most essential employees from start to end of the four-year contract.

Information has been extracted from files concerning several pertinent personnel on the project management team. These personnel profiles were identified as being of possible concern and interest to the risk management team. The following pages provides relevant information.

Other project employees will include the administrative staff for the various departments, product engineers, the computer programmers and analysts, electronic design and manufacturing personnel, and the machinery and assembly staff.

Project Team Personnel Profiles

Jerry Kazalinski, a principle with E. F. Electronics, has a B.A. degree from the University of Virginia (UVA) in economics (1965) and a Ph.D. in Business Administration from Columbia University. He worked for three years for the management consulting firm of Connors, Owens & Wilson early in his career, as a member of the economic policy division, where he prepared numerous research studies for Government clients. He has worked over the last nine years as Director of Government Programs for E. F. Electronics, Inc. Dr. Kazalinski will lead the project team.

Kim Lee Armstrong, also a principle in E. F. Electronics, will work in support of Jerry Kazalinski. Ms. Armstrong has a B.A. in business from Pennsylvania State University ("Penn State") and an M.B.A. from the Wharton Business School (1982). She was born in Japan, the daughter of American missionaries, but came to the United States after her high school graduation. She considers herself a Japanese-American in terms of the cultural heritage she learned while in Japan. She belongs to the national Japanese-American Cultural Friendship Society, and works closely with Japanese business personnel who visit the mid-Atlantic region of the United States. Ms. Armstrong is beginning to experience financial difficulties and has been having an increasingly difficult time keeping up with heavy credit debts. She is usually one month behind in her mortgage, but so far has managed to keep making this important payment. Ms. Armstrong realizes that she is overextended financially, but does not know how to solve her problems. Her husband cannot work due to a physical disability that requires continued monthly treatments, including a lot of physical therapy.

Selvinii Bavnkaar is the Chief Operations Officer, and earned a double degree from Princeton University in 1970, a B.A. in literature and a B.S. in optical laser electronics. He was selected to lead E. F. Electronics Industry's operations team for the satellite project because of its vital importance to the growth and stability of the company. Mr. Kazalinski, who is heading up the E. F. Electronics business development activities, and all other project team members, will report to Mr. Bavnkaar. Mr. Bavnkaar has been on the "fast track" ever since he joined E. F. Electronics, Inc. in 1982. He climbed to the position of Deputy Chief of Operations Officer after only nine years. Born in New Delhi, India, he is a naturalized U.S. citizen. Bavnkaar was married for several years between graduation from college until shortly after joining E. F. Electronics, Inc., when his marriage ended in a bitter divorce. He told colleagues that he had never remarried because his career was so important that he did not have time for any "extra baggage." This is only the second time that he has led such a major project. He likes to take mini-vacations around the United States, and always takes a two-week vacation to India each year to visit former college friends and business people in New Delhi. It has been noted recently that he has somewhat expensive tastes in automobiles and just acquired a lovely mansion outside of town, which has three servants and a full-time gardener.

Tom Ling, the Assistant Deputy Chief of Operations Officer, earned a B.A. in Psychology from North Carolina State in 1973. His whole career has been with E. F. Electronics, Inc. He has specialized in kicking off major projects and has successfully formed project teams for other more daring and innovative developmental ventures for E. F. Electronics, Inc. He is an expert in handling major project operations and prides himself on obtaining very sensitive business information that has given E. F. Electronics, Inc. a competitive edge. He feels that he should have been selected as the COO to head this project and believes that Selvinii Bavnkaar, although competent, doesn't have the "experience" to lead this critical project. He feels that Mr. Bavnkaar's selection has more to do with his Ivy-league education than his experience in the job market. He wouldn't mind seeing Bavnkaar trip up, since this would give him an opportunity to shine by salvaging the entire project.

PROJECT EQUIPMENT

The E. F. Electronics management team will require eight to ten networked personal computers and several laptops to perform the research design and development aspects of the satellite program, in addition to developing appropriate hardware and software that will be included within the satellite. Additional computers and software will be used by other divisions within the project. All in all, some sixty to eighty computers will be in use. The management team computers will comprise a small network, but the rest will be also be linked into a second networked system. The computers were purchased through J-Soft at excellent below market prices. (The E. F. Electronics contract requires J-Soft to have personnel available within an hour to resolve any hardware/software problems. Currently, DSS (Defense Security Service) is looking at J-Soft, concerned about the FOCI issue. (FOCI is foreign ownership, control or influence, and is of great concern where government classified, or sensitive information, or where advanced technology is concerned. It is necessary to ensure that businesses whose leadership—owned, controlled, or influenced—is foreign in nature, is not in a position to use our information and/or technology to their advantage and to the U.S. Governments detriment. As such, where there is a FOCI issue involved in a government contract, approvals and controls must be in place to limit their access to such information and technologies.) It is expected that the J-Soft contract will be dropped and a DSS-approved vendor will be selected to replace them. J-Soft are unaware of the DSS FOCI issue at the present.)

Specialized optical devices will also be computer-designed for the project. Other standard office equipment, such as telephones, photocopies, fax machines, and so forth, will also be required. E. F. Electronics has two paper shredders (1976 models) that can be used to shred official Government and proprietary information that is no longer needed for the project.

E. F. ELECTRONICS FACILITY SECURITY

Currently the Anytown facility has security in place. About eighty E. F. Electronics company employees are being brought in from other facilities for this sensitive classified Government project. Those personnel have worked on previous Government contracts and have current valid Secret security clearance. These positions are in addition to others that will be filled through regional newspaper and local hiring.

The security guard force at the facility main gate are concerned mostly about ensuring that vehicles entering on business have a company issued automobile decal; if not, individuals are directed to visitor parking behind the administrative building. Other entrance gate security personnel provide advice and directions to visitors. With several entrances for other organizations on the site, security will remain somewhat low at entranceways. Also, E. F. Electronics cannot deny access to individuals visiting other organizations or going to the restaurant.

The project buildings each have a security guard at their main entrance desk. All personnel must wear the E. F. Electronics Company Badge. All personnel working under the contract have a current Secret security clearance. The security guard maintains a personnel clearance roster for access. All visitors are escorted, whether or not they have a clearance. There is a roving guard at all times in buildings 4 and 4A.

In addition to the buildings 4 and 4A guards, there are two at the main gate to E. F. Electronics, Inc., and one at of the other rear gates to monitor those access points that are mostly used by employees from companies other than E. F. Electronics. The Guard force has six other personnel during the day shift, and three more for the evening, night, and weekend shifts.

The entire E. F. Electronics property was alarmed, but this was over twenty-five years ago. Within the past year E. F. Electronics has installed an alarm system that uses card reader/PIN technology for buildings 4 and 4A. These buildings also have door and window contacts, a series of heat and water sensors in the manufacturing area, and motion detectors in the first floor hallways pointed towards the entrance doors to both buildings. The system is monitored in the E. F. Electronics security office. Response time to an activated sensor is two to three minutes from the continually roving patrol guards for 4 and 4A. With radio backup, other security force personnel can be at an incident site within five minutes.

The E. F. Electronics fire department can respond immediately to any incident. It has three trucks, an ambulance, and twelve qualified personnel on each shift. All are EMT (Emergency Medical Technician) trained.

CONTRACTED SYSTEM GENERAL DESCRIPTION

The following information was extracted from the DoD contract with E. F. Electronics, Inc. Also, information concerning the threat, national threat issues, and critical technologies relative to the project have been included below.

Background

The world's military-political situation has become increasingly volatile and unpredictable. The rivalry between the former East-West superpowers that set the context for nearly all other conflicts has ended, and in its place new alliances have formed. The result is a world where the dual threats of Soviet expansion and nuclear holocaust have been replaced with a continuum of threats ranging from terrorism and regional conflict to conventional war.

The threat continuum has unquestionably been expanded. For example:

- The "nuclear club" membership has been expanded by three former republics of the Soviet Union who inherited nuclear weapons. In addition, other previously nonnuclear nations—India and Pakistan in particular—have recently developed and tested nuclear weapons.

- The opportunity for "outlaw" organizations (e.g., terrorist groups and criminal organizations) to obtain nuclear weapons has increased due to a lessening, or elimination in some cases, of control formerly exercised by Moscow for the central Soviet Government. The theft and sale of nuclear materials to rogue nations or transnational terrorist groups is now a very real possibility. Within the past two years, several incidents of nuclear materials being smuggled into western Europe have been detected and the perpetrators caught.

The U.S. Army and Air Force, in conjunction with other National agencies, have perceived that a technology breakthrough in the area of satellite construction, controls, capabilities, and reentry vehicle characteristics has presented a means to take a quantum leap forward in U.S. capability to deliver precision strikes. Participants in this program strategy, and also the Navy, and Defense Intelligence Agency (DIA), have also identified rapid technological advances in C^3I (Command, Control, Communications, and Intelligence) systems and precision-guided munitions.

Satellite Features.   The satellites feature the use of a multisensor performance with real-time synchronic capability, allowing the satellite to be a platform for observation and deployment of a variety of precision-guided weapons to be used against targets on the Earth's surface. Intelligence collection and targeting support is also provided by a space-based multisensor intelligence collection platform.

System Features.   The system features include twenty-four-hour, all-weather look-down capability for all included sensors for observation, photo-reconnaissance, and intelligence-gathering, when ordered by the National Command Authority (NCA).The system provides visible detail to a range of four meters. The unit is self-contained with a mini-reactor. The system will use UHF, VHF, and advance meteor burst communications for receiving and transmission of data.

Militarily Critical Technologies.

- Expertise to design, develop, and produce specific signature-reducing materials and structures.
- UHF, VHF, and AMB transceivers.
- Use of artificial intelligence in design, guidance computers, and associated proprietary software.
- Advanced minireactor design and shielding.

Critical Elements of Information.

- Use of a multiperformance capability. The orbiting satellite is a platform for observation and deployment of a variety of weaponry.
- Unit is self-contained with a minireactor using advanced design and shielding.
- Use of artificial intelligence in design, guidance computers, and associated proprietary software.

National Security Threat Issues

Initial threats would result from a reduced capability to preempt, defuse, or respond to an overseas crisis. The U.S. no longer has a robust capability to take swift action without the involvement of troops.

The loss of overseas bases, reduced troop forces, and limited supplies and materials for a sustained battle are also somewhat limited. These elements, plus the shifting international political climate, necessitates that under certain circumstances it would be unacceptable for military involvement to be traceable back to the United States.

Threats to E. F. Electronics Facility

Any initial threats to E. F. Electronics R&D/production facilities are similar to those facing any other advanced technological research and/or production facility.

When the announcement of this contract by *Commerce Business Daily* (CBD) appears within two weeks, the threat potential will probably rise. The concerns here are that various international organizations and/or companies, with or without their governments' support, are expected to target E. F. Electronics, Inc. to obtain early-on data as to specific technologies, electronics, computer designed programs, weaponry, communications, and other items. It is expected that personnel will also be targeted, since E. F. Electronics has been advertising through technology and business trade magazines for specialized personnel. Such advertising provided interesting reading for the uninitiated, not to mention personnel having an interest from an intelligence or advanced technology standpoint.

There is a significant danger that a potentially hostile country or other potential adversary nation might react to the discovery of this system by attempting to develop a similar system of their own. No other country is currently capable of fielding a system with all the characteristics of this particular satellite platform. A number of countries, however, are capable of using existing satellite technology to field a crude, but less robust version.

Refer to the attached Intelligence Letter Report, which can provide more detailed information on the Foreign Intelligence Threat.

> **THIS NATIONAL DEFENSE DOCUMENT IS CLASSIFIED SECRET FOR TRAINING ONLY—ACTUALLY UNCLASSIFIED**

SUBJECT: Intelligence Letter Report—Foreign Intelligence Threat

1. Background. A mission need was established to address required advanced design satellite capabilities. The need was to acquire, maintain, and improve a capability to deliver a variety of payloads from an airborne platform. This system must respond to a crisis worldwide within four hours of National Command Authority decision.

2. The U.S. Army Space and Strategic Defense Command (USASSDC), Huntsville, Alabama, is monitoring two concurrent contract efforts: Space Products Corporation, Beverton, Oregon, and E. F. Electronics, Inc., Anytown, YourState. This report will focus on E. F. Electronics, Inc., which has been awarded the satellite development and manufacturing contract, and is expected to be recommended for continuation of a follow-on contract. This report provides a preliminary Foreign Intelligence Threat Report.

3. General. While preliminary evaluations show no direct evidence of specific targeting of program, the threat environment is rated as a high level. This level is assigned due largely to the fact that advanced weapons systems are traditionally rated as a top priority for Foreign Intelligence Service (FIS) collection efforts.

4. Methodology. This report was developed through an evaluation of open source literature, historical intelligence files, and known foreign intelligence collection effort priorities.

5. HUMINT. The threat from human intelligence collection sources is assessed as HIGH. While no direct targeting of E. F. Electronics, Inc. is known to exist, foreign intelligence agents have sufficient opportunity and access to program locations. Expanded media coverage of this viable contract assures that the E. F. Electronics, Inc. project is a likely collection source.

   a. Priority Intelligence Requirements. Known priorities that may affect the effort include:
      — information on satellite systems with military applications
      — integration and assembly features
      — advanced munitions
      — technical manuals on prototype and major weapon systems

    b. Foreign Intelligence Collectors. Known FIS (Foreign Intelligence Service) collectors have given U.S. research and development (R&D) their first collection priority. In addition:
- FIS agents (Russia, India, Japan, and Korea) have unimpeded access to several program locations to include the prime contractor;
- loosening of travel restrictions by the U.S. Government has eliminated several barriers to travel and has made it more difficult to track possible intelligence collection agents;
- the FBI estimates that 30 to 45 percent of official foreign mission personnel from the former Warsaw Pact and Third World countries have intelligence backgrounds;
- increased competitiveness for state-of-the-art technologies dictates that there is a large presence of known FIS collectors at trade shows and conferences; and
- the collection of economic intelligence is prevalent among foreign countries (witness the recent exposure of French intelligence agents targeting U.S. business people). The FBI has stated there has been a large surge in foreign economic espionage in the United States during the last twelve months.

    c. Official Travel. All work areas associated with this project are well traveled, affording collection opportunities through easy highway access. Permanently assigned foreign embassy, mission, and consulate staff members were required to notify and receive permission from the Department of State prior to travel outside a specific radius. The location of E. F. Electronics, Inc. is within the specified radius.

    d. Hostile Establishments. There are no known hostile establishments in the Anytown, YourState area that could possibly pose a HUMINT threat.

6. LITINT. Much of the intelligence collection in the area of literature intelligence (LITINT) is performed through surveys of open source literature and through exploration and exploitation of the Internet via online resources. Within the past five years, volumes of materials have been published relating to:
- low observable technology
- Air Force sponsored R&D efforts
- state-of-the-art missile and space technology
- strategic missile systems
- space weapons systems

7. IMINT. Imagery intelligence (IMINT) can be gathered either through space-borne collectors, overhead flights, or hand-held cameras. A significant threat exists during open-air testing due to the exposure to prepositioned collection systems. While in a contained environment, the primary threat will be from hand-held devices. Treaty compliance

inspections and visits also present an imagery threat, particularly the Open Skies overflights.

8.   SIGINT. Signal and communications intelligence collection may be direct threats to the development of the project satellites.

    a.   Ground-based SIGINT will focus primarily on the microwave links found in strategic test scenarios at the contractors' locations. Major collection points have also been found in Washington, D.C., San Francisco, New York, and Yuma, Arizona.

    b.   Space Borne Platforms. Satellite communications are easily intercepted.

    c.   Collection monitoring from off-shore surveillance is predominantly from the Russian Auxiliary General Intelligence (AGI) ships frequenting both East and West coasts. Since the primary contractor and USASSDC are highly susceptible to having their communications electronically monitored, this is assessed as a high threat environment.

    d.   A SIGINT threat also arises from the ease in which economic competitors can monitor the signals and communications of E. F. Electronics, Inc. using off-the-shelf technology.

9.   Conclusion. The project resides in a HIGH threat environment; however, *no known targeting by FIS* <u>*can be documented*</u> *at this time.*

    a.   HUMINT and SIGINT are the primary threats to the program due to the accessibility of information and collection opportunities, as well as a traditional high level of interest in the critical elements of the program from friend and foe alike.

    b.   No open source literature was found detailing specific project development. Several articles highlighted U.S. Army and U.S. Air Force work in space-based systems.

10.   Point of contact is Aimee B. Goode, Satellite Project Development Office.

THIS NATIONAL DEFENSE DOCUMENT IS CLASSIFIED SECRET FOR TRAINING ONLY—ACTUALLY UNCLASSIFIED

Aeronautical Systems Division
Department of Defense Satellite Office
Anytown, ThisState 00000

*****DATE*****

Security Classification Guide
for
Advanced Satellite Project

Applicability: This guidance applies only to the above stated satellite project.

Scope: The guidance provided in this document relates only to this project.

INFORMATION REVEALING	CLASSIFICATION
1. General Information revealing the fact that:	
a. Program description.	C
b. Specific capabilities, availability, and mission of planned operational systems.	S
c. General capabilities, availability, and mission of planned operational systems.	S
2. Communications Links:	
a. The fact that there are three different transmission/receiving capabilities with specific bandwidths.	S
b. The fact that the satellite uses various communication sensors.	S
c. The fact that communication transmissions are encrypted.	U
d. Company project number or contract numbers.	U
e. A list of contractors and/or subcontractors associated with the satellite and application to a military system.	U
3. Design and Specifications:	
a. External view.	U
b. Weights, power, size, other physical parameters that did not reveal satellite vulnerabilities.	C
c. Design or test information which reveal satellite vulnerabilities.	S
d. General design concept for multiple modules *excluding* any electrical or electronic features	U
e. Transmitted or received signal amplitudes and frequency ranges.	C
4. Launch program:	
a. Launch locations	U
b. Launch dates	C (U after launch)
c. Test flight objectives/results (general or specific)	C
5. Design & Manufacturing Concepts and Techniques:	
a. Physical principles associated with specific techniques	C
b. Detailed designs	S
c. Demonstration data analysis &/or performance reports	S
d. Manufacturing (processing or operating) techniques that represent an advance in the state-of-the-art technology.	S
6. Satellite system Computer Codes	
a. If data has been encrypted	U
b. Encryption codes, data, process, etc.	S
c. Calculation routines implementing mathematical models.	U
d. Computer codes that are generic and based on classical, unclassified physics laws.	U

> **THIS NATIONAL DEFENSE DOCUMENT IS CLASSIFIED SECRET FOR TRAINING ONLY—ACTUALLY UNCLASSIFIED**

PRACTICAL EXERCISE #1

Purpose: This three-part exercise is designed to *identify and prioritize assets* that need protection.

Part 1A: Critical Asset Identification

In each of the categories listed below, identify critical assets in need of protection by means of security countermeasures:

a.   Activities
b.   Information
c.   Equipment
d.   Facilities
e.   Personnel

Directions: Review the scenario. Make a list of the assets that E. F. Electronics, Inc. will need to protect. Your first priority is to identify assets in actual need of protection; there may, though, be other assets that could or should require some level of protection outside the typical protection provided for any organization, government or private.

ASSET ASSESSMENT
Personnel
Information
Equipment
Facilities
Activities

Part 1B: Undesirable Events Relating to Critical Assets

Objective: To identify potential undesirable events that could cause loss or damage to the assets identified in part 1A.

Directions: Use the information on critical assets developed in Part 1A, and review the updated list of assets and the memoranda on the pages that follow. Identify potential undesirable events that could cause loss or damage to the assets identified. Use the Impact Assessment Chart provided to list these events for each asset.

Dated three weeks ago

MEMORANDUM FOR:	Risk Management Group
FROM:	Robert K. Leister, II, President,
	E. F. Electronics Inc. — Anytown
SUBJECT:	Security Requirements for the Anytown
	Satellite Project

We recently won the contract order with the Department of Defense to provide a series of satellites. This contract is valued at over $135,000,000 during the next four years. It represents a significant accomplishment for our company and, with the potential for an add-on (continuing) contract, we foresee a 35% increase in the size of our defense operations. Spin-offs from the contract into the commercial sector may well boost the increase upwards to 60%.

Please assess the risk levels of the various threats to our assets at the Anytown site, determine the risks associated with our new operation, develop a series of security countermeasure options, and recommend a single option. The Board of Directors for E. F. Electronics, Inc. requires a thorough review of the threats, vulnerabilities, and risks present in our new operation at Anytown.

As you may have already heard, the local area is somewhat unstable and, during the initial contract period, I do not foresee it becoming much better. Threats and known criminal activity and a certain amount of politically-motivated violence against local, much less major business personnel and corporations, are increasing. I have made arrangements to obtain a broad range of regional social, political, and economic information, a majority of which is known only to select members of the regional Governments and law enforcement personnel. Please note that it is imperative that we protect our investment and protect the assets we will have at the Anytown facility.

The project administrative office will be located in the main administration building just inside the front gate (to the left) at Anytown. I will forward a floor plan to you shortly. In the meantime, please look over the facility and note the co-located companies, of which Kasko Oil owns their property (purchased a number of years ago from E. F. Electronics), while all others have long-term rental agreements.

Three members of the project team will be focusing on new business development (those spin-offs I mentioned earlier) and responding to requests for proposals. The remaining members will perform project oversight in addition to several classified or sensitive studies as called for under our new contract.

Attached is a copy of a letter I think you should review.

Robert L. Bergstrom
E. F. Electronics, Inc.
3211 Industry Drive
Anytown, YourState
Robert K. Leister, II, *President*
John Amos, *Ph.D., Principle*
Ranni Bavnkaar, *M.B.A., Principle*

Dr. J. Chavden
Micro-Electro-Optic Systems, Inc.

Dear Dr. Chavden:

E. F. Electronics, Inc., a petrochemical company for over thirty years, has, during the past decade, expanded into several new fields that now involve major Governmental contracts. We recently won a contract to provide a number of specialized satellites and several studies of a sensitive and classified nature to the Department of Defense.

We have converted and expanded our Anytown site, with a large amount of specialized equipment, some of which came from Micro-Electro-Optic Systems, Inc. At this juncture, we will be sub-contracting with you and others to provide some specialized electronics and computer expertise in support of this new contract. I have laid the groundwork for this with Mr. Powers of your contracts department, and he is in possession of the final contract, which I will be down to sign next week.

Anytown is but one of several sites that we have in mind for Government contract work; others will be opened at the beginning of the next calendar year, thus allowing for a expanding business base for product R&D and various studies. As I had mentioned to Mr. Powers, your company's past performance is such that we intend to work exclusively with you in a variety of capacities. We will be opening a branch office somewhere in the Washington, D.C. area, probably in the northwest area, but quite possibly in Silver Spring. I would like to meet with you personally next week to learn of any major projects or contracts that you plan during the next several years that could impact on our doing business together.

Yours very truly,

_____

IMPACT ASSESSMENT CHART

Critical Assets	Potential Undesirable Events	Impact Level
Information		
Equipment		
Facilities		
Personnel		
Activities		

Part 1C: Critical Asset Loss Impact

Objective: Estimate the impact of the loss of or damage to the assets identified in Part 1A.

Directions: Use all the information on critical assets and undesirable events developed in Parts 1A and 1B. Also, review Job Aid 1: Asset Assessment (see below). Consider the consequence of each undesirable event and rate the impact on the company if the event were to occur. Determine whether the impact level is critical, high, medium, or low. Use the impact rating criteria in Job Aid 1 as the basis for your decisions.

Materials Needed: Information and forms from Parts 1A and 1B, Job Aid 1: Asset Assessment, and the reporting form.

JOB AID I: ASSET ASSESSMENT

To determine the **impact level**, answer the following three questions:

1. Could significant damage to national security or loss/injury to human life occur as a result of this event?
2. Could ongoing operations be seriously impaired/halted?
3. Could costly equipment or facilities be damaged or lost?

Use the answers to these questions and the matrix below to determine the impact level. This decision matrix demonstrates an approach that can be used to help make judgments regarding impacts. There are six general types of impacts identified across the top of the matrix. The ratings, defined in the chart below, are rough relative estimates and can be used when a monetary impact assessment is not required, or is too difficult to determine.

1	2	3	4	5	6	
Loss or Injury to Human Life	Loss of Top Secret or Secret	Loss of Confidential Data	Loss of Sensitive Unclassified Data	Impaired or Halted Operations	Damage or Loss to Costly Property	Overall Impact Level
YES	Yes/No	Yes/No	Yes/No	Yes/No	Yes/No	Critical/ High
No	**YES**	Yes/No	Yes/No	Yes/No	Yes/No	High
No	Yes/No	**YES**	Yes/No	YES	Yes/No	High
No	Yes/No	Yes/No	**YES**	YES	Yes/No	High
No	No	No	No	**YES**	Yes/No	Medium
No	No	No	No	Yes/No	**YES**	Medium
No	No	No	No	No	No	Low

Impact Rating Criteria

Critical—Indicates that compromise to the assets targeted would have grave consequences leading to the loss of life or serious injury to people.

High—Indicates that a compromise to assets would have serious consequences resulting in the loss of classified or highly sensitive data that could impair operations affecting national interests for an indefinite amount of time.

Medium—Indicates that a compromise to the assets would have moderate consequences resulting in the loss of confidential, sensitive data, or costly equipment/ property that would impair operations affecting national interests for a limited period of time.

Low—Indicates little or no impact on human life or the continuation of operations affecting national security or national interests.

IMPACT ASSESSMENT CHART

Critical Assets	Potential Undesirable Events	Consequence of Event	Impact Level
Information			
Equipment			
Facilities			
Personnel			
Activities			

PRACTICAL EXERCISE #2

Purpose: This two-part exercise is designed *to identify threat sources, specific threats, and the threat level* for each asset and undesirable event identified in Practical Exercise 1.

Part 2A: Identifying Potential Threats to Critical Assets

Objective: Determine the source of the threat and specific threats to critical assets.

Directions: Read the information presented on the pages that follow, including:

A memorandum for the Risk Management Group from the president of E. F. Electronics, Inc.

Copies of cables.

Newspaper clippings.

Also review the profiles of the project employees provided in the Case Study scenario and any additional threat information provided.

Using all the available information, identify the (a) threat category and (b) specific threats related to each asset and undesirable event identified in Practical Exercise 1. Make a list of specific threats within each category. Use the charts provided to organize the information on insider, terrorist, foreign intelligence service (FIS), and criminal threat according to the adversary's intent, capability, and history.

Suggestion: Before starting the exercise, review previously provided information that applies to this exercise.

Materials Needed: Information and forms used in Practical Exercise 1; memoranda, cables, newspaper clippings, employee profiles, Threat Assessment Chart, and any other information provided.

(Dated 30 days ago)

Memorandum for:	Risk Management Group
FROM:	Robert K. Leister, II,
	President, E. F. Electronics, Inc.
SUBJECT:	Anytown Risk Management

The Board of Directors is demanding information about our exposure to risk in opening the Anytown facility. They are considering scrubbing the entire project at the facility and moving to one in the midwest that—while it is secure—would cost E. F. Electronics, Inc. an inordinate amount of funds to either rent long-term or purchase outright. I think it would be best if you could send me weekly updates on the progress your team is making as you conduct the risk assessment. Specifically, I plan to brief the board on the threats we anticipate, the level of each threat, and our level of vulnerability to the specific risks we face.

Attached are some items of information that recently were provided by our U.S. Government contracting liaison. I had previously contacted both of the organizations concerned to see if they could be of any help. This is all they sent me. I have also enclosed a photocopy of a newspaper clipping my secretary saw in this morning's paper. This information should help in your assessment of the threat environment.

Keep me appraised!

/s/

Robert K. Leister, II

Attachments
RKL/cr

REUTERS NEWS SERVICE

Page: 0079

(DATED LAST TUESDAY)

FM RNS, FIELDS DISTRICT, YOURSTATE

SERIAL: IN2307155396

BODY:

COUNTRY: UNITED STATES

SUBJ: CRIMINAL ACTIVITIES AGAINST BUSINESS; THIRD TAKE — UPDATE

TEXT:

DURING THE PAST WEEK YOURSTATE TELEVISION REPORTED THE FOLLOWING EVENTS:

TWO AMERICAN BUSINESSMEN, JOHN C. CARPENTER AND HARRY RASHAD, WERE ABDUCTED BY A CRIMINAL ORGANIZATION IN THE CORDOVA SUBURB NEAR SULFER SPRINGS, YOURSTATE. THE ORGANIZATION IS BELIEVED TO BE COMPOSED OF INDIVIDUALS IDENTIFIED IN THE PAST AS WORKING WITH SEVERAL UNDERWORLD CRIMINAL ELEMENTS TIED TO PREVIOUS THEFTS OF HIGH-TECH MATERIALS AND PRODUCT DESIGNS. INITIALLY, THE GROUP DEMANDED THE RELEASE OF THREE OF ITS JAILED MEMBERS AND NEARLY $2,000,000 (U.S.), OR IT THREATENED TO HARM THE TWO BUSINESSMEN.

THREE INTERNATIONAL BUSINESSPERSONS, TWO NEW DELHI, INDIA WOMEN, AND ONE GERMAN, WERE ASSAULTED ON MERIDAN BOULEVARD, JUST OUTSIDE OF ANYTOWN, YOURSTATE, BY A GANG OF TEENAGERS WHO DEMANDED MONEY, JEWELRY, AND CREDIT CARDS. THE GERMAN BUSINESSMAN RESISTED AND WAS SHOT. HE IS CURRENTLY IN THE HOSPITAL IN EAST INDEPENDENCE, YOURSTATE, IN SERIOUS BUT STABLE CONDITION. BOTH THE WOMEN WERE BRUTALLY BEATEN EVEN AFTER THEY COOPERATED AND WILLINGLY HANDED OVER THEIR VALUABLES. SEVERAL OF THE GANG MEMBERS SHOUTED AND SCREAMED A VARIETY OF ANTI-FEMALE SLOGANS AS THEY PUNCHED AND KICKED THE WOMEN, TELLING THE WOMEN TO LEAVE THE AREA AND LET MEN DO THE JOB, AND THAT WOMEN ARE ONLY GOOD FOR HOUSEKEEPING AND BEARING CHILDREN. ALSO, IN THE ATTACK, TWO PERSONAL COMPUTERS WERE TAKEN THAT HELD CORPORATE FINANCIAL AND PROJECT MATERIALS.

AN ENGLISH TOURIST'S CAR WAS HIJACKED BY TWO YOUTHS ON THE OUTSKIRTS OF A METROTOWN SUBURB, IN YOURSTATE. THE

YOUTHS ASSAULTED THE DRIVER AND SPAT ON MEMBERS OF HIS FAMILY AFTER FORCING THEM OUT OF THE AUTOMOBILE AT GUNPOINT.

THE ATTACKS ON FOREIGNERS, WOMEN, AND SOME BUSINESS INDIVIDUALS SEEM TO BE ON AN UPSWING. THIS ESCALATING CRIME PATTERN HAS BEEN IDENTIFIED IN AREAS WHERE BUSINESSES ARE EXPANDING AND REGRESSING, BUT PRIMARILY IN AREAS WHERE THERE IS A HIGHER THAN NORMAL PERCENTAGE OF POVERTY-LINE INCOME, FEW JOBS, AND BUSINESS VENTURES BRINGING IN INDIVIDUALS FROM THE OUTSIDE TO THE DETRIMENT OF LOCAL CITIZENS.

UNCLASSIFIED

(ROUTINE MSG — DATED 60 DAYS AGO)

FROM: AMEMB CZECHREP

SUBJECT: CRIMINAL ACTIVITY IN CZECH REPUBLIC/LOCAL POLICE PROTECTION

1. OFFICIAL GOVERNMENT STATISTICS ON CRIME INDICATE THAT CONTINUED HIGH LEVELS OF UNEMPLOYMENT HAVE FUELED CRIME IN COMMUNITIES WHERE U.S. CITIZENS RESIDE. IN GENERAL, CRIME HAS SHOWN A MARKED INCREASE AND IS BECOMING MORE VIOLENT. OFFICIAL REPORTS SHOW THAT AS MANY AS 279 MURDERS AND 385 KIDNAPPINGS WERE REPORTED DURING THE FIRST FIVE MONTHS OF 1996. ACTIVITY ACCOMPANYING CRIME IS ON THE UPSWING.
2. THE CZECH REP GOVERNMENT ALSO REPORTED THAT POLICE FORCES THAT PATROL MAJOR CITIES AND INDUSTRIAL COMPLEXES AND BUSINESS FIRMS, ESPECIALLY THOSE WITH FOREIGN TIES, HAVE RECENTLY BEEN EQUIPPED WITH PATROL CARS WITH TWO-WAY RADIOS. THE POLICE CAN BE CONTACTED 24 HRS A DAY, AND THEIR AVERAGE RESPONSE TIME VARIES BETWEEN 30-90 MINUTES.
3. LOCAL RADIO BROADCASTS INDICATED THAT ABOUT 8% OF POLICE OFFICERS WERE IMPLICATED IN CRIMES SINCE START OF THE YEAR.
4. FOREIGN OFFICES, INDIVIDUALS, AND ORGANIZATIONS BEING TARGETED BY CRIMINAL ACTIVITIES INCLUDE ELECTRONICS, COMPUTERS, AND OTHER TECHNICAL MANUFACTURING ORGANIZATIONS THAT HAVE A LOW TO MEDIUM PROFILE, BUT ARE LIKELY TO HAVE LARGE AMOUNTS OF CASH OR SPECIALIZED HIGH TECHNOLOGY (TO THE CZECHS), PRODUCTS THAT CAN BE SPIRITED AWAY AND SOLD ON THE BLACK MARKET.
5. THERE IS ALSO A GROWING NEED FOR PATENTS, PROCESSES, PROCEDURES, AND OTHER UNCLASSIFIED BUT SENSITIVE BUSINESS INFORMATION. A CERTAIN AMOUNT OF THIS IS BEING BARTERED WITH OTHER CRIMINAL ENTERPRISES TO FAR EASTERN AND INDIAN GOVERNMENTS. RECENTLY, FRENCH INTEL SERVICE AGENTS WERE ARRESTED IN CONJUNCTION WITH A LOCAL CRIMINAL GANG THAT DEALT IN SPACE ELECTRONICS. IT WAS LEARNED THAT MICRO-ELECTRO-OPTIC SYSTEMS, INC., WAS THE SOURCE OF THE TECHNICAL INFORMATION AND ELECTRONIC COMPONENTS THAT WAS PROVIDED. AS NOT YET DETERMINED BY CZECH FEDERAL INVESTIGATORS IS: WHO PROVIDED INFORMATION AND/OR PRODUCTS? IS THIS A ONE-TIME

OR CONTINUING CRIMINAL ENTERPRISE? ARE CZECH INDIVIDU-
ALS INVOLVED DIRECTLY WITH MICRO-ELECTRO-OPTIC SYS-
TEMS, INC.? OR IS INFORMATION BEING OBTAINED VIA
INTERNET? (TWO COMPUTERS WITH INTERNET CAPABILITY
WERE CONFISCATED BY CZECH AUTHORITIES; ONE HAD DISKS
CONTAINING COMPUTER MATH MODULES USED IN COMMUNI-
CATIONS, WHILE TWO OTHER DISKS CONTAINED INFORMATION
AND CAD SCHEMATICS PURPORTING TO BE LOW-EMISSION
ELECTRONIC TRANSMISSION DESIGNS FOR SOME SORT OF COM-
PACT TRANSMISSION UNIT—AS YET UNDETERMINED. BOTH
DISKS' DATE ARE CONSIDERED PROBABLY STATE OF THE ART.)

6. IT IS PRESUMED THAT WHILE CZECH OFFICIALS RETURN DATA
TO AMEMB FOR FORWARDING TO MICRO-ELECTRO-OPTIC SYS-
TEMS, INC., WE CAN ASSUME THEY HAVE MADE COPIES AND
PROVIDED TO CZECH BUSINESSES AND GOVERNMENT ORGANI-
ZATIONS HAVING SUCH INTERESTS.

Washington Post (DATED 4 DAYS AGO)

Crime on Upswing in YourState

Pendington (AP)—The Pendington Police reports another increase in crime. Capt. Bunter says that Government officials must increase spending on law enforcement matters, but will continue to battle on with existing forces and limited funding in attempts to decrease crime on all fronts.

Homicide increased 6% over the previous year, while reported rape incidents increased from 43 to 72. Robbery increased 20% from last year's total of 480. Aggravated assault was nearly unchanged at 465 incidents. Burglary increased 14% from 528 to 602 incidents. Bomb threats decreased 7% to 35 incidents. Demonstrations and disturbances, especially in low employment areas, were unchanged. All this represents an 8% increase over the previous year.

Pendington (YourState) Daily Journal

(DATED 1 DAY AGO)

Micro-Electro-Optic Systems, Inc. to Close Plant; 392 Jobs Lost

Pendington—Micro-Electro-Optic Systems, Inc., the area's largest employer, announced they are closing their doors within the next sixty days, citing the high costs of training and maintaining employees. This was unusual since, at the time, they had a number of new Government contracts to provide high-tech electronic modules for a variety of Government systems. NASA's Johnston Space Center in Texas said they were aware of the plant closing, but it will not affect the three satellite contracts it now holds with Micro-Electro-Optic Systems, Inc. (MEOS). MEOS had assured NASA that the contracts were still on schedule, as a duplicate plant had been set up in India where they were producing the modules for NASA, with a variation being available to other countries.

Micro-Electro-Optic Systems, Inc. president Dr. Ray Chavden said in a press release that while they regretted the closing of the plant and the loss of jobs, the company's worldwide commitment necessitated a new plant overseas, since much of their business was international in scope. In the past, contracts with Romania, the Czech Republic, and even the Republic of China, have led to further contracts. He also indicated that a new factory will be built in the far east—country unspecified—to support a ten-year project that will provide gyroscopic and a satellite-based ground location system.

The Huntington Chamber of Commerce and Mayor Lindsey's office of business development are now preparing a job fair in conjunction with other businesses in the area to obtain what employment they can for the now unemployed personnel.

Major Lindsey himself has called upon other businesses to consider the economic and tax advantages of doing business in the Huntington region. He has moved up several business trips aimed at increasing the Huntington business base. Just last year, he was able to convince E. F. Electronics, Inc. to reopen parts of their plant that had been closed when the oil storage area was sold off. Also, a young, but aggressive Japanese software design and development company was enticed to the area, eventually settling in at one of E. F. Electronics's vacant buildings.

(see related articles on A-4, B1-2)

Technical Professionals

Micro-Electro-Optic Systems, Inc. is an employee-owned business founded in 1970. We are focused on the DoD Intelligence/Security, Weapons, and Satellite Systems marketplace, and committed to *Securing America's Future*. MEOS has immediate openings for experienced, career motivated technical professionals who like to work hard and have fun!

All positions require an active TS clearance.
>   Network Engineers
>   Senior Software Test Engineers
>   Senior computer Scientists
>   Programmers
>   Technical Writers
>   Printed Circuit-Board Designers.

Submit resume and cover letter for consideration to:

Micro-Electro-Optic Systems, Inc.
8213 Ringer Drive
Silver Spring, MD

E. F. Electronics, Inc.

3211 Industry Drive Anytown, YourState

E. F. Electronics is seeking to identify qualified technical professionals in any of the following areas *within the next 60 days:*

Signal Processing	Satellite Systems
Weapons Systems	C++ UNIX
Software Engineer	SONNET ATM
Technical Writer/Editor	Application Programmer Analysts
Computer Scientist	System Architect
Senior Engineer	Technical Architect
Systems Analysts	
Interface & communications	
Programmers	

E. F. Electronics is seeking to identify qualified technical professionals in the following areas *within the next 30 days:*

Satellite/Communications Engineer: Seeking the right individual with 5–8+ years in frequency and spectrum engineering. Will analyze satellite communications system, perform interference analysis and simulations among satellite systems. Deeply involved with program decision-making at the highest levels. M.S. in EE, Astro, or Systems Engineering with some experience in satellite communication or orbit analysis.

Geoscientist: Must have extensive knowledge of NIMA-type products and detailed production activities. Will be involved in the extraction of definition of soft-copy photogrammetric products for National defense. Rqmts include 8+ years in production activities, B.A. degree in a related field, ability to lead requirements definition activities, and manage product tasks.

Senior Communications Programmer: B.A. in computer science or equivalent work experience; 8+ years with VTAM, MVS, LANS, others desirable. Also, 2+ years of integrated circuitry installation experience a plus.

U.S. citizenship required for all positions. Applicants selected may be subject to a security investigation and must meet eligibility requirements for access to TS/SCI information. Current SBI a strong plus!

If you are cleared in any of the above mentioned areas and looking to explore new and exciting opportunities, please mail to DoD Project Manager.

THREAT ASSESSMENT CHART

Threat Category	Intent (Interest/ Need)	Capability (Methods)	History (Incidents/ Indicators)	Overall Threat Level
Foreign Intelligence Threat	HUMINT:			
	TECHNICAL:			
Terrorist				
Criminal				
Insider				

Part 2B: Undesirable Events and Related Threat Levels

Objective: Determine the *threat level for each asset and undesirable event.*
Directions: Use all available information, including Job Aid II: Threat Assessment (see below), and estimate the threat level for each asset identified. Weigh the adversary's intent, capability, and history in relation to each asset to determine whether the threat level is critical, high, medium, or low. Use the threat-rating criteria in Job Aid II as the basis for your decision.
Materials Needed: All information from previous exercises, Job Aid II: Threat Assessment.

JOB AID II: THREAT ASSESSMENT

To determine the threat level for a specific threat, answer the following three questions for each potential source of threat. *Does the threat source have a:*

1. Motivation or the intention to mount this specific threat?
2. Capability to pose this specific threat?
3. History of attempting to mount, or successfully mounting, this specific threat?

After you determine simple "yes" or "no" answers to the three questions above, use the chart below to determine the threat level. The threat level is a relative rating based on best available information from your sources. To determine the relative degree of threat, a criteria should be developed to allow for consistent rating of threat levels. Below is an example of a decision matrix with an explanation of each of the four rating categories.

Intent	Capability	History	Threat Level
Yes	Yes	Yes	Critical
Yes	Yes	No	High
Yes	No	Yes/No	Medium
No	Yes	No	Low
No	No	No	Low

Impact Rating Criteria

Critical—Indicates that a definite threat exists against the assets and that the adversary has both the capability and intent to launch an attack, and that the subject or similar assets are targeted on a frequently recurring basis.

High—Indicates that a credible threat exists against the assets, based on our knowledge of the adversary's capability and intent to attack the assets, and based on related incidents having taken place at similar facilities.

Medium—Indicates there is a potential threat to the assets based on the adversary's desire to compromise the assets and the possibility that the adversary could obtain the capability through a third party who has demonstrated the capability in related incidents.

Low—Indicates little or no credible evidence of capability or intent, with no history of actual or planned threats against the assets.

PRACTICAL EXERCISE #3

This exercise is conducted to *identify the vulnerability* of assets to loss or damage.

Objective: To determine the vulnerability levels related to each undesirable event.

Directions: Review the information gathered during your asset and threat assessment and in the attached vulnerability data to include the facility description, floor plan, and area map. Then identify related vulnerabilities for each undesirable event to include vulnerabilities in the following areas:

- Operational/procedural
- Physical
- Technical

Use the Existing Countermeasure Assessment Chart to identify and evaluate the effectiveness of existing countermeasures.

Complete the Vulnerability Assessment Chart using the information previously documented. To determine the relative level of vulnerability, you need to have a good understanding of the effectiveness of any existing countermeasures and the environment surrounding the assets you are protecting.

Materials Required: Facility description, floor plan, and area map; Vulnerability Assessment Forms; and Job Aid III.

Time: This exercise should take approximately one hour to complete.

E. F. Electronics, Inc. Office Buildings & Property Management

E. F. Electronics, Inc. maintains several buildings at the Anytown facility, some of which are corporate owned and leased out, and others that have been sold off. All buildings are currently occupied.

Skelly Oil owns its entire section of the E. F. Electronics site. The chemical plant is still wholly owned by E. F. Electronics, Inc.

J-Soft, a computer design company, occupies the second floor (8,000 sq. ft.) and part of the third floor (6,500 sq. ft.) of the old plans building. The first floor is a full-service cafeteria still run by E. F. Electronics, Inc. Wanker County Environmental Coalition leases the rest of the third floor. Note that both ends of the second and third floors of the buildings will have a series of windows put in, with J-Soft performing the installation, with no cost to E. F. Electronics, Inc.; since there was no cost, E. F. Electronics approved the building modifications.

The following information has been obtained and may be of interest to the RM Team:

- There are no fire alarms or sprinklers in buildings 4, 4A, or 3 at this time.
- Security personnel are limited for the entire facility; buildings 4 and 4A have a security guard force required under the DoD contract. Skelly Oil locks their gates at night with no night watchman present. J-Soft uses their own security force, who are Japanese and non-English-speaking.
- There is no central air conditioning in buildings 2, 3, 4, 4A, 5, and 5A, although individual window units can be installed.
- Electricity comes in from the outside to the facility. J-Soft and Skelly have their own backup generator units. Buildings 4 and 4A are subject to power failures due to age.
- Access to buildings 4 and 4A is controlled. Building 7 is manned continuously. Building 6 has no access control other than the lock and key and a receptionist inside the front entrance during business hours.

A site map will be provided for reference.

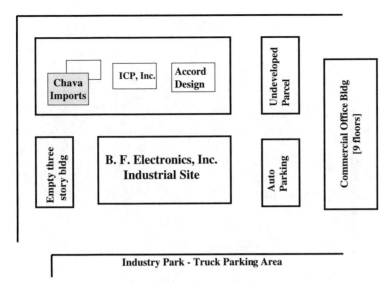

Figure A.1   Area Map.

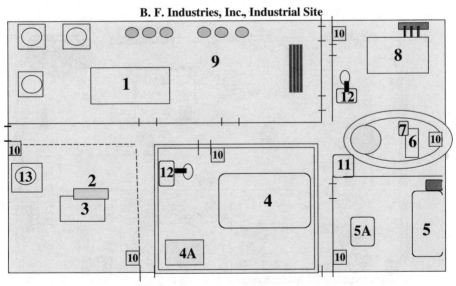

1. Kasko Oil Hq	6. Administration & Personnel Offices
2. Restaurant	7. Security Dept & SGF Alarm Station
3. J-Soft/Environmental Hqs	8. Chemical Production Bldg
4. Satellite mfg plant	9. Kasko Oil distribution facility
4A. Computer/electronics R&D bldg	10. Faclity security guard booths
5. Project supply warehouse storage	11. Facility fire department
5A. Other storage & supply	12. Heating/power plant

NOT TO SCALE

Figure A.2   Site Map.

Building #4

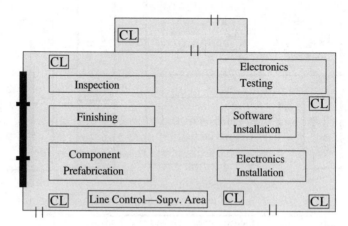

NOTES: 1. CL = computer link
2. Left end of bldg has warehouse size double doors and the three louvre areas [4 X 22 feet] above the doors for ventilation. Most of the louvres are broken out.
3. Bldg #4 is made of wood; over 20 years old.

Figure A.3   Facility Description.

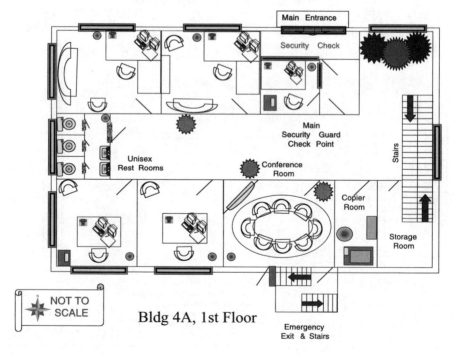

Figure A.4   Building 4A—First floor.

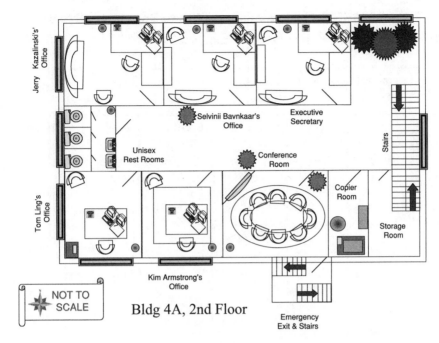

Figure A.5   Building 4A—Second floor.

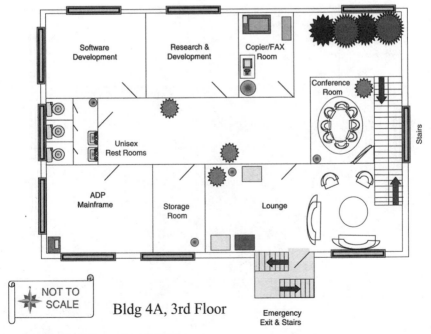

Figure A.6   Building 4A—Third floor.

STEP 3 WORKSHEET: Linking Vulnerabilities to Undesirable Events

(Identify the Effectiveness of Existing Countermeasures)

Vulnerabilities	Undesirable Events				
	Event 1	Event 2	Event 3	Event 4	Event 5

STEP 3 WORKSHEET: Vulnerability Assessment Chart

(Determine Vulnerability Level)

Critical Assets	Potential Undesirable Events	Vulnerability Identification	Vulnerability Level	Vulnerability Rating

JOB AID III: VULNERABILITY ASSESSMENT

To determine the **vulnerability level** for a given asset, answer the following three questions:

1. Is the asset made vulnerable by a single (as opposed to multiple) weakness in the security protective system?
2. Does the nature of the vulnerability make it difficult to exploit?
3. Is the vulnerability of the asset lessened by multiple, effective layers of security countermeasures?

After you determine simple "yes" or "no" answers to the three questions above, use the chart below to determine the vulnerability level.

Vulnerability through One Weakness	Difficult to Exploit?	Multiple Layers of Countermeasures	Vulnerability Level
Yes (single)	Yes	Yes	Low
Yes	Yes	No	Low
No (multiple)	Yes	Yes	Low
Yes	No	Yes	Medium
Yes	No	No	Medium
No	No	Yes	High
No	Yes	No	High
No	No	No	Critical

Vulnerability Rating Criteria

Critical—Indicates that there are no effective countermeasures currently in place and all known adversaries would be capable of exploiting the asset.

High—Indicates that, although there are some countermeasures in place, there are still multiple weaknesses through which many adversaries would be capable of exploiting the asset.

Medium—Indicates that there are effective countermeasures in place, however one weakness does exist that some known adversaries would be capable of exploiting.

Low—Indicates that multiple layers of effective countermeasures exist and few or no known adversaries would be capable of exploiting the asset.

Existing Countermeasures Assessment Chart

Existing Countermeasures	Undesirable Events			
	Surreptitious Entry by FIS	Theft of Equipment	Bomb Attack by Anyone	Communication Intercept by Local Adversary Group
	Effectiveness Rating	Effectiveness Rating	Effectiveness Rating	Effectiveness Rating

Rating Scale = 1 (ineffective) – 10 (effective)

Vulnerability Assessment Chart

The chart below provides an overview of vulnerability in relation to assets and undesirable events. It also provides the assessed level of vulnerability in relation to each asset you are trying to protect.

Critical Assets	Potential Undesirable Events	Vulnerability Description	Vulnerability Level
Activities			
Information			
Facilities			
Equipment			
People			

PRACTICAL EXERCISE #4

This exercise is conducted to *identify impact and risk levels and to prioritize and classify risks.*

Objectives: Estimate the impact, threat, vulnerability, and risk levels of potential undesirable events.

Directions: During the previous exercises, you identified the assets requiring protection, their loss impacts, threat sources, specific threats, threat levels, and the vulnerability of critical assets to damage/loss. Review the attached revised list of assets provided by the E. F. Electronics, Inc. Board of Directors, then identify the following information for any of the assets you identified earlier:

- impact level for loss/damage to each asset
- threat level
- vulnerability level
- risk level for each asset
- classification of risks as acceptable, unacceptable, or conditionally acceptable

Use the Board's prioritized list of assets to validate the assets for which you will determine the impact and risk levels. In any case, select assets for which you have already identified the threat and vulnerability levels. Work to identify the needed information.

Materials: Revised list of assets, Risk Assessment Form, Job Aid IV.

RISK ASSESSMENT CHART

Critical Assets	Potential Undesirable Events	Impact Rating	Threat Rating	Vulnerability Rating	Overall Risk	Risk Acceptable Yes/No?
Activities						
Information						
Equipment						
Facilities						
People						

JOB AID IV: DETERMINE THE LEVEL OF RISK

To determine the risk level, you can use the following matrix based on your team's determination of the likelihood of threat and vulnerability and the impact levels.

Threat Level	Vulnerability Level	Impact Level	Risk Level
High	High	High	Critical
High	High	Low	Medium
High	High	Medium	High
High	Low	High	Medium
High	Low	Low	Low
High	Low	Medium	Medium
High	Medium	High	High
High	Medium	Low	Low
High	Medium	Medium	Medium
Medium	High	High	High
Medium	High	Low	Medium
Medium	High	Medium	Medium
Medium	Low	High	Medium
Medium	Low	Low	Very Low
Medium	Low	Medium	Medium
Medium	Medium	High	Medium
Medium	Medium	Low	Medium
Medium	Medium	Medium	Medium

Low	High	High	Medium
Low	High	Low	Low
Low	High	Medium	Medium
Low	Low	High	Low
Low	Low	Low	Very Low
Low	Low	Medium	Very Low
Low	Medium	High	Medium
Low	Medium	Low	Very Low
Low	Medium	Medium	Medium

E. F. Electronics, Inc.
3211 Industry Drive
Anytown, YourState
Robert K. Leister, II, *President*
John Amos, *Ph.D., Principle*
Ranni Bavnkaar, *M.B.A., Principle*

Here's a list of assets . . . the way the Board sees it!

Prioritized List of Assets for Anytown DoD Project

1. 10–15 Staff members ($ unmeasurable)
2. DoD satellite contract activities: Initial contract: $135,000,000; Follow-on: $925,000,000
3. Office equipment: ($1,420,000)
    a. Special technical equipment ($800,000)
    b. Vehicles (with telephone, fax hook-up)
    c. AIS equipment (desktop, laptop, and printers)
    d. 2 Copy machines (1 color) ($17,500)
    e. Scanners (2) ($23,000)
    f. Fax machines (office areas) ($3,600)
    g. Cellular phones ($5,000)
4. Sensitive unclassified and classified DoD Government documents ($ unmeasurable)
5. Proprietary E. F. Electronics, Inc. data ($1,750,000)
6. Staff principals, R&D (computer, etc.) personnel and other members' personal property (home computers, etc.) and E. F. Electronics, Inc. connectivity equipment used at home in support of satellite project ($800,000)

PRACTICAL EXERCISE #5

This exercise is being conducted to *identify countermeasure options* that could be used to protect the company's assets.

Objective: Identify two or three countermeasure options to reduce risk in the critical areas previously identified.

Directions: Review the attached list of undesirable events to ensure that they have all been addressed in your assessment. Identify countermeasures that reduce the risk relative to each undesirable event. Then, determine the effect of each countermeasure in terms of reducing the risk level and estimate the cost of each individual countermeasure.

Next, develop two or three countermeasure options to protect against the risks that your group identified as unacceptable.

Finally, determine the overall cost for each countermeasure option.

Materials: Revised list of assets, revised list of undesirable events.

E. F. Electronics, Inc.
3211 Industry Drive
Anytown, YourState
Robert K. Leister, II, *President*
John Amos, *Ph.D., Principle*
Ranni Bavnkaar, *M.B.A., Principle*

Dear Risk Management Group:

Attached is a copy of the Board of Director's sense of the undesirable events that we should be doing our best to protect ourselves against. Please identify up to three countermeasure options to protect us against these undesirable events, determine the effect of each countermeasure and countermeasure option in terms of reducing the risk level, estimate the cost of each individual countermeasure, and the overall cost for each countermeasure option.

Prioritized List of Undesirable Events

1. Harm to our employees due to criminal, FIS, or other activity.
2. Exposure of activities that may lead to impaired operations.
3. Loss of credibility resulting in inability to obtain new business opportunities from nondefense organizations.
4. Loss/leakage of sensitive, official U.S. Government documents due to theft from inside company.
5. Loss of revenues resulting from our inability to fulfill our contractual obligations under this contract.
6. Harm to our office equipment due to deliberate damage or theft.
7. Compromise of critical information due to computer emanations attack.
8. Compromise of critical information due to communications intercept.
9. Compromise of critical information due to surreptitious entry/technical implant.

/s/ Bob

E. F. Electronics, Inc.
3211 Industry Drive
Anytown, YourState
Robert K. Leister, II, *President*
John Amos, *Ph.D., Principle*
Ranni Bavnkaar, *M.B.A., Principle*

Memorandum to: Risk Management Team

The Board of Directors has reviewed your weekly reports and the progress that your team is making on identifying risks for the Anytown facility.

As a whole, the Board has authorized the expenditure of up to $50,000 for security upgrades to the facility under this particular DoD contract.

Mindful of the importance of this project and the final constraints that we are under, you are directed to provide the Board with a short presentation this Friday. The presentation should provide some background, highlight (as necessary) the areas covered, and also include various option packages that the Board may consider for implementation to adequately secure the E. F. Electronics facility satellite area.

Robert K. Leister, II

Countermeasures Identification Chart

Undesirable Events	Potential Countermeasures and Costs		
	Procedures	Equipment	Manpower

Countermeasure Effectiveness Chart

Below is a format that can be used for tracking countermeasure effectiveness against potential threats or undesirable events. Depending on the level of detail required, the matrix can either be used to link countermeasures to undesirable events, or it can also be completed with a numerical rating indicating a relative level of effectiveness for each countermeasure. In the example below, a ten-point scale was used with "1" being "extremely low" and "10" being "highly effective."

Possible Counter-measures	Undesirable Events			
	Effectiveness Rating (1–10)	Effectiveness Rating (1–10)	Effectiveness Rating (1–10)	Effectiveness Rating (1–10)

COUNTERMEASURE OPTIONS CHART 1: MOST EXPENSIVE

Undesirable Events	Countermeasures	Risk Level Reduced From/To	Cost
Overall Risk/Total Cost			

COUNTERMEASURE OPTIONS CHART 2: LEAST EXPENSIVE

Undesirable Events	Countermeasures	Risk Level Reduced From/To	Cost
Overall Risk/Total Cost			

COUNTERMEASURE OPTIONS CHART 3: RECOMMENDED

Undesirable Events	Countermeasures	Risk Level Reduced From/To	Cost
Overall Risk/Total Cost			

PHYSICAL SECURITY COUNTERMEASURES

Physical security countermeasures are the various measures taken that will enhance the security posture of a facility. Such measures can be procedural in scope, increased manpower, or the addition of specific items of equipment. The following are typical countermeasures that can be included. Possibly the reader may know of or wish to consider others; please do so.

Terrorism Countermeasures

Vehicular Suicide
- Compound with curved entrance, Jersey barriers/fence and vehicle barriers
- Bollards, large rocks, or low walls around building
- Building designed with no first floor windows and main entrance high with special steps and landscaping
- Special glass, Mylar film, or heavy drapes on windows

Vehicle Parked
- Controlled compound
- Building set back from parking lots
- Registration of all vehicles
- Specially designed visitor parking area with blast wall deflection, etc.
- Controlled loading dock area
- Special glass, Mylar film, or heavy drapes on windows

Small Bomb
- Compound
- Exterior building inspections/patrols
- Package inspection program

Shooting
- Compound
- Opaque windows
- Secure lobby configuration
- Ballistic construction

Technical Countermeasures

Surreptitious Entry
Visibility
- Illumination of building
- Clear view of building entrances and windows (no vegetation)
- CCTV with motion detection activation

Controlled Compound
- Perimeter barrier (fence/wall) with controlled gates
- Perimeter detection system
- Roving patrols
  Building Control
- 24-hour human presence
- Perimeter entrances have substantial doors, inside locking hardware, and IDS
- Substantial perimeter wall construction and window protection
- Compartmented secure areas (true vault construction)
- Combination locks
- GSA-approved security containers
- Internal IDS with immediate response into secure areas
- Roving patrols
  Tempest Attack
- Tempest equipment
- Controlled compound
- Controlled building
- Wall and window applications
- Shielded enclosures
  Other Stand-Off Attacks
- Controlled compound
- Window Blinds and curtains closed (laser)
- Roving patrols around building
  Technical Implant
- ALL ITEMS LISTED UNDER SURREPTITIOUS ENTRY
- Escort program for unauthorized personnel
- TSCM inspection program
- Construction security program

Criminal Countermeasures (Outsider)

Crimes Against People
- Compounds/controlled parking lots
- Roving patrols of armed protective personnel
- Exterior illumination
- Panic buttons and intercom in parking areas
- CCTV with motion detection capabilities
  Crimes Against Property
- ALL ITEMS LISTED UNDER SURREPTITIOUS ENTRY
  Unauthorized Entry
- ALL ITEMS LISTED UNDER SURREPTITIOUS ENTRY
- 24-hour human presence
- Access control equipment
- Proper lobby and building design

- Security escort program
- Combination locks
  Unauthorized Removal of Classified Materials
- Personnel security program
- Counterintelligence awareness
- Protective force personnel

HUMINT Countermeasures

Building Observation
- Create a police state
- Military type compound (large, many other buildings)
- High wall around compound
  Employee Observation
- Military type compound (large, many other buildings)
- Parking garage with direct access to building
- Employee disguises, fake license plates

Criminal Countermeasures (Insider)

Crimes against People (workplace violence, stalking, assault, etc.)
- Metal detectors
- Prohibited items policy
- Employee Assistance Program
- Panic Buttons
- Awareness Training
  Crimes against Property (theft, sabotage)
- Property passes
- CCTV at entrances
- Theft-reporting procedures
- Baggage checks

IDS Components by Cost

Control Equipment	$1,000.00 total
Magnetic contacts (building perimeter doors)	$400.00 per sensor
Magnetic contacts (building interior doors)	$200.00 per sensor
Motion detection sensor	$600.00 per sensor
Panic Switch	$200.00 per switch
Window detection equipment (glass breakage sensor)	$300.00 per window
Central station monitoring (no 24-hour presence)	$2,000.00 per year

Physical Security Components by Cost

24-hour armed guard force	$150,000.00 per year
12-hour armed guard force	$75,000.00 per year
24-hour unarmed guard force	$100,000.00 per year
12-hour unarmed guard force	$50,000.00 per year
10-foot high fence	$50.00 per foot
6-foot high fence	$30.00 per foot
Earthen berm	$10.00 per foot
Lighting	$1,000.00 per light pole
Card controlled gate	$5,000.00 each
Delta vehicle barrier	$20,000.00 each
Barred windows	$500.00 per window
Ballistic glass guard post	$25,000.00 each
Dog patrol, night only	$1,000.00 per month
Generator and Diesel fuel tank	$30,000.00

CCTV Components by Cost

Interior video cameras, fixed	$1,000.00 per camera
Exterior video cameras, fixed	$2,000.00 per camera
Video camera, pan, tilt, and zoom	$8,000.00 per camera
Video/intercom	$3,000.00 each
Video monitor, simple	$1,500.00
Video monitor, controllable	$3,000.00
Video monitor, controllable and recorded	$5,000.00

Security Cost Breakdown

Security Cost Element	Estimated Cost
Personnel Security:	
Clearance Program	
Initial Investigations	
Adjudication	
Reinvestigations	
Polygraph	
Physical Security:	
Physical Security Equipment	
Protective Forces	
Physical Security for Personnel	
Physical Security for Organizations	
Intrusion Detection and Assessment	
Barriers/Controls	
Vital Components and Tamp-Safe	
Monitors	
Access Controls/Badging	
Visitor Control	

continued next page

Information Security:	
Classification Management	
Electronic Security/Info. Tech. Systems	
Compromising Emanations/(TEMPEST)	
Technical Surveillance Countermeasures	
Communications Security (COMSEC)	
Sensitive Unclassified Information Mgmt.	
Operations Security (OPSEC)	
Awareness Programs:	
County Threat Briefings	
Travel Briefings	
Employee Assistance Programs	
Personal Protection Training	
Security Policies & Procedures Briefings	
Other Security Costs:	
Total Security Costs:	

THE FRAMEWORK FOR ESTIMATING SECURITY COSTS

The following provides a detailed summary of the many categories of security activities involved in protecting classified or corporate sensitive (including R&D) information. It provides a framework for reporting protection and security-related expenditures in budget documents.

Security and Safeguards Estimates

I.   General

The intent of this common framework is to establish departmental/agency/organization best resource estimates for domestic and overseas security. Counterintelligence resources are not included in the security and safeguards estimates. If 51 percent or more of a resource is devoted to security or safeguarding, it should be included in this estimate.

II.   Primary Categories
A.   Personnel Security
B.   Physical Security
C.   Information Security
1. Classification Management
2. Electronic Security/Information Technology Systems
3. Sensitive Unclassified Information Management
D.   Professional Education, Training, and Awareness
E.   Security Management, Oversight, and Planning

III.   Department/Agency Unique Categories

(Major responsibilities for some departments/agencies that are not reported in Primary Categories above.)

IV.   Definitions

The following definitions will serve as guidance to aggregate resource estimates for each primary category. Estimates should be developed to be reported at the Category level only.

In the Primary Categories below, the Departments/Agencies/Organizations should report an estimate for Personnel Security, Physical Security, and so on. The exception to this rule is that under Information Security, separate estimates will be reported for Classification Management, Electronic Security/Information Technology Systems, and Sensitive Unclassified Information Management.

Primary Categories

1.   Personnel Security: A series of interlocking and mutually supporting program elements that initially establish a Government or contractor employee has eligibility, and ensure suitability for the

continued access to Government classified, sensitive unclassified, or proprietary sensitive information.

a. Clearance Program: Personnel and activities to determine eligibility and suitability for initial or continuing access to classified or sensitive unclassified information or activities for Government programs.

b. Initial Investigations: Completing and reviewing Personnel Security Questionnaire, initial screening, filing data in Central Personnel Database, forwarding to appropriate investigative authority and the investigation itself.

c. National Agency Check: (self-explanatory)

d. Adjudication: Screening and analysis of personnel security cases for determining eligibility for access authorizations and appeals process.

e. Reinvestigations: Periodic recurring investigations of Government and contractor personnel.

f. Polygraph: Substantive examinations in security screening process.

2. Physical Security: That portion of security concerned with physical measures designed to safeguard and protect personnel, facilities, and information, domestic or foreign.

a. Physical Security Equipment: Any item, device, or system that is used primarily for the protection of Government property and resources, personnel, installations and facilities, and classified or sensitive unclassified information.

b. Protective Forces: All personnel and operating costs associated with protective forces to include but not limited to salaries, overtime, benefits, materials and supplies, equipment and facilities, vehicles, helicopters, training, communications equipment, and management,

c. Physical Security for Personnel (Anti-Terrorism/Low Intensity Conflict): Physical security equipment and portable security systems that, as defensive measures, may be used to protect personnel or property when deployed to or operating in geographic areas where the threat of violence is high or in which limited politico-military conflict is occurring. It can include, but is not limited to, special equipment such as armored cars, bullet-resisting materials, clothing and upgrade of quarters, vehicles and communications equipment for personnel.

d. Physical Security Organizations: Those military, civilian, and contractor organizations whose primary mission, domestic or foreign, is the conduct of the physical security function, as compared to criminal counterintelligence investigations. It excludes organizations whose primary mission is outside the scope of physical security protection or who perform security duties in addition to normal functions. (Report construction estimates attributable to security requirements.)

e. Intrusion Detection and Assessment: Alarms, sensors, protective lighting and their control systems, and the assessment of the reliability, accuracy, timeliness, and effectiveness of those systems.

f. Barrier/Controls: Walls, fences, barricades or other fabricated or natural impediments to restrict, limit, delay, or deny entry into a designated area.

g. Vital Components and Tamper-Safe Monitoring: Personnel and operating activities associated with the monitoring of tamper-indicating devices for containers, doors, fences, and so forth, which reveal violations of containment integrity and posting and monitoring of anti-tamper warnings or signs.

h. Access Controls/Badging: Personnel and hardware such as badging systems, card-readers, turnstiles, metal detectors, cipher locks, CCTV, and other access-control mechanisms to ensure that only authorized persons are allowed to enter or leave a facility, and that they do not introduce prohibited articles into or remove property from a facility.

i. Visitor Control: Personnel and activities associated with administering visitors for classified and unclassified visits as well as assignment by foreign nationals.

3. Information Security: (As stated above, estimates for the Information Security Category will be captured at the level of the three main subcategories, i.e., Classification Management, Electronic Security/Information Technology Systems, and Sensitive Unclassified Information Management.)

a. Classification Management: The system of administrative policies and procedures for identifying and controlling from unauthorized disclosure, classified information, the protection of which is authorized by executive order or statute. Classification management encompasses those resources used to identify, control, transfer, transmit, store, and retrieve inventory or archives and declassify or destroy classified information.

b. Electronic Security/Information Technology Systems: Measures and controls that ensure confidentiality, integrity, and availability of the information processed and stored by a computer or information technology system. It can include, but is not limited to, the provision of all security features needed to provide a system of protection for computer hardware and software, and classified, sensitive unclassified, or critical information, material, or processes in automated systems.

c. Compromising Emanations (Tempest): Investigation, study, and control of compromising emanations from telecommunications and automated information systems.

d. Technical Surveillance Countermeasures (TSM): Personnel and operating expenses associated with the development, training, and application of technical security countermeasures, such as nondestructive and destructive searches, electromagnetic energy searches, and telephone system searches.

e. Communications Security (COMSEC): Measures and controls employed to deny unauthorized persons information derived from telecommunications and to ensure the authenticity of such communications planning or scheduling verification of the acceptability and validity of existing facility approval, status-granting facility approval, terminating facility approval, maintenance of facility data and approval records, identification, tracking and closure, or findings of deficiencies noted during inspections, presurveys, surveys, or assessments, development of reports to identify security program deficiencies, status and corrective actions.

Sensitive Unclassified Information Management: The system of administrative policies and procedures for identifying and controlling from unauthorized disclosure, sensitive unclassified information. Sensitive Unclassified Information Management encompasses those resources used to identify, control, transfer, transmit, store, retrieve, inventory, archives and destroy sensitive unclassified information.

f. Operations Security (OPSEC): The process of denying to potential adversaries information about capabilities and/or intentions by identifying, controlling, and protecting evidence of the planning and execution of sensitive activities. It can include, but is not limited to, the process of analyzing friendly actions and activities to (a) identify those actions that can be observed by adversaries, (b) determine indicators adversaries might obtain that could be interpreted or combined in time to be useful to adversaries, and (c) select and execute measures that eliminate the vulnerabilities of National Foreign Intelligence Program programs.

4. Professional Education, Training, and Awareness: The establishment, maintenance, direction, support and assessment of a security training and awareness program; the certification and approval of the training program; the development, management, and maintenance of training records; the training of personnel to perform tasks associated with their duties; and the qualification and/or certification of personnel before assignment of security responsibilities.

5. Security Management, Oversight, and Planning: Development and implementation of plans, procedures, and actions to accomplish policy requirements, develop budget and resource requirements, oversee organizational activities, and respond to management requests.

   a. Research, Test, and Evaluation: The development, management, and oversight of an acceptance and validation testing and evaluation program, corrective action reports, and related documentation that addresses safeguards and security elements. The examination and testing of physical security systems (construction, facilities, and equipment) to ensure their effectiveness and operability and compliance with applicable directives.

   b. Surveys, Reviews, Accreditation, and Assessments: Personnel and activities associated with surveys, reviews, accreditations, and assessments to determine the status of the security program and to evaluate its effectiveness, development, and management of a facility survey and approval program, facility presurvey, and information technology system accreditation.

   c. Special Access Program: A program established for a specific class of classified information that imposes safeguarding and access requirements that exceed those normally required for information at the same classification level. (Unless specifically authorized by the President, only the Secretaries of State, Defense, and Energy and the Director of Central Intelligence may create a special access program (SAP). Sensitive Compartmented Information (SCI) programs are not included as SAPs for the purpose of these estimates, rather, SCI security costs are integrated and estimated throughout all categories as appropriate.)

   d. Security and Investigative Matters: The investigation of security violations, criminal matters not included in counterintelligence, law enforcement, or defensive security programs.

   e. Industrial Security (Noncontractor Costs): Those measures and resources directly identifiable as Government activities performed for the protection of classified and sensitive unclassified information to which contractors and their subcontractors, vendors or suppliers have access or possession. Examples of such activities are industrial security reviews, surveys, and granting facility clearances.

   f. Foreign Ownership, Control, or Influence (FOCI): The development and management of a foreign ownership, control, or influence program; evaluation of FOCI submissions; the administration and monitoring of FOCI information; and the development of FOCI notifications.

Forms Used in the Risk Management Process

Asset Identification Chart

Assets
People
Activities
Information
Facilities
Equipment

Asset Impact Assessment Chart

Critical Assets	Potential Undesirable Events	Impact Level
People		
Activities		
Information		
Facilities		
Equipment		

Threat Assessment Chart

Critical Assets	Potential Undesirable Events	Threat Category/ Adversary	Threat Level
People			
Activities			
Information			
Facilities			
Equipment			

Vulnerability Assessment Chart

Critical Assets	Potential Undesirable Events	Vulnerability Description	Vuln. Level
People			
Activities			
Information			
Facilities			
Equipment			

Risk Analysis Matrix for Identifying Unacceptable Risks

Potential Undesirable Events	Impact Rating	Threat Rating	Vuln. Rating	Overall Risk	Risk Acceptable?

Linking Countermeasure Options to Vulnerabilities

Undesirable Events	Existing Risk Level	Related Vulnerabilities	Countermeasure Options	New Risk Level
1.				
2.				
3.				
Etc.				

Impact Level Decision Matrix

1	2	3	4	5	6	
State undesirable events, from highest (1) to the lowest (6); add others, as appropriate						OVERALL IMPACT LEVEL
Yes	Yes/No	Yes/No	Yes/No	Yes/No	Yes/No	Critical/High
No	Yes	Yes/No	Yes/No	Yes/No	Yes/No	High
No	Yes/No	Yes	Yes/No	Yes	Yes/No	High
No	Yes/No	Yes/No	Yes	Yes	Yes/No	High
No	No	No	No	Yes/No	Yes	Medium
No	No	No	No	Yes	Yes/No	Medium
No	No	No	No	No	No	Low

Asset Assessment Chart

Critical Assets	Potential Undesirable Events	Consequence of Event	Impact Level

Adversary Intent Determination Chart

ADVERSARY	INTENT		
	Needs	Wants	Indicators

Adversary Capabilities Determination Chart

Adversary	Capabilities						
	State capabilities as determined						

Adversary Incident Frequency Chart

ADVERSARY	HISTORY		
	Suspected Incidents	Attempted Incidents	Successful Incidents

Threat Information Tracking Sheet

Adversary	Intent (Interest/Need)	Capability (Methods)	History (Incidents)

Threat Level Decision Matrix

Intent	Capability	History	THREAT LEVEL
Yes	Yes	Yes	Critical
Yes	Yes	No	High
Yes	No	Yes or No	Medium
No	Yes or No	No	Low

Threat Assessment Summary Chart

Critical Assets	Potential Undesirable Events	Threat Category/ Adversary	Threat Level

Effectiveness of Existing Countermeasures

Current Countermeasures	Undesirable events stated for each column						

Vulnerability Level Decision Matrix

Vulnerable thru One Weakness?	Difficult to Exploit?	Multiple Layers of Countermeasures?	VULNER-ABILITY LEVEL
Yes (Single)	Yes	Yes	Low
Yes	Yes	No	Low
No (Multiple)	Yes	Yes	Low
Yes	No	Yes	Medium
Yes	No	No	Medium
No	No	Yes	High
No	Yes	No	High
No	No	No	Critical

Vulnerability Assessment Chart

Critical Assets	Potential Undesirable Events	Vulnerability Identification	Vuln. Level

Risk Assessment Matrix - Part 1 - Impact

Critical Assets	Potential Undesirable Events	Impact Rating	Threat Rating	Vuln. Rating

Risk Assessment Matrix - Part 2 - Threat

Critical Assets	Potential Undesirable Events	Impact Rating	Threat Rating	Vuln. Rating

Risk Assessment Matrix - Part 3 - Vulnerability

Critical Assets	Potential Undesirable Events	Impact Rating	Threat Rating	Vuln. Rating

Linking Countermeasure Options to High Priority Vulnerabilities

Undesirable Events	Existing Risk Level	Related Vulnerabilities	Countermeasure Options	New Risk Level

Risk Assessment Matrix - Part 4 - Overall Risk

Critical Assets	Potential Undesirable Events	Impact Rating	Threat Rating	Vuln. Rating	Overall Risk

Risk Assessment Matrix - Part 1 - Impact

Critical Assets	Potential Undesirable Events	Impact Rating	Threat Rating	Vuln. Rating	Overall Risk	Risk Acceptable?

Countermeasures Matrix

Current Countermeasures	INDICATE UNDESIRABLE EVENTS IN THESE COLUMNS			

Identifying Option Costs

Undesirable Events	Procedures	Equipment	Manpower

Countermeasure Option Package 1 - Most Expensive

Undesirable Events	Countermeasures	Risk Level Reduced From/To	Cost
OVERALL RISK/ TOTAL COST			

Countermeasure Option Package 2 - Least Expensive

Undesirable Events	Countermeasures	Risk Level Reduced From/To	Cost
OVERALL RISK/ TOTAL COST			

Countermeasure Option Package 3 - Recommended

Undesirable Events	Countermeasures	Risk Level Reduced From/To	Cost
OVERALL RISK/ TOTAL COST			/

Appendix C

Are You Safeguarding the Crown Jewels? Determining Critical and Sensitive Information

Donald R. Peeples, Ph.D

Author's Note: The first step in safeguarding your Crown Jewel information is determining exactly what information is really critical. This Appendix should be used as a continuing reference on determining what information are your Crown Jewels and, hence, worth safeguarding, as well as the sources of such critical information. Dr. Peeples is a mathematician and Risk Analyst, and he developed this very unique and most valuable reference aid for the U.S. Government.

INTRODUCTION

For nearly 2,000 years the pharaohs of Egypt were "sent on to the next life" surrounded by everything from household goods and faithful retainers to the Crown Jewels. However, only one such collection has remained unpilfered to this day. The others have been attacked by grave robbers, who only need one piece of information to wreak havoc—the location of a tomb. Thus, the Critical Information for safeguarding these tombs is the location. Said another way: "The safeguarding of King Tut's Crown Jewels depended on the safeguarding of the Critical Information: location."

The same is true for an organization involved in adversarial or competitive activities: the Crown Jewels of the organization are its critical and sensitive information. For instance, Patton was ready for Rommel "because he read Rommel's book." Also, the U.S. steel industry lost its world leadership role, in part, because it could not legally keep foreign competitors from using proprietary resources. Not only is information important, safeguarding an organization's Crown Jewels is an absolutely essential part of future success.

Common sense tells us that not all information warrants safeguarding. The discipline of Operations Security (OPSEC) employs an analytic method to support decision-makers of programs or activities in determining what Critical Information to safeguard, and how best to safeguard these Crown Jewels.

Contents

In addition to the OPSEC discipline, this Appendix steps through a case study loosely based on a real company that was forced out of business due to not safeguarding its Crown Jewels: critical information. For each step of the procedure presented, the following chart applies the concept of this step to the case-study example. The "Quick Guide" is a one-page rapid reference to guide the reader in selecting various generic categories in which the identification of critical assets may be determined. The Appendix continues with an example and the various procedures.

This Appendix is as much a training manual as it is a reference guide on how to determine which information is worth safeguarding and the sources of such information. In terms of content, this guide steps through a case study loosely based on a real company that was forced out of business due to not safeguarding its "Crown Jewels"—its critical information. For each step of the procedure presented on the left side of the guide, the corresponding right side applies the concept of this step to the case study example. After walking though the step-by-step case study example, the reader has available a number of generic operation categories which will assist you in the identification of critical information related to an organization, program, or project.

Quick Guide

Organizational Boundaries. Work unit(s) with associated support and management whose information's sensitivity is in question.

Operations. An organization's activities, projects, and programs to be considered.

Adversaries, with Goals, and Objectives.

Adversary and Goals. An entity, personal or corporate, whose goals are in conflict with the Good-Guy's goals.

Objectives. Strategy to cause short- or long-term harm, damage, or loss of operational effectiveness.

Generic Operation Categories. For each combination of a Good-Guy Operation and an Adversary with a Bad-Guy objective Operation, choose the best Generic Category from Appendix C.I, "Generic Operation Categories."

Critical Information Components (CIC).

Appendix C.II. For each choice of a Generic Operation Category, find the section in Appendix C.II, "Critical Information Components of Generic Operation Categories."

Tailor and Screen. Disregard CIC that do not apply. Tailor to Operation. Check on possible CIC being actually CIC: Could knowledge of this Critical Information Component (CIC) about this Good-Guy Operation be of value to the Adversary in causing any Bad-Guy objectives?

The Critical Information.

Aggregate and Edit CIC. Aggregate with "ANDs." Edit.

Sufficiency Check. Check on possible Critical Information actually being The Critical Information: Could knowledge of The Critical Information by the Adversary be sufficient to allow the Adversary to initiate actions that would lead to short-term or long-term harm, damage, or loss of operational effectiveness? If not "YES", then additional CIC needed. Obtain more. Continue repeating until both questions get "YES" responses.

Sources of Information. Make a list of "medium," "event," and "other phenomenon" Sources of Information for each Operation-Adversary pair.

Major Vulnerabilities. Considering each location/functional area, list the Major Vulnerabilities (especially access-control, personnel, computer, and communications).

Sources of Sensitive Information (Indicator Categories).

Events and Other Phenomena. Make a list of the "event" and "other phenomenon" Sources of Information from the previous section.

Media. For each "medium" Source of Information, add to the list each Source "that mentions or refers to"
- the "events" (again!),
- the "other phenomena" (again!),
- Major Vulnerabilities (previous section), and
- Critical Information Components.

RISK MANAGEMENT PRODUCT EXAMPLE

Project Background

The Product. A Chemical company is about to start a project to develop a new plastic glove. Research has shown that the use of a new catalyst—Catalyst Y, extracted from the root of a somewhat rare Philippine shrub—in manufacturing produces a plastic glove that is twice as thin as any known plastic glove, costs about the same, and has the same properties of gripping, strength, and so forth, as the best selling gloves. The value of thinness is better tactile sensitivity, in particular for health care professionals. This new glove will probably capture the market.

People, Production, and Marketing. The people involved in the project are the project manager, the clerical staff, and the chemists working on the project at a suite on the third floor of Building 3 in the company's main complex in the Midwestern city of Metrotown. They plan to make 20,000,000 gloves initially, to be released in six months. Each pair will cost $1.99 per pair and will be marketed in the eastern United States by a saturation publicity campaign.

Concerns. The lead chemist, who is virtually irreplaceable in this project, has an alcohol problem and is susceptible to "loose lips" after a few drinks at the local pub. Also, the rear laboratory emergency door has no provision for escorts or monitoring. Any visitor, repair person, or others, could unlock this door for future use or accomplice access to the lab. Upon access through this door, a knowledgeable competitor could easily discover most of the Critical Information.

The Competition. Finally, the other plastic glove manufacturers, to increase their market-share of the plastic-glove market, may decide to take actions to:

- make raw materials unavailable;
- render key personnel unavailable;
- make manufacturing facilities unusable;
- release a similar new product at about the same time as glove release;
- float a major advertising campaign to counteract release of the new glove, and/or have a saturation give-away campaign of gloves to decrease initial sales.

PROCEDURE

Determine Boundaries and Operations

Set Organizational Boundaries.   Determine   which   work   unit(s), including associated support and management, uses the information whose sensitivity is in question. Call this group the Organization—occasionally called the Good-Guy.

Determine Operations.   Determine which of the organization's activities, projects, and programs will be considered. One possibility is to consider all of the organization's operations. Another possibility is to choose only one. Name all of those chosen the Operations.

Determine Adversaries, with Goals, and Objectives

Adversary and Goals.   Each Operation may have several Adversaries. An Adversary—occasionally called the Bad-Guy—is a group, country, set of countries, company, set of companies, and so on, whose Goals are in conflict with the Good-Guy's goals.

Objectives.   An Adversary's Objective is an action intended to inflict harm, damage, or loss of operational effectiveness to the Operation based on knowledge of the Good-Guy's objectives. An Objective may be a short-term or long-term attempt at lowering the Good-Guy's effectiveness but must be a specific action.

To fully understand who the Adversaries to an operation are, the decision-maker needs to know the intentions of any entity that is a possible Adversary. Because intentions (Goals and Objectives) in most instances are known only through capabilities, detailed information may be needed to understand capabilities and analyze them as intentions. The decision-maker may need further help in gathering and analyzing possible Adversarial information, consultation with personnel having intelligence expertise may be in order.

Choose Generic Operation Categories.   For each combination of a Good-Guy Operation and an Adversary with a Bad-Guy Objective to impact the Operation, choose the best Generic Category that applies. Appendix C.I provides a list of Generic Categories into which an Operation might fall.

EXAMPLE

Determine Boundaries and Operations

Set Organizational Boundaries.   The Organization is the project manager, the clerical staff, the chemists working on the project along with associated support personnel and management.

Determine Operations.   The Operation to be analyzed for critical and sensitive information is only this new plastic glove project even though the chemists are working on many other projects.

Determine Adversaries, with Goals, and Objectives

Adversary and Goals.   All the other plastic glove manufacturers are Adversaries in this Operation. The Goal for each is to increase their market-share by cutting into the Good-Guy Organization's market-share.

Objectives.   The following are examples of Bad-Guy Objectives against the Good-Guy Operation:

- raw materials made unavailable;
- key personnel made unavailable;
- manufacturing facilities made unusable;
- similar new product released by another manufacturer about the same time as glove release;
- major advertising campaign by another manufacturer to counteract release of the new glove; and
- saturation give-away campaign of gloves by another manufacturer to decrease initial sales.

Choose Generic Operation Categories. (Refer to Appendix C.I.) .
There are two possibilities. The Operation clearly fits Generic Category III: "Research, Development, Testing, Evaluation (RDTE), and Production of Sensitive Technology." Also, the lead chemist is virtually irreplaceable in this project; therefore, the Operation also fits into Generic Category XIa: "Safety of Important Personnel—Permanent Site." However, this person really could be replaced (and there is an insurance policy); therefore, Generic Category III is the best choice.

PROCEDURE

Determine Critical Information Components (CICS)

Appendix C.II. For each combination of a Good-Guy Operation, an Adversary, a Bad-Guy Objective to impact the Operation, and choice of a Generic Operation category, find the section in Appendix C.II, "Critical Information Components of Generic Operation Categories," that applies to the category.

Tailor and Screen. Disregard each possible Critical Information Component (CIC) listed in this section that does not apply to the Operation. Then write a short tailored statement of the remaining possible dc.

Author's Note: The CIC in Appendix C.II are intended only to stimulate thought. Do not use CIC that do not apply to this Good-Guy Operation. There may be additional CIC of a Generic Operation Category. Include any other CIC that also yields a positive response to the question above. Imagination may be required.

Terms: The author is aware of at least three ways that the term "Critical Information" is used by OPSEC professionals. Hence, for the sake of clarity, the terms "Critical Information Components" and "The critical Information" are introduced in this section and the next.

Clarification: Readers with an intelligence background will notice that these components are similar to the steps in a Hostile Intelligence Service Collection Strategy—HOIS Collection Strategy. In fact, the components listed in Appendix C.II probably look like a generalized statement of a HOIS Collection Strategy.

EXAMPLE

Determine Critical Information Components

See Generic Operation Category III in Appendix C.I.

Tailor and Screen

EXISTENCE: a research, development, testing, evaluation, and production product.

WHO: the company and, in particular, the project manager, clerical staff, and chemists.

TYPE: a plastic glove project.

LOCATION: A suite on the third floor of building 3 in the company's main complex in the Midwestern city of Metrotown.

LOCATION'S TIME FRAME: from now until the product release in six months.

CONCEPTUAL DESIGN: none.

CAPABILITY: thinness of the new plastic glove.

VULNERABILITY: none.

BREAKTHROUGH: the use of Catalyst Y extracted from the root of the rare Philippine shrub in the manufacturing of the plastic.

INTEGRATION TECHNIQUE: none.

MANUFACTURING TECHNIQUE: none.

QUANTITY: 20,000,000.

PRICE: $1.99 per pair.

TARGET MARKET: eastern Untied States.

MARKETING STRATEGY: saturation publicity campaign.

UNRELIABLE OR LOST PRODUCTION: not applicable.

CUSTOMER LOSS: not applicable.

PROCEDURE

Determine Critical Information Components (continued)

Tailor and Screen (continued)

Finally, using the statement ask the following question to decide if a possible CIC is actually a CIC:

> *Could knowledge of this Critical Information Component (CIC) about this Good-Guy Operation be of value to the Adversary in causing any Bad-Guy Objectives?*

Determine the Critical Information

Aggregate CIC.   For each Operation and Adversary, aggregate the Critical Information Components into one sentence connected with "ANDs."

EXAMPLE

Determine Critical Information Components (continued)

Tailor and Screen (continued)

The preceding list is reviewed for criticality relative to the following tailored question:

> *Could knowledge of this Critical Information Component (CIC) about the new plastic glove project be of value to any of the competitors in hurting the release and sales of the new plastic gloves?*

The possible CIC—Quantity—is excluded because it would not be of value to the competitors to know that the quantity of gloves produced is 20,000,000.

Determine *The* Critical Information

Aggregate CIC.   Aggregation of the list of Critical Information Components yields a possibility for The Critical Information:

There is a research, development, testing, evaluation, and production project,

AND The project manager, clerical staff, and chemists are doing the project,

AND The project is a plastic glove research, development, testing, evaluation, and production project,

AND The location of the Organization's project is a suite on the third floor of Building 3 in the company's main complex in the Midwestern city of Metrotown,

AND Product release is in six months,

AND The product is twice as thin as any industry product,

AND Catalyst Y from the root of a somewhat rare Philippine shrub is the new feature of the manufacturing process,

AND The price will be $1.99 per pair,

AND The target market is the eastern seaboard,

AND The marketing strategy is a saturation publicity campaign.

PROCEDURE

Determine The Critical Information (continued)

Edit Aggregated CIC.   Edit the sentence so that it is easier to read and to understand.

Sufficiency Check.   Using the aggregated and edited statement, ask the following question to decide if the possible Critical Information is actually The Critical Information:

> *Could knowledge of The Critical Information by the Adversary be sufficient to allow the Adversary to initiate actions that would lead to harm or damage or lower operational effectiveness?*

If the answer to this question is not "YES," then additional Critical Information Components (CIC) are needed; go back to the previous section to determine additional CIC. Continue repeating these two sections until (1) each CIC gets a "YES" response to the question in the previous section, and (2) the aggregated Set of CIC, The Critical Information, gets a "YES" response to preceding question in this section.

This completes the sections that produce The Critical Information. In summary, The Critical Information for an operation is information that, if learned by the Adversary, could allow the Bad-Guy Objectives (short-term or long-term harm or damage to the Operation or loss of operational effectiveness).

EXAMPLE

Determine The Critical Information (continued)

Edit Aggregated CIC. The edited version of this possibility for the Critical Information is:

> In the company suite the project manager, clerical staff, and chemists are engaged in the research, development, testing, evaluation, and production of a new plastic glove. The plastic glove is twice as thin as any other industry product due to manufacturing with Catalyst Y — from the root of a somewhat rare Philippine shrub. The saturation publicity Campaign of the two-dollar glove will be in six months.

Sufficiency Check. Check this possibility against the following tailored question:

> Could knowledge by competitors of this information be sufficient to allow them to initiate actions leading to damaging our projected glove release?

If the answer yields a "YES," then the preceding is a statement of the Critical Information.

PROCEDURE

Determine Sources of Information

For each Operation-Adversary pair, make a list of the "medium," "event," and "other phenomenon" Sources of Information involved—in the Operation that might contain or indicate any Critical Information Components about the Operation. Examples of Sources of Information are:

Media

radio messages (voice and data)

telephone messages (voice, data, facsimile)

stored machine data

paper documents

nonpaper documents

chalk/dry/bulletin boards

interpersonal conversations, including meetings

Events

predictive activities

unusual activities

Other Phenomena

physical signatures and profiles

physical residuals (includes odors, sounds, seismic waves, etc.)

intentional and unintentional electromagnetic emanations

For the last five Sources of Information, the existence of the Source of Information is, in fact, really information. On the other hand, for the first seven, the information is, in some sense, embedded in or imprinted on the Source of Information.

Determine Major Vulnerabilities

For each Operation-Adversary pair and location the Operation is conducted, list each Major Vulnerability, a weakness (not known by the Adversary; see notes below) in the safeguards system protecting the location and functional area from the Adversary. Particular attention should be given to access-control, personnel, computer, and communications Vulnerabilities.

Notes: (a) If the Adversary knows a vulnerability, there is no need to call it "sensitive information." (b) A Major vulnerability exists even if there is no Adversary capable of exploiting it. Successful completion of this step may require expertise in the security disciplines of Physical, Personnel, Computer, and Communications Security.

EXAMPLE

Determine Sources of Information

The sources of Information that exist due to the plastic glove project are:

Media

telephone messages
facsimile messages
stored machine data in two computers and on floppy disks
paper documents
vugraphs
chalkboards, dryboards, and bulletin boards
interpersonal conversations, including meetings

Event

unusual activities

Other Phenomena

physical residuals

Determine Major Vulnerabilities

Major Vulnerabilities in the safeguards system protecting the suite from the competitors are:

the rear laboratory emergency door, and
the lead scientist's alcohol problem.

PROCEDURE

Determine Sources of Sensitive Information (Indicator Categories)

Events and Other Phenomena.   Make a list of the "event" and "other phenomenon" Sources of Information from the previous section.

Media.   For each "medium" Source of Information, add to the list each Source "that mentions"

- the "events" (again!)
- the "other phenomena" (again!)
- Major Vulnerabilities (previous section)
- Critical Information Components

This concludes the procedure for determining Critical Information and Indicator Categories.

EXAMPLE

Determine Sources of Sensitive Information (Indicator Categories)

The Sources of Sensitive Information (Indicator Categories) are by category:

Event

- Delivery of packages from the Philippines
- Other Phenomenon
- manufacturing waste liquids contain traces of Catalyst Y

Media

- telephone messages mentioning:
  Critical Information Component
  the Philippine packages
  the traces of Catalyst Y in waste liquids
  the rear lab door situation, or
  the lead scientist's alcohol problem
- facsimile messages transmitting or referencing:
  a Critical Information Component
  the Philippine packages
  the traces of Catalyst Y in waste liquids
  the rear lab door situation, or
  the lead scientist's alcohol problem
- computers or floppy disks storing or referencing:
  Critical Information Component
  the Philippine packages
  the traces of Catalyst Y in waste liquids
  the rear lab door situation
  the lead scientist's alcohol problem
- paper documents mentioning:
  Critical Information Component
  the Philippine packages
  the traces of Catalyst Y in waste liquids
  the rear lab door situation
  the lead scientist's alcohol problem
- vu-graphs, slides, or other projection media mentioning:
  Critical Information component
  the Philippine packages
  the traces of Catalyst Y in waste liquids
  the rear lab door situation
  the lead scientist's alcohol problem

- chalkboards, dryboards, and bulletin boards mentioning:
  Critical Information Component
  the Philippine packages
  the traces of Catalyst Y in waste liquids
  the rear lab door situation
  the lead scientist's alcohol problem
- interpersonal conversations and meetings mentioning:
  Critical Information Component,
  the Philippine packages,
  the traces of Catalyst Y in waste liquids
  the rear lab door situation
  the lead scientist's alcohol problem

This concludes the example.

TIPS FROM OPERATIONS SECURITY

Tips

The discipline of operations security (OPSEC) offers the following perspectives to support the effective use of this Appendix.

Dissemination. The decision-maker may want to order dissemination of (1) each Critical Information Component, (2) the time frame of protection of that Component, and (3) Sources of Sensitive Information (Indicator Categories) to each employee working on the sensitive operation with the following restriction:

Each Critical Information Component and each Major Vulnerability will be disseminated only to those workers who have a "need to know" or whom the decision-maker determines must be granted "accepted accessibility." In the latter case a nondisclosure statement may be helpful.

Time. The timing or phasing of an operation may change the critical and the sensitive information in the operation. In particular, as the operation progresses through time, certain Critical Information Components may be discovered, exposed, leaked, and so forth; trying to protect this information afterwards may be deemed unwise. This piece of information would no longer be "critical" nor would any information referring to this former Critical Information Component be sensitive.

Also, the use of this Appendix gives a perspective on a "slice in time"; the decision-maker may want to evaluate the operation using the procedure in this Appendix at appropriate times during the operation.

Planning. In particular, experience has shown that the best time to start protecting critical and sensitive information is in the planning stages of an operation. I highly recommend that the decision-maker develop a plan for such protection during operation planning stages.

Suggestion. A useful planning technique used by Operations Security (OPSEC) practitioners is to put the different phases of the operation next to a timeline. Then, as each Critical Information Component is determined, the time frame during which protection of that Component is needed is also marked. The resulting graph is a presentation of how the Critical Information Components in the Operation change over time.

CONCLUSION

Being able to effectively identify the instances of sensitive information that "mention" or "refer" to Critical Information Components, Sources of Information, or Major Vulnerabilities is not a simple task. In fact, it takes Operation Security (OPSEC) practitioners years of study and practice to become proficient in this identification. The decision-maker who needs further help in protection of critical and sensitive information should contact an OPSEC practitioner for assistance.

APPENDIX C.I—GENERIC OPERATION CATEGORIES

The Generic Operation Categories are:

I. Interception and Interdiction of Adversary (Mobile Operation)
II. Sensitive Movement of personnel, Vehicles, or Materials (Troops, Planes, Hostage Rescue, Hostage Taking, Assassination)
III. Research, Development, Testing, Evaluation, and Production of Sensitive Technology (or Commodities)
IV. Operational Strategic or Sensitive Military Weapons
V. Protection at Transportation Stations or Nodes
VI. Communications Network Relationship
VII. Undercover Personnel
VIII. Conduct of Sensitive Negotiations
IX. Intelligence Gathering
X. Presence of Important Personnel at a Site
XI. Safety of Important Personnel
    a. Permanent Site
    b. Temporary Fixed Site (Conference Center, Hospital, Airport, Hotel)
    c. Fixed Route Mobile Tour (and Safe Movement of Sensitive Materials)

In order to illustrate the choice of the best Category, let's say that the Operation is the protection of a General or other VIP departing an airport. One of the threats is a terrorist attack. Both Generic Categories V (Protection at Transportation Stations) and XIb (Safety of Important Personnel at a Temporary Fixed Site) apply. However, the latter is a closer statement of the Operation mission. Hence, only Generic Category XIb would be chosen for this Operation.

APPENDIX C.II—CRITICAL INFORMATION COMPONENTS OF GENERIC OPERATION CATEGORIES

Each page is devoted to one of the Generic Operation Categories listed in Appendix C.I. Included is a list of possible Critical Information Components of that Generic Operation Category. The list may not be complete; there may be Critical Information Components for the Operation-Adversary pair that are not listed under that Generic Operation Category. Also, there may be listed Critical Information Components that are not of value to the Adversary in causing Bad-Guy Objectives to the Operation. Choose only those listed Critical Information Components for which "YES" is the answer to the following question:

> Could knowledge of this Critical Information Component (CIC) about this Good-Guy Operation be of value to the Adversary in causing any Bad-Guy Objectives?

GENERIC OPERATION CATEGORY I:
INTERCEPTION AND INTERDICTION OF ADVERSARY
(MOBILE OPERATION)

Possible Critical Information Components

Existence. The existence of a mobile force to intercept and interdict the adversary.

Who. Organizations that have an objective to intercept and interdict the Adversary.

Profiles. List of characteristics of the Adversary's operations (if one of these PROFILES is observed, the Organization will more probably move assets for possible interception and interdiction).

Profile Detection Capability. Capability of the Organization's surveillance system to detect Profiles.

Profile Detection. Organization's intelligence findings in identifying an Adversary operation as fitting a Profile.

Position Detection. Organization's intelligence findings of the location of the Adversary relative to a PROFILE.

Asset Location. Location of the Organization's assets that could be used to intercept and interdict the Adversary.

Asset Quantity. The quantity of the Organization's assets that could be to intercept and interdict the Adversary.

Time to Intercept. Amount of time needed to move assets to Adversary's Detected Position.

Chase Speed. Velocity of Organization's assets during chase.

Chase Agility. Agility of Organization's assets during chase in changing directions, velocity, and so forth.

Weapon Capability. The capability of the Organization's weapons that could be used to interdict the Adversary.

Access Capability. The capability of the Organization to gain rapid physical access to the place where the Adversary is present.

Capability to Detect Spoofing. The capability, including sources and methods, of the Organization to detect Adversary spoofing.

Intelligence about Spoofing. The intelligence gathered about Adversary spoofing.

Interdiction Regulations.   Regulations affecting the Organization's ability to interdict, confiscate, arrest, and successfully prosecute the Adversary after an Interception.

GENERIC OPERATION CATEGORY II:
SENSITIVE MOVEMENT OF PERSONNEL VEHICLES, OR MATERIALS

(Troops, Planes, Hostage Rescue, Hostage Taking, Assassination)

Possible Critical Information Components

Existence. The existence of an operation to secretly move personnel, vehicles, or materials.

Who. The organization to whom the personnel, vehicles, or materials belong, or with whom they are associated.

Identities. The identities of the transported items—personnel, vehicles, or materials (may need to be specific).

Quantity. Quantity of identified (previous component) transported items.

Planned Route to Destination. The route planned for transportation of the personnel, vehicles, or materials to the destination.

Method of Transport to Destination. Type of carrier (boat, car, plane, and so forth) for the personnel, vehicles, or materials to the destination.

Planned Route from Destination. The route planned for transportation of the personnel, vehicles, or materials away from the destination.

Method of Transport from Destination. Type of carrier (boat, car, plane, and so forth) for the personnel, vehicles, or materials away from the destination.

Identity of Transport. Identity of particular carriers of the personnel, vehicles, or materials.

Route Security. Security in place to protect personnel, vehicles, or materials along the Planned Route.

Departure Time. Time of departure of personnel, vehicles, or materials. Time at which the personnel, vehicles, or materials will be expected to be points along the Planned Route.

Destination. The final destination of the moved personnel, vehicles, or materials.

GENERIC OPERATION CATEGORY III: RESEARCH, DEVELOPMENT, TESTING, EVALUATION (RDTE), AND PRODUCTION OF SENSITIVE TECHNOLOGY (OR COMMODITIES)

Possible Critical Information Components

Existence. The existence of a research, development, testing, evaluation (RDTE), and production project of sensitive technology (or commodities).

Who. Organizations who are involved in the RDTE process.

Type. The type of RDTE product; for instance, weapon, vehicle, computer, software, and so forth (also, wheat, beef, etc.).

Locations. Locations of the Organization's work areas on the RDTE and production project.

Locations' Time Frames. Time frame during which the Organization is working on the RDTE and production project at each Location.

Conceptual Design. Engineering, science, computer science, and mathematics used as conceptual framework for the RDTE and production project (genetics).

Capabilities. Technological (growth, resistance) capabilities of the produced RDTE project (may be several).

Technical Vulnerabilities. Known or discovered technical vulnerabilities in the performance, effectiveness, and reliability of the RDTE and production project.

Breakthroughs. Technological breakthroughs in the RDTE and production project that will make the item better, or able to be produced faster, and so forth (e.g., insecticide, growth hormone).

Integration Technique. A new method of integrating two or more technologies.

Manufacturing Technique. A new or special manufacturing process for producing the sensitive technology (planting, fertilizing, applying insecticide).

Quantity Produced. Quantity of particular pieces of sensitive technology produced at particular times.

Price. Price or volume price of each piece of sensitive technology at particular times.

Target Market. Prospective customers of the sensitive technology.

Marketing Strategies.   Strategies used by the Organization to try to sell a sensitive technology.

Unreliable/Lost Production.   Production of the sensitive technology diminished or unreliable due to unreliability or loss of factors such as resources, suppliers, technical expertise.

Customer Loss.   Loss of customers of the sensitive technology.

GENERIC OPERATION CATEGORY IV:
OPERATIONAL STRATEGIC OR SENSITIVE MILITARY WEAPONS

Possible Critical Information Components

Existence.   The existence of operational strategic or sensitive military weapons.

Weapon Locations.   Location where the Organization positions its weapon assets.

Target Locations.   Adversary's locations at which the Organization's weapons are targeted.

Weapons' Vulnerabilities.   Known or discovered vulnerabilities in the performance, effectiveness, and reliability of the weapons.

Types.   Types of strategic weapons used by the Organization against the Adversary.

Weapon Capability.   Capabilities of each TYPE of weapon used by the Organization against the Adversary.

Quantity.   Quantity of each TYPE of weapon used by the Organization against the Adversary.

Time of Delivery.   The time at which weapons are delivered or fired toward the Adversary.

Delivery Procedures.   The delivery or firing procedures for weapons used against the Adversary.

Delivery Control Procedures.   The procedures for the authorization and the procedures for the communication of the authorization for the delivery of weapons used against the Adversary.

GENERIC OPERATION CATEGORY V:
PROTECTION AT TRANSPORTATION STATIONS

Possible Critical Information Components

Portals. The location of each of the entrance and exit portals to the transportation media—ship, airplane, train, automobile (may be several).

Portal Security. Security in place at each Portal.

Non-Portal Security. Security at places other than Portals.

Baggage Procedures. Procedures in place to check baggage for unauthorized materials.

Other Checking Procedures. Procedures in place to check all non-baggage-transported items (mail, food, etc.) for unauthorized materials.

Baggage Security. Security in place to protect baggage from unauthorized access.

Special Equipment Types. The existence of special detection equipment types.

Special Equipment Locations. The location of each type of special detection equipment.

Special Equipment Capability. The technological detection capabilities of each type of special equipment.

Presence of Hazmat. The presence of hazardous materials at the station.

Locations of Hazmat. The locations of hazardous materials at the station.

Hazmat Itinerary. Time frame during which the hazardous materials will be at the station.

GENERIC OPERATION CATEGORY VI:
COMMUNICATIONS NETWORK RELATIONSHIP

Possible Critical Information Components

Existence.   The existence of a communications net.

Net Structure.   The existing communications links between pairs of nodes in the network.

Position of Command Node.   Identification of the Command Node from among the other nodes in the network.

Identity of Nodes.   Identity of individual members of the network (may be several).

Location of Nodes.   Physical location of net nodes.

Net Frequencies.   For radio nets, the frequencies over which the net communicates.

Net Time Schedule.   The times during which the net communicates.

Vulnerability in Network.   A known vulnerability in the network, such as load capability.

Capability to Detect Spoofing.   The capability, including sources and methods, of the Organization to detect Adversary spoofing of the network.

Intelligence about Spoofing.   The intelligence gathered about Adversary spoofing of the network.

GENERIC OPERATION CATEGORY VII:
UNDERCOVER PERSONNEL

Possible Critical Information Components

Existence.   The existence of an undercover personnel operation to gain information or evidence.

Targeted Operation.   The specific Adversary operation targeted by the undercover personnel (counter) operation.

Affiliation.   The Organization for which the undercover personnel work.

Identity.   The names of the undercover personnel.

Personnel Importance.   The positions of the undercover personnel.

Known Intelligence.   Organization's intelligence findings about the Adversary's operations.

Communication System.   The method of communication of undercover personnel with superiors.

Communication Schedule.   The scheduled times when communications between superiors and undercover personnel is planned.

Support System .   The support system in place to provide logistical funds and so on to undercover personnel.

Special Assets and Means.   Special assets and means used by undercover personnel.

Escape Plan.   Contingency plans for "blown" cover.

Undercover Regulations.   Regulations or procedures affecting the Organization's ability to gather information about the Adversary, to gather evidence against the Adversary, to arrest the Adversary, and to successfully prosecute the Adversary during an undercover operation.

GENERIC OPERATION CATEGORY VIII:
CONDUCT OF SENSITIVE NEGOTIATIONS

Possible Critical Information Components

Negotiators.   Identity of negotiators.

Negotiators' Locations.   Locations of the negotiators.

Negotiators' Itinerary.   Times at which the negotiators will be at specific locations.

Locations' Security.   Security in place at the negotiators' locations.

"Bottom Line" Negotiation Posture.   The negotiation posture either generated or given to the negotiators by their superiors of a "bottom line" position.

Other Negotiation Posture.   The negotiation posture, other than "bottom line," either generated or given to the negotiators by their superiors.

Document Existence.   The existence of documents (paper, nonpaper, software) containing details of the negotiation posture.

Document Security Posture.   The procedures, equipment, and so forth, in place to guarantee the security of the documents (paper, nonpaper, software) containing details of the negotiation posture.

Intelligence Sources and Methods.   The sources and methods in place to collect intelligence about the Adversary's negotiation posture.

Intelligence Known.   The previously collected intelligence about the Adversary's negotiation posture.

Capability to Detect Spoofing.   The capability, including sources and methods, of the Organization to detect Adversary spoofing of Operation negotiation posture.

Intelligence about Spoofing.   The intelligence gathered about Adversary spoof of Operation negotiation posture.

GENERIC OPERATION CATEGORY IX: INTELLIGENCE GATHERING

Possible Critical Information Components

Existence. The existence of an operation to secretly gather intelligence.

Who. Organizations that have an objective to collect intelligence against the Adversary.

Requirements. List of the intelligence requirements against the Adversary against which the Organization is authorized to collect.

Collection Methods. Methods used by the Organization against the Adversary relative to an intelligence requirement.

Vulnerabilities. Known or discovered vulnerabilities in the performance, effectiveness, and reliability of collection assets.

Types. Types of collection assets used by the Organization against the Adversary.

Collection Asset Capability. Capabilities of each TYPE of collection asset used by the Organization against the Adversary.

Target Identity or Locations. Locations of the Adversary where collection is targeted.

Collection Locations. Location where the Organization positions its collection assets.

Time Frame. Time during which collection against the Adversary is done.

Collection Regulations. Regulations affecting the Organization's ability to collect intelligence against the Adversary.

Fulfilled Requirement. The degree of fulfillment of an intelligence requirement against the Adversary.

Capability to Detect Spoofing. The capability, including sources and methods, of the Organization to detect Adversary spoofing.

Intelligence about Spoofing. The intelligence gathered about Adversary spoofing.

GENERIC OPERATION CATEGORY X:
PRESENCE OF IMPORTANT PERSONNEL AT A SITE

Possible Critical Information Components

Identity.   The names of the important personnel.

Importance.   The positions of the important personnel.

Affiliation.   The organizations to which the important personnel belong.

Site.   Site at which the important personnel will be present.

Scheduled Places.   Particular rooms or areas within that Site at which the important personnel are scheduled to be.

Itinerary.   Time frame during which the important personnel will be at particular Scheduled Places.

GENERIC OPERATION CATEGORY XIA:
SAFETY OF IMPORTANT PERSONNEL—PERMANENT SITE

Possible Critical Information Components

Who.   The names and positions of the important personnel.

Site.   Permanent site at which protection is planned for the important personnel.

Scheduled Places.   Particular rooms or areas within that Site at which the important personnel are scheduled to be.

Itinerary.   Time frame during which the important personnel will be at particular Scheduled Places.

Scheduled Places' Security.   Security in place at Scheduled Places to prevent harm to the important personnel.

GENERIC OPERATION CATEGORY XIB:
SAFETY OF IMPORTANT PERSONNEL—
TEMPORARY FIXED SITE (CONFERENCE CENTER, HOSPITAL,
AIRPORT, LODGING, ETC.)

Possible Critical Information Components

Who.   The names and positions of the important personnel.

Site.   Site at which protection is planned for the important personnel.

Arrival Area.   Area at the Site at which the important personnel arrive.

Entrance Portal.   The portal at the Arrival Area at which the important personnel enter the Site facility.

Arrival Time.   Time at which the important personnel will arrive at the Arrival Area.

Arrival Area Security.   Security in place at the Arrival Area to prevent harm to the important personnel.

Exit Portal.   Exit used by the important personnel when leaving the Site.

Departure Area.   Area at the Site at which the important personnel depart.

Departure Time.   Time at which the important personnel will depart from the Site.

Departure Security.   Security in place at the Departure Area to prevent harm to the important personnel.

Scheduled Places.   Particular rooms or areas within the Site at which the important personnel are scheduled to be.

Itinerary.   Time frame during which the important personnel will be at particular Scheduled Places.

Scheduled Places' Security.   Security in place at Scheduled Places to prevent harm to the important personnel.

GENERIC OPERATION CATEGORY XIC:
SAFETY OF IMPORTANT PERSONNEL—FIXED ROUTE MOBILE
TOUR (AND SAFE MOVEMENT OF SENSITIVE MATERIALS)

Possible Critical Information Components

Who. The names and positions of the important personnel (kind of sensitive material).

Planned Route. The route planned for transportation of the important personnel (sensitive material).

Method of Transport. Type of carrier (boat, car, plane, etc.) of the important personnel (sensitive material).

Identity of Transport. Identity of particular carriers of the important personnel (sensitive material).

Vehicle Security. Security in place to prevent unauthorized personnel from tampering with vehicles used to transport the important personnel (sensitive material).

Route Security. Security in place to protect important personnel (sensitive material) at departure, along the Planned Route, and at destination.

Departure Time. Time of departure of the important personnel (sensitive material).

Itinerary. Time at which the important personnel (sensitive material) will be expected to be at certain points along the Planned Route.

Destination. The final destination of the moved important personnel (sensitive material).

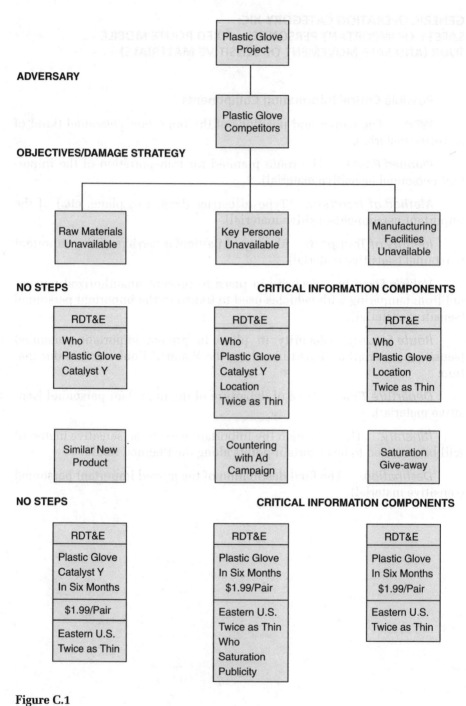

Figure C.1

Appendix D

Obtaining Asset Information: Conducting Interviews

Some of your greatest sources of asset information, which are important in terms of identifying what is critical to the organization, are your customers. "Customers" in this sense are those people within your own organization for whom you are performing a risk assessment in order to protect various critical assets. It is the individuals who work closest to the project, material, or information of concern who can provide you with needed information. You need information; they have it.

SOURCES OF ASSET INFORMATION

Asset information comes from a variety of sources.

Site Personnel Interviews

Interview those individuals close to, or supporting, the project, program, or operation for which the risk assessment is being conducted. Some of the types of individuals to be interviewed were identified in Chapter 4, "Asset Identification," but there are others within the organization. The person you least expect may well be interviewed. During the course of any assessment, other names crop up or are freely given to you. Don't dismiss them out of hand. They may have just that one piece of information you need to complete your data collection.

Also, be aware that, if you are working on the asset assessment, you will probably uncover information relating to threats and vulnerabilities. Why? Because when a person talks about a specific asset, and they realize that it requires protection, their mind will gravitate towards some of the possible or known threats and vulnerabilities associated with the asset. Use such information; never discard it just because you were not at that particular step in the asset process.

Rosters

Every organization keeps a variety of lists; lists of what they have, what has been ordered, what is lost, and so forth. There are lists of documents relating to a project or program; lists detailing equipment required for the program or project; personnel rosters associated with the program; access control for certain sensitive or controlled areas; and other lists. They abound in the larger organizations. Use these lists to determine assets, who within the organization "owns" (has control over) the assets, who has access or works with the assets, and who performs maintenance on the assets.

Surveys

Over a period of time various types of surveys or audits may have been performed in the organization. Take a look at them. Most will be found in the administration, security, supply, legal, or financial auditing sections of the organization. In some cases, such reports have been centralized. If so, your job has just been made much easier in terms of tracking them down. The surveys are important for several reasons, and you require access to them in order to ensure the risk assessment is performed adequately. Information within the reports will detail assets, areas of risk, areas of vulnerability, problems and concerns that have surfaced in the past, and various recommendations. The recommendations area of the report should be carefully checked. The risk manager is checking to determine if the recommendations were implemented, or discarded, and if discarded, why.

Existing Security Plans

Security plans detail the current security posture of the physical plant for the organization. Any master security plan should covers all aspects of security. In most organizations, there is a myriad of smaller plans, such as the physical security plan, the information protection security plan, the computer security plan, emergency or crisis management, financial, and other plans that may be in place. Some may be outlines, others may have been created to fill a requirement (and thus, probably, mostly worthless), while others still may be overly detailed. Compare the security plans and what they are supposed to accomplish and protect against the various survey reports. Are there inconsistencies? Whether there are inconsistencies or not, review the plans as they relate to the risk assessment.

Mission and Functions Statements

Every program, project, or operations, not to mention the organization itself, has a purpose for being. Without it, it ceases to function. Review the mission and functions statements and determine how they apply to the risk assessment. Information in some statements are of value when they tell you something someone or some other document hasn't. In some cases, it is assumed that the risk manager and team are aware of the organization's mission and functions, so items within the statements are never discussed. Assumption is a poor excuse and a hindrance to good risk management procedures and practices.

Technical Reports

Technical reports usually lie with scientists, engineers, computer technicians, and the like. Because of the complexity of these reports, they have a limited distribution and readership. But, when they apply (or could apply) to a risk assessment, the risk team needs to be aware of them, who uses the report, and who can discuss the report. A team member may not understand the report, but the individual who uses it certainly can, providing information from the technical report relative to various assets, possible threats, and any known or suspected vulnerabilities.

INTERVIEWS

The risk manager and the risk assessment team will perform a number of interviews within, and sometimes outside, the organization. This section outlines various items of concern when interviews will be conducted. No fancy words or phrases, "just the facts," and nothing else.

Why Interview?

- To determine objective facts, and to solicit opinions and interpretations
- To gain insights into organizational relationships
- To validate observations
- To identify additional information leads

Interview Attitudes

- Be straightforward and professional
- Establish a cooperative relationship

- Assume each interview will provide important, essential information
- Recognize and avoid imposing personal prejudices and tendencies

Preparing for the Interview

- Know the interview's goals: What Do You Want?
- Prepare an interview guide
- Know the interview setting
- Know the subject

Interview Guides

Interview guides provide a systematic method of addressing the various questions to be posed. Such guides ensure that all subject areas are covered in the required depth. Any interview guide used with a risk assessment needs to be standardized, with all personnel on the risk assessment team using the same guide, thus providing assurance that each interview conducted maintains a level of standardization throughout the interview process. As such, the standardized interview guides aid in the elicitation of the specific information from:

- Management, command, and supervisory personnel
- Planning and operations personnel
- Technical, engineering, and scientific personnel
- Support personnel

Interview guides aid in the elicitation of critical information data from:

- Program and organizational personnel
- Intelligence and other government agencies
- Technical community personnel

Interview guides aid in the elicitation of adversary and threat data from:

- Intelligence agency and/or other government agency personnel
- State, local, and government law enforcement personnel
- Other knowledgeable personnel

When developing an interview guide:

- Keep the format flexible; tailor it to meet current needs.
- Allow space for notes.

- Prepare a list of areas to be covered. List critical data items for each area.

CONDUCTING THE INTERVIEW

Interview Setting

- Consider Protocol
- Schedule appointments well in advance; think about "logistical" arrangements.
- Arrange for privacy.
- Discuss nonattribution of information.

Know the Subject

- Learn as much as possible about the interviewee's job functions.
- Avoid conveying preconceptions.
- Do not attempt to impress with your knowledge.
- Be empathetic.

The Interview Process

- Put the interviewee at ease.
- Establish rapport.
- Plan your time.
- Identify additional leads for further information.
- Listen.

Controlling the Interview

- Stay on track.
- Keep interview objectives in mind.
- Stay positive and nonjudgmental.
- Allow interviewee to express options, attitudes, and beliefs.
- LISTEN.

Note-Taking

- Tell interviewee why names are taken.
- Notes should not be taken by interviewing team member. Have another team member available, or delay note-taking, if possible.
- Allow time to transcribe notes.
- In your notes, evaluate and filter.
- Indicate key points (circle, checks, underline); allow space to add information later; use abbreviations.
- Take notes in your own words.
- Expand as soon as possible.
- Be straightforward and professional.

Things "Not to Do"

- Avoid asking "yes" or "no" questions.
- Never answer a question for the interviewee.
- Never interrupt a fellow team member while questioning.
- Never assume the intent of vague answers.
- Never cut an interviewee short.

STRUCTURING YOUR INTERVIEW QUESTIONS

There are four types of interview questions commonly used in survey interviews:

- Closed
- Leading
- Open-ended
- Probe

Closed Questions

Closed questions are commonly used by inexperienced interviewers. These are the lowest level of the four types of questions and generally seek to elicit specific information and facts. Closed questions allow little room for expansion, for example, "What did the project cost?" "Do you process travel vouchers?"

You want to encourage short, specific answers, not long drawn-out answers. Typically, the interviewer should be talking about 60 to 70 percent of the time.

Leading Questions

- Almost always "closed"
- Embeds an answer within the question
- May confuse the interviewee
- Suggests an expected/desired answer: "You do use the secure phone when discussing the project, don't you?" "Planning documents are controlled, aren't they?"

Be careful with leading questions. The interviewee may well bias an answer to please the interviewer, basically saying what he or she believes the interviewer wants to hear. This can create friction, though not necessarily at the initial stages of the interview.

Open-Ended Questions

- Most effective type of interview question
- Generates highest level of information
- Allows the interviewee latitude
- Tends to provide general perspectives and information
- Serves as the basis for subsequent probe questions: "How are operations plans disseminated?" "What is the process for shipping equipment to test sites?"

With these questions, you allow the interviewee to decide what and how much to say. When using open-ended questions, you require careful advance planning in specific question development. Using these types of questions, the interviewee will do 60 to 80 percent of the talking.

Probe Questions

Probe questions are used to lead the interviewee to the next level of detail in order to elicit additional information and clarification. Such questions can help to bring to the surface the attitudes of the interviewee or others within his sphere of influence. These questions should be a planned part of the general strategy.

The Funneling Technique

Whenever possible, use a combination of questioning techniques to get the real specifics, the "meat" of the subject matter in interviews. This is referred to as "funneling," as illustrated below:

Open question: "Tell me about the project."

More directive question: "What are your tasks in the project."

More direct: "What success measures have you devised?"

Closed questions: "Who determines if the project is successful?"

Follow-up questions should be prepared or at least anticipated by the interviewer.

A COUPLE OF SUGGESTIONS

Enhancing Your Interview Results

Nonattribution.   You get more information this way, and it will usually be unbiased and free from any organizational political concerns.

Whom to Interview.   Knowing whom to interview is just as important as knowing what questions to ask.

Facilities.   Have appropriate facilities available; a quiet room, quality furniture, good lighting, and possibly coffee or a light refreshment. When interviewing people from middle or senior management, select a location near their office area, never away. The more senior the person, the more likely you will be in their office for the interview. No matter what, don't be intimidated by the surroundings or location.

Scheduling.   Work your schedule around their schedule. You may be seen as a hindrance to the program or project, or a requirement they need to complete quickly. Take as little time as possible, but allow for another session if necessary. Be flexible.

Selecting Team Personnel.   All personnel on a risk assessment team should have some initial specialty area. It is hoped that they have background in other areas also. Avoid having personnel "volunteered" or appointed for you. The personnel should be easy to get along with, and easy to get along with each other. Their attitude is professional and concerned. They should all want to produce a quality product based on a thorough risk analysis. Foot-dragging and sloth are out.

Team Meetings.   At the start, meetings should be once a day, at the end of the day, to see what was accomplished and to plan for the next day. After a week, everyone should be able to meet more infrequently, perhaps one-on-one to pass data back and forth. Meet in an area free from distractions. Use a bulletin board to post notes. File information immediately for quick reference or further use. Type up notes daily. Maintain a work schedule and stick to it.

Appendix E

Technology Collection Trends in the U.S. Defense Industry

In order to protect various assets to their fullest, the risk manager needs to be acutely aware of the various technology collection trends that are ongoing. While many organizations do, in fact, hold government contracts, others do not. Even so, the collection trends against the U.S. Defense industries should be carefully read. What is not of national interest today may be tomorrow. Your organization may have no government contracts now, but in the near future, because of a program or project or an R&D venture that is currently taking place, a government contract could just be around the corner. Further, the Department of Commerce, like the FBI, is concerned about the loss the leading-edge technologies.

This Appendix is based on U.S. defense industry reporting of suspicious activity during 1996. The Defense Security Service (DSS), formerly the Defense Investigative Service (DIS), was now able to build upon previously observed trends of collection interest and activity by foreign companies *and* governments against U.S. industry. The collected data that was used and assessed to develop these trends is also used to provide threat data for national policy formulation. Referrals of potential economic espionage collection efforts help to educate industry, security, and counterintelligence personnel in the methods of operation (MO) being used against U.S. industry by foreign entities.

Personnel security investigation (PSI) and industrial security (IS) reports resulted in counterintelligence investigative and analytical referrals to the U.S. counterintelligence community, covering a wide range of issues. While using an intelligence officer (IO) to collect U.S. technology is a serious matter, it is not the most efficient means available.

The use of foreign scientists or engineers, working for foreign companies or institutions, is assessed to represent a more significant security challenge than the use of an IO. Visiting foreign scientists or engineers often gain access to U.S. facilities to collaborate on research. Once a foreign scientist or engineer has gained access to a facility, they have an advantage over an IO:

247

they know exactly what they want; there is less risk involved because of plausible cover; it is less expensive to develop bona fides; the technology can be collected more quickly; and the collected technology can be put into more immediate application in the foreign country.

Although traditional foreign threats continue their collection activities, DSS continues to observe the expansion of nontraditional foreign threat collection in industry. As the frequency and numbers of suspicious reports from cleared contractors continued to grow in 1996, an increase in the number of different countries involved in some form of suspicious contact also grew. A summary of the suspicious contacts reported in 1996 indicates that over forty different countries displayed some type of suspicious interest in one or more of the eighteen technology categories listed in the Militarily Critical Technology List (MCTL). These major technology categories include:

- Aeronautics Systems
- Armaments and Energetic Materials
- Chemical and Biological Systems
- Directed and Kinetic Energy Systems
- Electronics
- Ground Systems
- Guidance, Navigation, and Vehicle Control
- Information Systems
- Information Warfare
- Manufacturing and Fabrication
- Marine Systems
- Materials
- Nuclear Systems
- Power Systems
- Sensors and Lasers
- Signature Control
- Space Systems
- Weapons Effects and Countermeasures

One trend observed in 1996 was the relative significance or priority of technology collection interest. Of the eighteen MCTL categories, the three primary technology categories of suspicious foreign collection activity against the U.S. defense industry were Information Systems Technology, Sensor and Laser Technology, and Aeronautics Systems Technology.

A summary of suspicious contacts in 1996, reported by cleared defense contractors, indicates that foreign entities employed a variety of modus operandi in attempting to acquire information. Reported suspicious foreign contacts associated with various defense industry security countermeasures (SCM) concerns include:

- Unsolicited requests for scientific and technological (S&T) information
- Inappropriate conduct during visits
- Solicitation and marketing of services
- Targeting at international exhibits, seminars, and conventions
- Exploitation of joint ventures and joint research
- Outright acquisitions of technology and companies
- Co-opting of former employees
- Targeting cultural commonalities

Unsolicited requests for U.S. defense industry S&T program information are the most frequently reported MO associated with foreign collection activity. These requests generally reflect a wide range of interests, and often represent an information management problem for the U.S. defense industry. A growing number of incidents involve faxing, mailing, E-mailing, or phoning such requests to individual U.S. persons rather than corporate marketing departments. There are several reasons to explain the popularity of this MO: it is simple and low cost, nonthreatening to the recipient, and less risk to the collector. The growing popularity and expansion of the Internet is reflected in a significant increase in reports of SCM incidents. Using the Internet provides a direct method of communication for foreign collection efforts. Internet access to a company's bulletin board, home page, and employees provide a foreign collector many avenues to broaden a collection effort. The one factor that made the vast majority of reported unsolicited requests for information suspicious was the fact that the information frequently being requested was covered under the International Traffic in Arms Regulations (ITAR) and would require a license for export.

"Marketing surveys," faxed or mailed to U.S. companies by foreign consortiums or "consulting" companies of various types often may exceed generally accepted terms of marketing information. Often, there are strong suspicions that the "surveyor" is employed by a competing foreign company. Surveys may solicit proprietary information concerning corporate affiliations, market projections, pricing policies, program or technology director's names, purchasing practices, and types and dollar amounts of U.S. Government contracts. Customer and supplier bases for a company may also be surveyed.

Inappropriate conduct during visits was the second most frequently reported MO associated with foreign collection activity. While visits may be more costly and slightly more risky to the foreign entity, they usually gain access to the targeted facility. For this reason, this MO, while not the most frequently used, is assessed to be the most damaging form of collection activity because it can result in the loss of some technology as a result of the visit. Once in the facility, good collectors can attempt to manipulate the visit to address some, and perhaps all, of their collection requirements.

The one factor that made many foreign visits suspicious was the extent to which the foreign visitor would ask questions or request information outside the scope of what was approved for discussion. With few exceptions, security compromises reported from foreign visit incidents could have been prevented if U.S. personnel had been properly prebriefed as part of the risk management process. Potential exploitation methods include:

- Hidden agendas, as opposed to the stated purpose of the visit
- Last minute and unannounced persons added to the visiting party
- "Wandering" visitors who become offended when confronted
- Initiating conversations with escorts beyond the approved scope of the visit

Many of these techniques are specifically designed to produce potentially embarrassing incidents for the host, in order to obtain collection objectives as a result of the host attempting to be conciliatory.

Additionally, foreign-sponsored workshops, tours, and the like are potential responses to a disapproved visit request. Another variation involves the foreign activity attempting to exploit different visit procedures for U.S. Government-sponsored, nonsponsored, and commercial visits, using each category as an alternative mechanism to gain access to excluded and protected information.

Foreign individuals, with technical backgrounds, who were soliciting and marketing their services to research facilities, academic institutions, and even cleared defense contractors, were reported with greater frequency during the past year. Additionally, U.S. technical experts are often requested by foreign entities to visit the foreign country and share their technical expertise. U.S. defense industry reporting indicates that while many requests are routine and benign, some are viewed with suspicion and represent significant SCM concerns. Usually associated with alleged employment opportunities, there is also an increasing trend involving "headhunters" soliciting information from employees.

International exhibits, conventions, and seminars are rich collection-targeting opportunities for foreign collectors. These functions directly link programs and technologies with knowledgeable personnel. Consequently, U.S. defense industry reporting reflects that collection activity at these events is usually expected. Good risk management processes that accurately consider what information is being exposed, where, when and to whom is essential for implementing threat-appropriate, cost-effective, and rational security countermeasures to balance marketing requirements.

Joint ventures, joint research, coproduction and various exchange agreements potentially offer significant collection opportunities for foreign interests. As with frequent foreign visits and other international programs, joint efforts place foreign personnel in close proximity to U.S. personnel and afford potential access to S&T programs and information. Access can be intentional or unintentional, and for both, legal or illegal. More frequently, as the world market for defense products and services shrinks, the offer of a joint venture is sufficient to entice U.S. contractors to provide unusually large amounts of technical data as part of the bidding process, only to have their information taken when the contract is canceled. U.S. defense industry reporting of SCM concerns continues to indicate that assimilation of foreign personnel into the work environment, without security-sustainment training programs, usually results in a relaxation of security awareness, often resulting in a security compromise.

Foreign acquisition of technology and companies in the U.S. defense industry continues to generate significant SCM concerns regarding foreign access to U.S. markets or sensitive and proprietary information. Once a foreign entity gains ownership, control, or influence over a U.S. company with classified contracts, that ownership, control, or influence must be mitigated through an insulating instrument approved by the Defense Department. If such an approved insulating legal instrument is not implemented, the U.S. company and the foreign investor face the possibility of contract cancellations and loss of future classified contracts.

Incidents involving the co-opting of former employees who had access to sensitive proprietary or classified S&T or program information remains a potential counterintelligence concern. Frequently, targeting cultural commonalities to establish rapport is directly associated with the collection attempt. As a result, quite often foreign employees working for U.S. companies are specifically targeted by foreign collectors. Former employees may be viewed as excellent prospects for collection operations and considered less likely to feel obligated to comply with U.S. Government or corporate security requirements.

As the international political and economic environment continues to change and mature, U.S. defense industry strategic management processes will be increasingly challenged to balance international marketing and partnerships with sound security countermeasures. Good risk management practices will ensure that cleared employees are properly trained and empowered to recognize and report suspicious activity.

For government contractors, if you believe that any of the above situations apply to your company, you should immediately notify your DSS Industrial Security Representative through your company Facility Security Officer. Likewise, notify DSS if you have any indication that your company or any of your employees may be the target of an attempted exploitation by the intelligence service of another country. Reports of actual, probable, or possible espionage should be submitted to the FBI. All nongovernment organizations and companies should contact the nearest FBI office; the telephone number is in the telephone book under U.S. Government.

Appendix F

The Foreign Threat to U.S. Business Travelers

YOU ARE THE TARGET!

As a U.S. business traveler, you can be the target of a foreign intelligence or security service anytime, anywhere. Many foreign governments and businesses still place a high priority on U.S. technological and/or proprietary information, although the Cold War has ended. As you travel overseas, the risk of being an intelligence target increases.

Aside from being a potential intelligence target for the information you possess, foreign government scrutiny of you in another country also may occur by design or chance for some of the following reasons:

- Fitting a terrorism, narcotics-trafficking, criminal, or other profile. Involvement in black-market activity.
- Discovery by the host government of material on your person or in your luggage that is banned or strictly controlled.
- Associating with individuals the government labels as dissidents.
- Having language fluency, declared relatives, or organizational affiliations in the country you are visiting.

Usually, any intelligence activities directed against you will be conducted in an unobtrusive and nonthreatening fashion, although in some cases a foreign intelligence service may employ more aggressive provocation tactics. While most harassment incidents are intentionally obvious— meant to intimidate or "test" a traveler's reactions—many intelligence activities are conducted without the target's awareness.

Methods

Elicitation. A ploy whereby seemingly normal conversation is contrived to extract information about individuals, their work, and their colleagues.

- Puts someone at ease to share information.
- Is difficult to recognize as an intelligence technique.
- Is easily deniable.

Eavesdropping.   Listening to other peoples' conversations to gather information.

- Frequently done in social environments where attendees feel secure and more likely to talk about themselves or their work.
- Frequent venues include restaurants, bars, and public transportation.
- Eavesdropping can occur in a radius of six to eight seats on public transportation or ten to twelve feet in other settings.

Technical Eavesdropping.   Use of audio and visual devices, usually concealed.

- Relatively cost efficient and low risk.
- Concealed devices can be installed in public and private facilities, such as hotel rooms, restaurants, offices, and automobiles.

"Bag Operations."   Surreptitious entry into someone's hotel room to steal, photograph, or photocopy documents; steal or copy magnetic media; or download from laptop computers.

- Many times conducted or condoned by host government services.
- Conducted by foreign business operatives.
- Frequently done with cooperation of hotel staff.

Electronic Interception.   Increasingly conducted against modern telecommunications systems.

- Foreign carriers are particularly vulnerable because most are government controlled.
- Office, hotel, and portable telephones (including cellular) are key targets.
- Facsimile, telex, and computers can be electronically monitored.

How to Protect Yourself

Common sense and basic counterintelligence (CI) awareness can effectively protect you against foreign attempts to collect sensitive, proprietary, and other privileged information. Some security tips you should employ include:

- Arrange a pre-travel briefing from your corporate security office.
- Maintain control of sensitive documents or equipment. Do not leave such items unattended in hotel rooms or stored in hotel safes.
- Limit sensitive discussions; hotel rooms or other public venues are rarely suitable to discuss sensitive information.
- Do not use computer or facsimile equipment at foreign hotels or business centers for sensitive matters.
- Do not divulge information to anyone not authorized to hear it.
- Ignore or deflect intrusive inquiries or conversation about business or personal matters.
- Keep unwanted material until it can be disposed of securely—burn or shred paper and cut floppy disks in pieces and discard.
- Keep your personal computer as carry-on baggage—never check it with other luggage, and, if possible, remove or control storage media.
- If secure communications equipment is accessible, use it to discuss business matters.
- Report any CI incident to the relevant U.S. Government agency and your corporate security office.

Reporting Incidents

Referral of CI Incidents while Overseas.   When traveling overseas, suspect incidents should be reported to the Regional Security Officer (RSO) or Post Security Officer (PSO) at the nearest U.S. diplomatic facility.

Referral of CI Incidents in the U.S.   Incidents should be reported to your organization's appropriate security component immediately upon return from travel. Suspect incidents may be reported to any of the following agencies:

Federal Bureau of Investigation
Washington Metropolitan Field Office
(202) 278-2000
(Suspect incidents should be reported to your local FBI field office. Consult your local phone book for the telephone number.)

Department of State/Bureau of Diplomatic Security
(202) 663-0739

Defense Intelligence Agency
(703) 907-1307

National Security Agency
(301) 688-6911

Department of the Army
1-800-CALLSPY

Naval Criminal Investigative Service
1-800-543-NAVY

Air Force Office of Special Investigations
(202) 767-5199

Department of Energy
(202) 586-1247

U.S. Customs Service
1-800-BE-ALERT
(To report suspicious activities involving export of high-technology, munitions products, other commodities, narcotics, intellectual property, and U.S. currency)

Department of Commerce/Office of Export Enforcement
(202) 482-1208
(To report suspicious targeting of U.S. export-controlled commodities)

Defense Security Service (DSS)
(Defense contractors report suspect incidents to local DSS industrial security representative)

Pre-Travel Threat Information

The U.S. Department of State has a variety of threat information available by telephone, fax, and computer:

Department of State Citizens Emergency assistance to Travelers—Travel Advisories
Telephone: (202) 647-5225
FAX (202) 647-3000
Internet: http:www.state.gov

Consular Affairs Bulletin Board
Modem connect: (202) 647-9225

Overseas Security Advisory Council (OSAC)
Joint venture between State Department and private sector security professionals designed to exchange security-related information abroad. Contact your security officer or OSAC at (202) 663-0533.

Appendix G

Intelligence Organizations

Everyone wants information! It's not just a local, regional, or national competitor, nor is it someone looking to find out everything they can for a personal reason. Within our ever-shrinking world of industry, commerce, and rapidly advancing technology, international organizations and governments are also looking for information. The data they identify and want to know more about may be for political, military, or economic reasons. In some countries, the intelligence services support the government in obtaining information that can be used for their economic benefit. Further, the information—especially technological information—is also spread throughout the government where it will do the most good to enhance their economy, either regionally or globally.

Never assume that just because a given country, industry, or business arena is not interested in what you have, there are not others that take an interest in what you might have or do. Countries collect information, technical data, reports of new products, services, and technology to further some need or desire to know more about what you do. The long-term benefit for them may be to develop a new generation of a product before you do; to advance another technology; to sell it to a third party; or to use it for a political purpose. You only find out when it is too late to do anything about it.

Since not all countries engage in intelligence-gathering and economic espionage on a large scale, they may rely upon others to do it for them; or, a country's intelligence service collects the data and then passes it on to the business sector in order to enhance their economic base. The following discussion breaks out only some of the top countries of the world that use their intelligence services to collect information. Some are very specific in what they want; others use the vacuum-cleaner approach, collecting anything and everything and then weeding out the unnecessary.

The last item in this section concerns the use of intelligence gathering by drug cartels. They have, by far, extremely vast amounts of money to purchase specialized equipment; to hire others to operate the intelligence gathering equipment; or to hire others to perform the collection effort for them.

FRENCH INTELLIGENCE ORGANIZATIONS

The French have several organizations that make up its intelligence capability, but the service overall is considered by some to be less than professional. The primary organization tasked with supplying intelligence to the French Government is the General Directorate of External Security, or DGSE. The decree of April 2, 1982 that created the DGSE also defined the organization's role:

> The Direction Generale de la Securité Exterieure, in order to conduct its mission for the benefit of the Government and in strict collaboration with other organizations concerned, [is] to seek and exploit intelligence advantageous to the security of France, also to detect and disrupt, throughout the national territory, espionage activities directed against interests in order to prevent the consequences.

The DGSE has been heavily involved in economic and industrial espionage in support of its own economy as well as its international arms trade. The service has also been active in antiterrorism, Latin American politics, and North Africa. The DGSE has been active in at least two attempts to overthrow Mu'ammar Gadhafi.

The French SIGINT element is the Radio-Electric Communications Group, which, during the 1960s, targeted a U.S. air base in Morocco. The French operate at least four SIGINT stations within France itself, as well as seven stations spread around the world, from Guadeloupe to Africa.

The French armed forces and defense establishments operate a variety of defense and military service intelligence and security organizations. Subordinate to the Supreme Council of Defense is the National Defense Staff. Reporting to the Defense staff are the Security and Defense Division and the Second (Intelligence) Division. Within the Second Division are two intelligence centers: the Center for the Exploitation of Scientific and Technical Intelligence and the Center for Intelligence Exploitation. The Second Division is also responsible for coordinating the activities of the attachés who serve in French embassies.

To collect imagery, the French use a combination of aircraft and satellites. The 33rd Reconnaissance Wing of the French Air Forces has three types of airplanes with which to conduct aerial reconnaissance. The most capable is the Mirage WR, with its suite of optical sensors, infrared line scanners, and side-looking airborne radar. It can fly at 1,222 mph and has a range of 2,485 miles. France also operates ELINT aircraft, Gabriel C-1 60 Transalls, equipped with UHF and DF antennas.

The SAMRO satellite system is a derivative of a nonmilitary satellite called SPOT (Systeme Probatoire d'Observation de la Terre). In 1978, the French government decided to develop the SPOT to perform functions similar to that of the U.S. LANDSAT. The satellite's capabilities include 20-

meter (66-foot) ground resolution of color images in three (visible and near infrared) bands and 10-meter (33-foot) resolution of black-and-white images. So far five SPOT satellites have been launched, giving the French satellite reconnaissance capability well into the late 1990s. The SAMRO system was never developed into a satellite system, but a high-resolution camera was developed. The current French satellite system is called HELIOS and is based on the SPOT platform.

The DGSE has reportedly been upgraded with more highly qualified personnel and more funding in an attempt to increase its economic espionage. The agency reportedly tried to infiltrate European branch offices of IBM and Texas instruments for the purpose of passing secrets to a French competitor. The French Embassy in Washington also reportedly arranged for a team of French engineers to tour Lockheed in an attempt to gather information on the stealth technology used by American manufacturers of the F-117, B-2 and others.

In another incident in 1991, two men were spotted perusing the garbage outside a private house in a Houston suburb. An off-duty policeman noted the license number of the van, which was later traced to the French consulate. The house belonged to an executive of Texas instruments. DGSE compiled a secret dossier on proposals from U.S. and former Soviet aerospace firms involved in a fighter aircraft deal with India. This information was provided to France's Avions Marcel Dassault-Breguet Aviation, which produces the Mirage fighter. In another example, a French national, employed by Corning incorporated, sold fiber optic technology data to the DGSE, which offered the technology to competitors in France.

ISRAELI INTELLIGENCE ORGANIZATIONS

The primary Israeli intelligence organizations are the Central Institute for Intelligence and Special Duties (MOSSAD) and the Israeli Defense Forces Intelligence Branch (AMAN). The MOSSAD is responsible for human intelligence collection, covert action, and counterterrorism. Its principal function is to conduct operations *against* Arab nations and organizations and their official representatives and installations throughout the world, particularly in Europe and the United States. Other targets of MOSSAD operations are the United States and the United Nations. Its objectives are to determine foreign governments' policy towards Israel, dealing with the problem of Jewish emigration, and determining the extent and nature of other nations' assistance to Arab organizations and nations. MOSSAD also promotes arms deals and acquires military-related equipment to allow for analysis of the equipment in order to duplicate it or design countermeasures. In the United States, the MOSSAD seeks to collect scientific and technical intelligence, gain information about Arab military capabilities and acquire knowledge of U.S. policy decisions and intelligence operations regarding the Middle East.

Israeli military intelligence is responsible for the collection, production, and dissemination of military, geographic, and economic intelligence, particularly concerning nations of the Middle East.

The AMAN differs from the MOSSAD in that its primary focus is almost exclusively oriented towards the Arab countries, whereas the MOSSAD has a more worldwide mission. AMAN is responsible for overt and covert collection operations, including signal intelligence activities for the entire Israeli intelligence community. The Collection Division's Signals Branch gathers both communication intelligence and electronics intelligence via atmospheric and landline (use of telephone line [wire]tapping techniques to intercept telephone calls) interception. There have two reported instances of the Israelis planting bugs in U.S. official establishments in Israel, one in the office of the U.S. ambassador and one in the residence of the U.S. military attaché. In 1979, MOSSAD was tapping the telephone of then Ambassador to the U.N. Andrew Young as he tried to contact the PLO.

AMAN also controls Air Force Intelligence, which is equipped with a variety of aerial reconnaissance platforms: MOHAWK OV-ID, RF4E Phantoms, and the Mirage IIIRJ. The Israelis also have used Remotely Piloted Vehicles for aerial reconnaissance to obtain both imagery and SIGINT and for jamming enemy radar.

Relations between the Israeli intelligence services and the United States dates back to the early 1960s, when the U.S. supplied Israel with some classified computers used for crypto-analysis. Israel has supplied the U.S. with captured equipment from both the 1967 and 1973 wars, including Soviet ground-to-air missiles and antitank weapons. The U.S. matched that cooperation during the 1960s, when then Director of the CIA, Bill Casey, provided Israeli intelligence with reconnaissance satellite data, including the photos themselves. The U.S. also provided greater Israeli access to the product resulting from U.S. reconnaissance flights. However, that spirit of cooperation has been hindered somewhat by U.S. advancements in Arab relations as a result of Desert Storm, and by revelations of Israeli intelligence operations against the United States. Jonathan Pollard, a U.S. Navy analyst, was a recruited agent for an element of the MOSSAD, primarily focusing on providing military information. Another example of Israeli targeting of U.S. technology is the theft of documents from the Recon-Optical Company, which had been building a classified spy camera in cooperation with the Israeli government.

JAPANESE INTELLIGENCE ORGANIZATIONS

Japan's primary intelligence organization is the Cabinet Research Office (CRO), which is under the direct control of the Prime Minister and provides him with studies and analysis to aid in making foreign policy as well as defense decisions. The CRO receives its intelligence data from private news and business organizations, as well as military intelligence sources. Information may come from attachés, business travelers, or exchange students traveling in the target countries. The CRO publishes classified reports on various subjects, including a weekly report entitled *Military Information Data*. Most of the information and reporting deals with Russia, the People's Republic of China, and other members of the Pacific Rim.

The three Divisions of the Information Analysis, Research, and Planning Bureau are responsible for the collection, analysis, and distribution of information on international affairs, research, and surveys of foreign countries. Additional intelligence information is gathered by the various units that make up the Ministry of International Trade and Industry (MITI). The Japanese seem to have the ability to form ad hoc groups within MITI to target specific industries. For example, a Special Survey Group of the Information Room of the MITI Bureau of Heavy Industries was, at one point, set up to report on the U.S. computer industry.

MITI is the force behind several industrial espionage operations against U.S. companies and U.S. programs. As an example, employees of the Japanese companies Hitachi Limited and Mitsubishi Electric Corporation were recently arrested after allegations were made that they paid $650,000 for stolen data on the IBM 3081 computer. In April 1992, a rocket scientist from California was sentenced to prison for selling Strategic Defense Initiative and rocket technology to four Japanese companies for more than $700,000 during the 1980–1990 period. The four companies, Mitsubishi, Nissan, Ishiawaji-Harima, and Toshiba, have pledged to capture 20 percent of the aerospace market by the year 2000.

The Second Section, Investigative Division, Japanese Ground Self-Defense Forces, collects and analyzes information of interest to the military. Data from the thirty Japanese military attachés stationed at embassies around the world is funneled to this agency. The Intelligence Division, Maritime Staff Office, Japanese Maritime Self-Defense Forces is responsible for producing basic naval intelligence on the navies of Russia, China, and other countries in the Pacific Rim. This division also monitors foreign naval operations in the vicinity of Japan. To accomplish this mission, the Japanese employ several naval surveillance aircraft, including sixty-nine P-3 Orions and nine EP-3C ELINT planes. The Japanese also employ an extensive undersea listening array around their territorial waters. The Intelligence Division, Japanese Air Self-Defense Forces, produces intelligence on the air forces of the Pacific Rim countries. The unit also supervises the airborne imaging program for the Japanese military. The 501st Flight Squadron, located at Hyakuri air base, flies RFAE Phantoms equipped with side-looking radar, an infrared imaging system, and an optical camera.

Signals intelligence is provided by the Annex Chamber, Second Section, Investigation Division, Japanese Ground Self-Defense Forces. Japan's signals intelligence agency is called the Chobetsu and is directly responsible to the Cabinet Research Office. The Chobetsu has approximately 1,000 employees drawn from all three branches of the military as well as from the civilian populace. These personnel include experts in intercept operations, crypto-analysis, and foreign languages. There are ten ground stations around Japan, three out of four of which are equipped with DF arrays. The station at Hokkaido was heavily involved in the monitoring of Soviet Air Force communications during the 1983 Korean Air Lines shooting. The Japanese also operate several signal intelligence aircraft, including EP-2Js and C-I 30s, and have been known to mount some special operations to collect SIGINT in denied areas. In 1986 a Japanese-owned railway container filled with electronic surveillance equipment was discovered on the Trans-Siberian railroad.

For satellite imagery, the Japanese military has obtained photography produced by the civilian LANDSAT earth resources satellite. Since 1985, the Japanese government has been buying LANDSAT photography and passing it to the 101st Survey Battalion in Tokyo for analysis. Ocean surveillance is conducted by the Marine Observation Satellite (MOS-1), launched in 1987, and MOS-2, launched in 1991, both in a 564-mile sun-synchronous orbit. The MOS carries microwave, multispectral, thermal infrared and visible radiometers. Resolution on MOS-1 was believed to be 165 feet but may be improved on MOS-2. Japan has an intelligence-sharing agreement with the United States and has reportedly received either photographs or information derived from U.S. satellites.

RUSSIAN INTELLIGENCE ORGANIZATIONS

The Russian Intelligence Service still maintains a semblance of Directorate T, the second largest directorate in the old First Chief Directorate of the KGB. It was responsible for collection of scientific and technical intelligence, including the theft of high technology of all types. In addition to having been trained in all types of spying techniques and foreign languages, many Directorate T officers are scientists or engineers with advanced degrees. They attend international scientific symposia abroad as well as participate in scientific exchange agreements with all countries of interest. Such projects as the Kama River truck factory and the 1975 Apollo-Soyuz joint space shot are examples of technology transfer to the former Soviet Union.

According to several sources, the Soviets alone were able to gain access to billions of dollars worth of American high technology through multiple avenues—many of them by perfectly legitimate means, openly fostered by the U.S. Government, and many through illegal means, including:

- Over the counter purchase of U.S. consumer goods containing advanced technology.
- Legitimate exports from U.S. firms.
- Exports of U.S. technology from European firms.
- Technology publications.
- Establishment of bogus companies or front organizations with the pretext of obtaining lucrative Russian contracts or being involved in technology exporting.
- Extortion or bailouts of failing high technology firms. Reverse-engineering of U.S.-made products.
- Attendance at various engineering schools in the United States, especially those with DOD contracts.

The Russians still employ two agencies as collectors in the United States—the GRU (military intelligence service) and the SRV (foreign Intelligence Service). Both agencies have increased their collection efforts to obtaining scientific and high-technology secrets, both from civilian firms and the military. This data is needed to boost the efficiency of lagging Russian industry. Russia is targeting Western weapons systems, for example, in order to upgrade its surplus arms, which can then be sold abroad to earn hard currency. Some of the former Soviet republics are also in the process of setting up their own intelligence services with the help of former KGB operatives. Relaxed tensions between the former Soviet Union and the United States has allowed a flood of Russian academics, business executives, and tourists, providing many more opportunities for cover for HUMINT operatives than it had under the strict monitoring of the Cold War. The Russians may be even more active than before to make up for the loss of very capable operatives from the East European services that were subject to less surveillance than the KGB and GRU.

The GRU continues to maintain some of its original electronics intelligence (ELINT) satellites. These satellites are maintained in a constellation of six satellites spaced 60 degrees apart, and are used to detect and monitor the emissions of large pulsed radars, probably for the purpose of determined electronic order of battle (OB). These satellites are virtually useless for collecting research and development information. However, there are airborne systems, such as the "COOT" aircraft, that do collect intelligence information. The GRU and Soviet Navy also maintain a fleet of some 50 intelligence collection vessels; however, these ships have been grounded in port because of political and economic (fuel cost and availability) reasons.

The Russians have also operated various types of imagery satellites. The primary satellite systems in operation at this point are believed to be the third generation and fourth generation genre. The third generation has a two-to-three-week mission duration and may have a resolution of as much as eight inches at an altitude of 135 miles, its normal perigee. These third generation satellites are probably being phased out in favor of the fourth generation digital imaging system, which has a longer mission life and greatly increased capabilities for data collection.

CHINESE INTELLIGENCE ORGANIZATIONS

The Chinese Intelligence Service (the Ministry of State Security), unlike that of the former Soviet Union, does not depend upon its diplomats to do its intelligence collection. Most of China's agents are planted among the more than 50,000 Chinese students, academics, and business personnel in the United States. In China, the best scientists work for the military because that area is well funded. The Chinese use the following assets to perform its intelligence collection operations:

- 1,500 Chinese commercial and diplomatic representatives.
- 70 People's Republic of China (PRC) establishments and offices.
- 15,000 students arriving yearly.
- 10,000 representatives arriving in 2,700 delegations each year.
- A large ethnic Chinese immigrant community.

China targets high technology, particularly that with military applications, for incorporation into its extensive international arms sales business. Approximately 50 percent of almost 900 technology transfer cases on the West Coast involve the Chinese. Most of China's espionage efforts are directed at illegally acquiring mid-level technology that has not been cleared for export, using three basic operational patterns: (1) recruiting the co-optee in China and having him or her acquire the technology while abroad; (2) purchasing American companies with access to the desired level of technology; and (3) the purchase of high-technology related equipment through front companies in Hong Kong. In 1990, the Bush administration blocked the sale of a Washington state company to the China National Aerotechnology Import and Export Corporation, citing security reasons. The sale was stopped for fear that the Chinese would gain access to in-flight refueling technology. The threat to national security by visiting Chinese scientific and technical delegations was demonstrated by a Chinese visit to Lawrence Livermore National Laboratory in California, where the Chinese are believed to have obtained vital information for the development of a neutron bomb it tested in 1988.

Other Chinese intelligence organizations are the New China News Agency, which monitors foreign news and occasionally provides cover for intelligence operatives, and several research institutes. These institutes, based on the Soviet model, include the Party Research Office, the Institute for International Studies, the College of International Politics, and the Beijing Institute for International Strategic Studies.

The Military Intelligence Department, or MID, is responsible for basic order of battle (OB) intelligence, studies of foreign weapons systems, and analyses of foreign armies and their capabilities. The MID operates China's rather extensive imagery reconnaissance program. China has launched several photo-reconnaissance satellites of at least two types. Its first satellites were of the film-return type, in which capsules containing film were recovered on Chinese territory after the conclusion of the mission. The latest satellite is a digital imaging system, transmitting pictures to earth by radio signals. A ten-foot-diameter tracking dish for receiving such imagery was observed at the Xian Institute of Radio Technology. A follow-on system, based on the charged-coupled device technology used by the French in SPOT, is reportedly operational. The MID also operates five Gates Lear jets equipped with Long-Range Oblique Photography (LOROP) cameras as aerial reconnaissance platforms.

The Technical Department is the Chinese signals intelligence agency and operates the four SIGINT stations located on mainland China. Two stations, at Qitai and Korla in China, are primarily targeted against telemetry from the Russian Tyuratam and Sary Shagan test centers.

DRUG CARTEL INTELLIGENCE COLLECTION CAPABILITY

Although there is no centralized cartel intelligence collection capability, the various cartels do manage to conduct fairly sophisticated intelligence operations.

The *primary* source of Cartel intelligence is HUMINT. Cartels have the resources to bribe government personnel for information that will enable them to evade government interdiction efforts. The information they collect through HUMINT can then be further exploited through other, more technical, means.

Frequency lists of various law enforcement agencies have been found at cartel SIGINT collection facilities. Usually these SIGINT operations consist of rather unsophisticated signals collection equipment, but it provides the drug traffickers with most of the information they need to avoid arrest. Drug traffickers have been known to use aerial reconnaissance to determine where patrols are located or where aerostats are being employed. Recent indications are that the cartels are getting more sophisticated in their capabilities, even employing former intelligence experts to help them in their efforts.

We have evidence that a number of cartels are engaged in collecting information concerning government efforts to develop more high-tech drug detection equipment. The cartels are increasing their resources in this area so that they can develop countermeasures that will be in-place when these new systems are fielded.

As the cartels continue to increase their efforts in detection and countering of government initiatives, we can expect that their intelligence collection capabilities will continue to improve. With the resources they have at hand, there is little in the way of technology that they can't afford. Their efforts should be taken as seriously as any modern government intelligence collection program.

Appendix H

The FBI National Security Awareness Program

The Awareness of National Security Issues and Response (ANSIR) program is the FBI's National Security Awareness Program. It is the "public voice" of the FBI for espionage, counterintelligence, counterterrorism, economic espionage, cyber- and physical-infrastructure protection, and all national security issues. The program is designed to provide unclassified national security threat and warning information to U.S. corporate security directors and executives, law enforcement, and other government agencies.

It also focuses on the "response" capability unique to the FBI's jurisdiction in both law enforcement and counterintelligence investigations. Information is disseminated nationwide via the ANSIR-E-mail and ANSIR-FAX networks. Each of the FBI's fifty-six field offices has an ANSIR coordinator and is equipped to provide national security threat and awareness information on a regular basis to corporate recipients within their jurisdiction. The ANSIR-FAX was the first initiative by the U.S. government to provide this type of information to as many as 25,000 individual U.S. corporations with critical technologies or sensitive economic information targeted by foreign intelligence services or their agents.

ANSIR-E-mail increases the capacity for the number of recipients to exceed 100,000, which should accommodate every U.S. corporation who wishes to receive information from the FBI. Interested U.S. corporations should provide their E-mail address, position, company name, and address, as well as telephone and fax numbers to the national ANSIR E-mail address at ansir@leo.gov. Individual ANSIR Coordinators in the respective field divisions will verify contact with each prospective recipient of ANSIR E-mail advisories.

The FBI is the lead agency for a variety of national security concerns. With regard to foreign counterintelligence activity, theft of U.S. technology and sensitive economic information by foreign intelligence services and competitors has been estimated by the White House and others to be valued up to a $100 billion annually. It is therefore prudent and necessary that we provide information to those who are the targets of this activity. Critical infrastructure protection, both cyber and physical, is also a major focus of the FBI, and the ANSIR program helps to identify these infrastructures and ensure that communication with the FBI is established.

Each ANSIR coordinator in the FBI's fifty-six field offices is a member of the American Society for Industrial Security. This membership enhances public/private sector communication and cooperation for the mutual benefit of both. FBI ANSIR Coordinators meet regularly with industry leaders and security directors for updates on current national security issues.

The ANSIR program focuses on the "techniques of espionage" when relating national security awareness information to industry. Discussing techniques allows ANSIR representatives to be very specific in giving industry representatives tangible information to help them decide their own vulnerabilities. These techniques include compromise of industry information through "dumpster diving," where Foreign Intelligence Services and competitors may try to obtain corporate proprietary information in dumpsters or other garbage collection areas, or through the use of listening devices that may be as simple as using a police scanner to tune in the frequency of the wireless microphone being used in the corporate boardroom. Through the ANSIR program and the discussion of techniques of espionage, corporations are able to learn from the experiences of others, enabling them to avoid adverse results.

Along with awareness, the ANSIR program provides information about the FBI's unique "response" capability with regard to issues of national security. The FBI has primary jurisdiction for a variety of criminal and counterintelligence investigations that impact on national security. For instance, the recent passage of the Economic Espionage Act of 1996 opened up new areas of FBI response to the wrongful acquisition of intellectual property. It also encourages corporations to consider how best to protect their proprietary information or trade secrets from both domestic and foreign theft.

The FBI ANSIR Coordinator in the local field office is the point of contact for information about the FBI's national security programs; they also receive initial information that may result in a response from the FBI. U.S. corporations should also contact the local ANSIR Coordinator to receive ANSIR-E-mail or ANSIR-FAX information.

NATIONAL SECURITY THREAT LIST

The FBI's foreign counterintelligence mission is set out in a strategy known as the National Security Threat List (NSTL). The NSTL combines two elements:

- First, it includes national security threat issues regardless of the country of origin.
- Second, it includes a classified list of foreign powers that pose a strategic intelligence threat to U.S. security interests.

The issue threat portion of the NSTL was developed in concert with the U.S. Intelligence Community and key elements of the U.S. Government. As a result, the FBI identified eight categories of foreign intelligence activity that were deemed to be significant threats to U.S. National security interests. The FBI will investigate the activities of any country that relate to any of these eight issues.

The Key Issue Threats are:

1. Terrorism
2. Espionage
3. Proliferation
4. Economic Espionage
5. Targeting the National Information Infrastructure
6. Targeting the U.S. Government
7. Perception Management
8. Foreign Intelligence Activities

The following is an explanation of the above Key Issue Threats.

Terrorism

This issue concerns foreign-power-sponsored or foreign-power-coordinated activities that:

- involve violent acts, dangerous to human life, that are a violation of the criminal laws of the United States or of any State, or that would be a criminal violation if committed within the jurisdiction of the United States or any state;
- appear to be intended:
  to intimidate or coerce a civilian population;
  to influence the policy of a government by intimidation or coercion; or
  to affect the conduct of a government by assassination or kidnapping; and
  occur totally outside the United States or transcend national boundaries in terms of the means by which they are accomplished, the persons they appear intended to coerce or intimidate, or the locale in which their perpetrators operate or seek asylum.

Espionage

This issue concerns foreign-power-sponsored or foreign-power-coordinated intelligence activity directed at the U.S. Government or U.S. corporations, establishments, or persons, which involves the identification, targeting and collection of U.S. national defense information.

Proliferation

This issue concerns foreign-power-sponsored or foreign-power-coordinated intelligence activity directed at the U.S. Government or U.S. corporations, establishments, or persons, which involves:

- the proliferation of weapons of mass destruction to include chemical, biological, or nuclear weapons, and delivery systems of those weapons of mass destruction; or
- the proliferation of advanced conventional weapons.

Economic Espionage

This issue concerns foreign-power-sponsored or foreign-power-coordinated intelligence activity directed at the U.S. Government or U.S. corporations, establishments, or persons, which involves:

- the unlawful or clandestine targeting or acquisition of sensitive financial, trade, or economic policy information, proprietary economic information, or critical technologies; or
- the unlawful or clandestine targeting or influencing of sensitive economic policy decisions.

Targeting the National Information Infrastructure

This issue concerns foreign-power-sponsored or foreign-power-coordinated intelligence activity directed at the U.S. Government or U.S. corporations, establishments, or persons, which involves the targeting of facilities, personnel, information, or computer, cable, satellite, or telecommunications systems that are associated with the National Information Infrastructure. Proscribed intelligence activities include:

- denial or disruption of computer, cable, satellite, or telecommunications services;
- unauthorized monitoring of computer, cable, satellite, or telecommunications systems;
- unauthorized disclosure of proprietary or classified information stored within or communicated through computer, cable, satellite, or telecommunications systems;
- unauthorized modification or destruction of computer programming codes, computer network databases, stored information, or computer capabilities; or
- manipulation of computer, cable, satellite, or telecommunications services resulting in fraud, financial loss, or other federal criminal violations.

Targeting the U.S. Government

This issue concerns foreign-power-sponsored or foreign-power-coordinated intelligence activity directed at the U.S. Government or U.S. corporations, establishments, or persons, which involves the targeting of government programs, information, or facilities, or the targeting of personnel of the:

- intelligence community;
- foreign affairs, or economic affairs community; or
- defense establishment and related activities of national preparedness.

Perception Management

This issue concerns foreign-power-sponsored or foreign-power-coordinated intelligence activity directed at the U.S. Government or U.S. corporations, establishments, or persons, which involves manipulating information, communicating false information, or propagating deceptive information and communications designed to distort the perception of the public (domestically or internationally) or of U.S. Government officials regarding U.S. policies, ranging from foreign policy to economic strategies.

Foreign Intelligence Activities

This issue concerns foreign power-sponsored or foreign power-coordinated intelligence activity conducted in the U.S. or directed against the United States Government, or U.S. corporations, establishments, or persons, that is not described by or included in the other issue threats.

NATIONAL SECURITY BEGINS WITH YOU

You may be the target of foreign intelligence activity if you or your company are associated with critical technologies. Foreign powers may also seek to collect U.S. industrial proprietary economic information and technology, the loss of which would undermine the U.S. strategic industrial position. Foreign intelligence collectors target corporate marketing information in support of their nation's firms. Overseas travel, foreign contact, and joint ventures may further increase your exposure to the efforts of foreign intelligence collectors. If you suspect possible foreign intelligence activity, or have questions concerning the National Security Threat List strategy, please contact the FBI ANSIR Coordinator at the FBI Field Office nearest you.

Up to $500,000 Reward for Stopping Espionage

An amendment to Title 18, U.S.C., Section 3071, recently enacted, authorizes the Attorney General to make payment for information of espionage activity in any country that leads to the arrest and conviction of any person(s):

1. for commission of an act of espionage against the United States;
2. for conspiring or attempting to commit an act of espionage against the United States;
3. or which leads to the prevention or frustration of an act of espionage against the United States.

Specifics of this amendment can be obtained from any FBI ANSIR Coordinator. FBI Contact Numbers to report suspected illegal intelligence or terrorism activity against the interest of the United States. Telephone the ANSIR Coordinator at the FBI Field Office nearest you.

Appendix I

Economic and Espionage News for the Risk Manager

This Appendix contains an extensive variety of items of counterintelligence interest related to economic and other forms of espionage that concern the risk manager. The items span the entire globe, with a variety of countries discussed. Please note that espionage does not exist just against one country; it is ongoing between almost all of them. For this reason, many different views are presented, dependent upon the country and the type of espionage taking place. All are of great interest to the risk manager, who needs to know what is "out there" and may be affecting the security of the organization, product, or program.

As a risk manager, or any individual concerned and interested in the protection of assets—especially those in any advancing field of manufacturing, science, or technology, which are the areas of concern to adversaries seeking product or other types of information—the various cases that are discussed in the following pages will give you much food for thought. What an adversary is looking for, you may have. If you don't realize the threat and/or adversary, you are missing a great deal of information that should be in your risk analysis. Read with care, and where appropriate, determine steps to follow up on items that may relate to your organization.

In addition to general economic espionage and nation security espionage issues that are of interest from a protection viewpoint, case studies, lessons learned, and security countermeasures are also included. At the end is a compendium of Websites of economic espionage, intelligence, security, and counterintelligence interest.

Much of the material herein has been obtained from the National Counterintelligence Center (NACIC), a multiagency counterintelligence organization that provides national-level counterintelligence (CI) products and services for the U.S. Government and the U.S. private sector.

In a rapidly changing but still-hostile world, the NACIC coordinates the U.S. Government's effort to identify and counter foreign intelligence threats to U.S. national and economic security. Operating under the auspices of the National Security Council, the NACIC draws its staffing from counter-intelligence (CI) and security professionals from the FBI, CIA, DIA, NSA, the Office of Secretary of Defense, the military services, and the Departments of State and Energy.

The principal customers of the NACIC include:

- National policy-makers and advisers.
- Intelligence Community agencies.
- Law enforcement agencies.
- Military commands.
- Security community agencies.
- Private industry.
- Regulatory agencies.
- CI agencies.

CI information and analysis are essential for identifying, understanding, and neutralizing foreign intelligence threats. In the past, this information and analysis has been provided primarily to the U.S. CI community. With the creation of the NACIC, CI information now will reach the security countermeasures community, other U.S. Government agencies, and the U.S. private sector on a more frequent and timely basis.

These information items can assist the risk manager in the determination of (to the extent that is ever possible):

- Identifying foreign intelligence threats and understanding the collection capabilities and intentions of foreign governments.
- Better allocating strategic and tactical resources to neutralize threats.
- Identifying vulnerabilities or gaps in U.S. security programs.
- Implementing more cost-effective security procedures and counter-measures.
- Providing a foundation for foreign policy and operational decisions.
- Assessing the effectiveness of national CI programs.
- Advocating for the resources, policy, information, and guidance needed by the national CI community.

For further assistance and information, the risk manager should contact the National Counterintelligence Center, Program Integration Office: (703) 874-4122. Areas of coverage are:

- National strategy for CI operational programs
- CI support to private sector:
  — Regional Awareness Seminars.
  — CI News and Developments newsletter.
  — CI Awareness Working Group.
- Community training:

— Evolution of American CI Course.
— Community Training Working Group
— Specialized seminars

The NACIC Threat Assessment Office: (703) 874-4119. Areas of coverage are:

- Nationally mandated studies and reports:
  — Annual CI Effectiveness Report.
  — Strategic Intelligence Review for CI.
- Foreign intelligence threat assessments.
- National damage assessments:
  — "CI lessons learned."
- Communitywide support:
  — National CI Analytic Working Group.
  — CI Directory.
  — CI Production Catalogue.

The NACIC Executive Secretariat: (703) 874-4121. Areas of coverage are:

- Secretariat support to:
  — National CI Policy Board.
  — National CI Operations Board.
  — Special working groups.
- Policy review and resource issues.
- Special coordination activities.
- Executive agent for "INTELINK-CI.

FIRST CONVICTION UNDER ECONOMIC ESPIONAGE ACT

On April 18, 1997, Daniel Worthing, of New Kensington, Pennsylvania, became the first person in the United States to be convicted under the Economic Espionage Act. Convicted in February 1997 of conspiracy to possess and deliver trade secrets, Worthing was sentenced to five years of probation, with six months of home confinement. He was also ordered to complete 100 hours of community service and pay a special assessment of $100. The conspiracy case against Daniel Worthing's brother, Patrick Worthing, was sentenced in June 1997.

The plot involving the two brothers began unraveling in mid-November 1996 when the chief executive officer of Owens-Corning received a letter from "Dane Davis," offering to sell nineteen items of PPG Industries' trade secrets for $1,000. The trade secrets were later identified as customer lists, secret fiberglass formulas, videos of machine operations, blueprints, photographs, and product samples. Unknown to the sender, the Owens-Corning executive forwarded the letter to PPG officials, who contacted the FBI.

On December 3, 1996, the Owens-Corning executive received a three-page fax from "Dane Davis," outlining more PPG insider information. A small memo automatically typed on the fax by the sending machine identified it as being sent from PPG's offices.

The executive was asked to page the sender if he was interested. The sender turned out to be Patrick Worthing, who used his own pager number in the fax. Patrick supervised a maintenance crew of about fifty workers who cleaned PPG's fiberglass research center and supplied people to operate prototype machines in suburban Pittsburgh. The crew allegedly had complete access to every office in the facility.

On December 7, 1996, believing they were to meet with an Owens-Corning representative, Patrick and Daniel Worthing were arrested by the FBI. Daniel Worthing, a garbage hauler by trade, said he got involved to protect his brother and to get a percentage of the profits.

UNSOLICITED REQUESTS FOR INFORMATION

The Most Frequently Used Modus Operandi for Collection

The unsolicited request for information is the most frequently used modus operandi (MO) for foreign attempts to collect U.S. classified, unclassified, and proprietary technology information. Furthermore, a comparison analysis of 1996 suspicious incidents determined that the unsolicited request for information surpassed the use of other collection methods by nearly a three-to-one margin.

The Technique. The vast majority of suspicious unsolicited requests for information involved data covered under the International Traffic in Arms Regulations (ITAR) that could not be lawfully exported without a license. The unsolicited request for information may be as simple as a letter, facsimile, telephone call, or E-mail sent from a foreign entity to a cleared U.S. contractor. Several factors explain the popularity of this MO: it is simple, low-cost, nonthreatening to the recipient, and a low risk to the collector. Frequently, the requester represents a foreign company or institute with specific technological interest and objectives that may be detrimental to U.S. interests.

Many unsolicited requests are sent directly to corporate marketing offices and may not be recognized as a collection attempt. Because of this, marketing personnel may file or discard the request once it is determined that the requester does not possess an export license and has no intent in applying for one. It is important for marketing and security personnel to keep in mind that an unsolicited request for information may be an attempt to fulfill a foreign collection requirement.

Case Studies

The unsolicited request for information is a popular MO among "closed countries" that face embargoes imposed by the United States. It is also a popular MO among foreign individuals and companies who may attempt to disguise the end-user through the use of front companies, and who seek to circumvent U.S. export laws. Intermediary companies, incorporated in the U.S., may be used as front companies to hide the end-user. The following incidents are classic illustrations of this MO.

A cleared U.S. company determined to be the primary producer of small jet engines for most U.S. cruise missiles received a letter from an individual identified as a foreign military officer. In the letter, the military officer stated he was interested in obtaining specifications for the design and construction of a personal, sport, mini-jet aircraft. The military officer concluded his letter by stating that his request did not infringe on the current embargo of his country. The information desired by the foreign officer was clearly export-controlled under the ITAR. The employees of the U.S. company recognized the request as a foreign collection attempt and refused the release of any information.

In another incident, a cleared U.S. company received an E-mail from a foreign businessman who was a graduate student at a major U.S. university. The foreign businessman stated that he was interested in the U.S. company's command, control, communications, and intelligence (C3I) technology. C3I technology is controlled under the ITAR and is also on the Department of Defense Militarily Critical Technology List (MCTL). Additionally, the businessman attempted to use an intermediary company to arrange the purchase and transfer of the desired technology.

Lessons Learned

Unsolicited requests for information can potentially result in the loss of classified or sensitive technology to unauthorized foreign end-users. The investigation of an unsolicited request can provide a considerable amount of information to assist counterintelligence and security personnel in the implementation of security countermeasures. The request may indicate a foreign collection requirement and may identify the cleared company and its employees as a potential target. Unsolicited requests can also increase our awareness of future collection attempts by a particular country.

Indicators of suspicious activity may include: foreign requests for information and technology covered under the ITAR and unlawfully exported without a license; requests sent directly to a company employee; requests in which the end-user is hidden by a consultant or front company; requests that acknowledge the inability to receive the technology due to an embargo; or a request that solicits unclassified portions of a classified project.

Note: As recently as September 1998 I was contacted via the Internet by a foreign "student" wanting to know of any contacts or any specific information I might have or know that dealt with technical topics, or that dealt with sensitive materials that could have a possible military use. It was a most open and blatant attempt to secure technical data. I didn't succumb to the sender's entreaties, but others might have! Be aware of who is making the request, where they are from, and why they want it. Even the slightest suspicions should be reported. It's better to be safe, than sorry.

CO-OPTING FORMER EMPLOYEES

Whom Do They Work For?

The Defense Investigative Service has received several reports in the past year that highlight a modus operandi (MO) involving the co-opting of formerly cleared U.S. company employees working overseas. Reporting clearly indicates that foreign entities are attempting to collect classified, sensitive, or proprietary information using this MO. Often targeted are U.S. citizens with past U.S. clearances who currently work for a foreign company or institute in a field similar to that of their work in the United States. In an effort to obtain proprietary U.S. information, foreign nationals may attempt to recruit former U.S. employees who are typically expected to exploit their U.S. contacts. Foreign entities may view former U.S. employees as excellent targets for collection operations due to the belief that the employees will no longer feel obligated to comply with U.S. Government or corporate security requirements.

The Technique.   The export of defense articles and services, which includes both classified and unclassified technical data, is controlled under the International Traffic in Arms Regulations (ITAR). In an effort to collect information restricted under the ITAR, as well as other classified technical information, foreign entities may exploit a knowing or unknowing former U.S. employee during a visit to his or her previous U.S. employer. In such a case, a visiting former employee may take advantage of former coworkers by incorrectly convincing them that "unclassified" technical discussions are appropriate or authorized for further dissemination.

Case Studies

Some foreign countries, to include certain U.S. allies, have active research and development programs for many of the eighteen technology categories listed on the Department of Defense Militarily Critical Technology List (MCTL). These same countries may also have an interest in acquiring the equipment and/or technology found on the MCTL. The following two examples are classic illustrations of this MO.

In an effort to obtain a foreign government research grant, a formerly cleared U.S. engineer specializing in sensor-related, militarily critical technology, resigned from a U.S. company and began working in the same field at an overseas foreign university. While employed by this foreign institution, the engineer returned to his former U.S. employer in an attempt to obtain specific information related to the militarily critical technology. The information was clearly export-controlled under the provisions of the ITAR. Employees at the U.S. company recognized their former coworker's solicitation as a foreign attempt to collect export-controlled information and refused the release of any information.

In another incident, a formerly cleared U.S. defense program employee began work overseas in a foreign company. Several times a year, the employee returned to the U.S. to visit her former employer and to socialize with former coworkers. Although the nature of these relationships may have been benign, the foreign country to which the employee moved did not have an Industrial Security Agreement with the United States. In addition, the foreign country had a history of technology diversions and attempted exploitations of data exchange agreements (DEAs) to gain access to otherwise restricted U.S. technology and equipment. Due to these circumstances, security countermeasures at the U.S. company were re-addressed.

Lessons Learned

A former company employee with current or past clearances is not necessarily authorized to access classified or unclassified export-controlled information. Company security professionals should ensure that employees are able to recognize foreign collection methods to include the attempted co-opting of both current and former employees. Cleared or formerly cleared U.S. employees working overseas, particularly in their previous area of expertise, may be at risk from foreign efforts to wittingly or unwittingly co-opt such an individual. If an individual encounters such an approach, it should be reported to DIS Industrial Security Representatives and local FBI authorities.

SATELLITE ACTIVITY

According to several technical and other open source reports, Hitachi Ltd. has launched an image information supply satellite. Launched from Siberia on-board a Russian rocket, the satellite can provide imagery to be used for a satellite-image data-distribution service. The reports suggest that anyone with a credit card can order the imagery, which will have enough resolution to see activity ranging from backyard barbecues to research and development testing.

Elsewhere in the spy-in-the-sky world, the Microsoft Corporation has signed an agreement with Aerial Images Inc., a North Carolina company, to publish declassified satellite images taken by the Russian military. The images, with a resolution of about one meter, date back to the 1990s. The initial photos will show Los Angeles, Washington, D.C., San Francisco, Rome, and London. The satellite images were purchased from Sovinforsputnik, Russia's space association. Aerial obtained rights to the imagery after an executive order granted commercial rights to make and sell satellite high-resolution photos. Russia has been selling its satellite photos taken at lower resolution since 1987, while the U.S. has allowed lower resolution satellite photos to be taken and sold commercially since 1993.

These two items are illustrative of the rush by a number of companies to acquire and sell high-resolution satellite photos that were once the sole province of governments and intelligence agencies of advanced nations.

FRENCH ECONOMIC INTELLIGENCE COLLECTION ACTIVITIES

According to a French newsletter, "Le Monde Du Renseignement," France's Delegate General for Armaments (DGA) is creating an economic intelligence office called the Economic and Strategic Information Bureau (IES). This newly created office is under the purview of the Directorate for Cooperation and Industrial Affairs (DCIA) and should be fully operational within two years.

The office will be staffed with about thirty people from the DGA who will be placed in about twelve different offices throughout the organization. This network of personnel will track and collect open source information and circulate internal DGA information.

By creating this new Bureau, the DGA hopes to improve on the collection and circulation of economic information in an organization dominated by engineers who rarely focus on such commercial aspects. Once IES becomes fully operational, the chief of the DGA hopes to use it as a basis for an external information exchange mechanism with French armaments industries. The goal is to increase France's share of the international armaments market from 10 percent to 15 percent in the next six years.

The DGA, which is in charge of 80 percent of France's defense equipment purchases, has 48,800 employees. More than half of them are employed in purchasing, testing, training, and running technical centers. In late 1996, the DGA created three new directorates: the directorate for systems of force and development; the directorate of arms systems; and the directorate of programs.

Armed with this enhanced approach to collecting open source "economic intelligence," the French probably hope to improve their image in foreign markets, defend the interests of their companies in world competition, and counter U.S. initiatives.

CHINA IN TRANSITION

As the transition in China continues, U.S. policy-makers see a country intent on becoming a leader and influential player in the world economy, with a goal to be on a par with the United States by the middle of the twenty-first century.

As part of an effort to achieve this goal, China appears to be taking another look at its unreturned students, regarding them as potential elements of an international support network able to provide China with the R&D data it needs to enhance its competitiveness, according to Chinese media reports. Appeals to patriotism and financial inducements reportedly are being used to draw expatriate scientists working overseas on advanced projects into deepening levels of commitment to their native land.

China is trying to solve its "brain drain" problem and lay the groundwork for technological competitiveness in part by tapping the knowledge of expatriate Chinese involved in leading-edge research abroad, according to Chinese press reports. Facing what the December 1997 Tianjin *Kexuexue yu Kexue Jishu Guanli (KKJG)*, a leading journal on S&T (Science and Technology) management, called a "serious shortage" of homegrown talent in science and technology, China has sought to supplement this shortfall and build up a cadre of young scientists by sending students abroad for study. Many such students have returned to play important roles in China's science establishment. For example, according to the December 1997 *KKJG*, China's 80,000 returned scholars are the "backbone" of Chinese science, and have assumed leadership posts and are responsible for what pioneering work China has accomplished. However, the majority reportedly opt to remain abroad, fostering concern among China's S&T managers about the country's high-tech drive.

There are indications in the Chinese press, however, that China has begun to regard this diaspora of scientific talent as a national asset and is taking steps to exploit these unreturned scholars to further China's research agenda. According to the February 14, 1997 edition of English language Beijing *China Daily*, most of the 170,000 Chinese students who have stayed overseas "are focused on engineering and technology" and are working on research projects with their foreign counterparts, a trend that the State Education Commission "plans to reinforce." In an article by a member of the State Natural Science Foundation Committee, *KKJG* argued that China must "face the fact" that the majority of its students remain abroad and turn this liability into an advantage.

The *KKJG* article went on to acknowledge that complex factors under-lie Chinese students' decision to remain abroad and stated "we cannot sim-ply conclude that the scholars are unpatriotic for not returning to China." Instead of abandoning them, the article said, China must recognize that

> the broad number of Chinese studying overseas are highly patriotic and hope for a continuing increase in the strength and prosperity of the motherland. Although their bodies are overseas, their hearts favor the motherland. They understand China's national conditions, are strongly patriotic, and are willing to serve the motherland in various ways.

The Communist Party and government agree on the need to "utilize this resource fully, effectively, and in a timely manner," the article observed. The journal cited various pronouncements by high-level officials exhorting Chinese students overseas to "serve the motherland by multiple means." For example, at the 15th party congress, Chinese President Jiang Zemin made a statement encouraging "personnel studying overseas to return home to work or serve the motherland in other appropriate ways." The journal noted that party and government policy now is to encourage students who have gone overseas to serve China while abroad. This "enlightened policy" has received the "enthusiastic support of the broad number of Chinese studying abroad," the journal claimed.

One example of this move to exploit expatriate talent is a program adopted by the State Natural Science Foundation Committee in August 1992 "to subsidize the return of overseas students for short periods to work and give lectures." The journal called the program "highly effective," credit-ing it with attracting some 1,300 expatriate researchers back to China tem-porarily to share their knowledge and provide "services of various kinds." Participants in the program, many of whom have graduated and taken up research positions in their host countries, are expected to "continue striving for new achievements" while overseas and "serve the motherland in various ways according to their individual circumstances and capabilities." The journal also suggested that China's own research priorities are adjusted according to the information these overseas scholars can provide, noting that "an effort is made to combine domestic requirements with the capabili-ties of those doing research abroad."

In disbursing financial support, China reportedly takes into account "the question of how to draw overseas scholars in the service of China into a deeper and more lasting type of exchange" that goes "beyond a general, superficial level." One such method, according to the journal, is the so-called two-bases pattern through which overseas scholars who cooperated for brief periods in the past are given higher subsidies that allow them to "carry out cooperative research and exchanges on a deeper level with greater continuity." Those selected for this more intense program return to China once or several times a year to coordinate with parallel groups set up in China. When not in China, they stay in "frequent contact" with their sponsoring organization via "E-mail, fax, and telephone." Their contributions reportedly enable Chinese science to "leap over stages" and quickly reach international standards.

Recipients of long-term subsidies are usually at the assistant professor level or higher or hold an equivalent rank in a research lab of their host country. They must work overseas in projects that are technically more advanced than in China and maintain "good cooperative connections" with their Chinese contacts. Expatriate researchers with less need for financial subsidies are encouraged nonetheless to steer their research toward China's domestic needs and "not abandon their foreign bases," even if they return to China. "Science has no national boundaries," the journal observed. It is not important where the scholars work, as long as they are "serving China."

SOUTH KOREA'S INFORMAL TECHNOLOGY ACQUISITIONS

South Korea is responding to economic difficulties by increasing its efforts to obtain foreign proprietary technology via indirect channels, according to Seoul media reports. Mechanisms through which enhanced collection activity has been reported include "joint research," recruitment of foreign nationals, outposts located in high-tech regions abroad, expatriate scientists, and the nation's intelligence apparatus. In addition, the Republic of Korea (ROK) Government reportedly is forming a new committee to systematize foreign technology collection and expand the number of overseas collectors.

The South Korean press has reported an intensification of the country's efforts to obtain foreign technology through informal channels, which is attributed in part to recent strains in the ROK economy. While earlier collection efforts had been motivated by what the media described as a shortage of "wellspring technology," other factors such as "snowballing" royalty payments, as reported in the August 5, 1997 and September 30, 1997 issues of *Chonja Sinmun*, and the current financial crisis are now cited as cause for renewed emphasis on this practice.

According to the January 10, 1998 *Chonja Sinmun*, South Korea's national laboratories have been tasked by the government to "help domestic industry overcome the economic crisis" by rendering "practical" support for new product development and by "internationalizing their research activities." Examples of the latter include the Korea Institute of Science and Technology's (part of the Ministry of Science and Technology—MOST) program to "conduct personnel exchanges, information interchange, and joint research with 57 institutions in 19 countries." The newspaper also reported the Korea Institute of Machinery and Metals' (another MOST affiliate) plans to set up joint R&D centers at Stanford University and MIT to "acquire leading future technologies."

According to a January 14, 1998 *Yonhap* report, South Korea is seeking U.S. Government backing to expand these "cooperative exchanges" across a wide range of "state-of-the-art technologies."

European countries have also been increasingly targeted as sources of new technology. On October 9, 1997 the *Chonja Sinmun* reported that South Korean science officers stationed at ten ROK Government-funded research centers in Europe and Russia met in Paris to discuss ways to boost their research activity, described by one officer as the "systematic gathering of information on [host country] research institutes, technologies, and personnel."

Direct exploitation of overseas scientists by ROK Government institutions, an approach noted in earlier reporting, is being stepped up by expanding the "brain pool" project, now in its fifth year, according to an Internet posting by the Korea-American Scientists and Engineers Association (KSEA) read on February 2, 1998 through a mirror site in Seoul. Administered by MOST and executed through eight national chapters (U.S., Canada, U.K., France, Germany, Japan, China, and Australia) of the Seoul-based General Federation of Korean Science and Technology Organizations, the project offers salaries and expenses to "outstanding scientists and engineers from overseas" to share their knowledge in "all fields of science and technology" with their counterparts at ROK national and corporate laboratories. In previous years, the notices capped the number of positions to a few dozen, whereas this year's solicitation appears to be open-ended.

ROK companies likewise are increasingly eager to tap the expertise of foreign scientists. According to the September 30, 1997 *Chonja Sinmun*, the major groups' electronics subsidiaries "have launched aggressive 'head hunting' operations" overseas aimed at scientists and engineers in electronics and information science. Samsung Electronics reportedly held briefing sessions and recruitment exhibitions "at major universities and research institutes in the United States and Europe." Samsung's efforts were matched by LG Electronics, Hyundai Electronics (through use of an Internet-based "manpower management program"), and Daewoo Electronics. The newspaper noted that Daewoo in particular "is securing competent employees overseas by using Korean students studying abroad on company scholarships, its overseas branches, and its own research institutes established in the U.S., Japan, and Europe as an information network." The September 27, 1997 *Hanguk Kyongje Sinmun* reported that overseas recruitment of scientific talent is being pursued at the group level and focuses not only on established scientists but also on new graduates of prestigious U.S. technical universities.

Besides these company-led efforts, South Koreans are establishing independent "consulting firms" overseas whose function is to "scout out technical manpower for Korean companies" and broker the transfer of "core technologies" to ROK producers, according to the September 9, 1997 *Maeil Kyongje Sinmun*. One such company reportedly was set up in Moscow by "specialists engaged in technology transfers from Russia on behalf of large Korean businesses." The same newspaper reported on December 5, 1997 the establishment of offices in Moscow and Los Angeles by another South Korean consulting firm to "recruit high-tech personnel in data communications." The newspaper quoted a personnel officer from an ROK company to the effect that fees of $100,000 are not considered excessive for the services of a top foreign scientist and speculated that "hiring advanced specialists from foreign countries will increase."

The United States' Silicon Valley is becoming a favorite venue for informal technology transfers through ROK Government-backed outposts for marketing and "information exchange." According to a Ministry of Information and Communications press release of November 17, 1997, South Korea is funding the creation of "incubators" in Silicon Valley designed both to promote the sale of ROK software products and conduct "technology exchange activities." On November 14, 1997, *Maeil Kyongje Sinmun* reported that Korea Telecom, a public corporation, would create a capital fund with ROK communications equipment manufacturers to support Silicon Valley-based "American venture enterprises in advanced data communications." In January 1998, the same newspaper noted the establishment in Silicon Valley of a semiconductor equipment manufacturing firm funded by the Korea Advanced Institute of Science and Technology (a MOST subsidiary) and run by expatriate Koreans. The firm reportedly is designed to allow ROK graduate students "to acquire technology at the same time they earn dollars" by performing research with world-class engineers.

Coordinating S&T collection efforts and integrating collection targets with the needs of ROK manufacturers—long a "bottleneck" in South Korea's informal technology transfer programs—will enter a "new dimension" as a result of programs undertaken by MOST's Science and Technology Policy Institute (STEPI), the December 10, 1997 *Chonja Sinmun* stated. According to a report released by STEPI on December 9 and cited by the paper, the separate collection programs run by the Ministries of Foreign Affairs, Trade and Industry, National Defense, and Science are to be brought together under a "Science and Technology Foreign Cooperation Committee" meant to systematize collection strategy, integrate local operations, and avoid duplication of effort. The committee reportedly will be divided into groups of specialists by geographical region who will interact with a council composed of working-level personnel from organizations such as the Korea Trade Promotion Agency (KOTRA) and STEPI on the one hand, and national labs, universities, and ROK companies on the other.

Reportedly formed to counter the "increasing reluctance of advanced countries to transfer their science and technology," the program entails establishing local "Korea Centers" to collect foreign S&T information and setting up overseas branches of government bodies, national labs, and companies "to provide information on foreign S&T," according to the December 10, *Chonja Sinmun*. Moreover, in order to "strengthen overseas S&T collection" and build an information system that will link ROK organizations to overseas sources of technology, STEPI reportedly will create an "Overseas Science and Technology Information Center" that integrates the S&T information collected by "overseas Korean scientists and engineers associations, Korean diplomatic and consular offices in foreign countries, large Korean trading companies, and the overseas offices of national labs."

In this connection, the Korean-U.S. Science Cooperation Center, an ROK Government-funded S&T collection facility and host to the KSEA, celebrated its first anniversary this February, according to a posting on its Internet Website (accessed via a Seoul mirror site). Items posted recently on the site include a comprehensive directory (with hot links) of major U.S. Government technology centers, national laboratories, and professional scientific organizations, along with an invitation for proposals to create new programs designed to promote S&T cooperation and to help "Korean and American scientists develop and maintain permanent S&T networks." KSEA, for its part, is currently promoting on its Website STEPI's "Creative Research Initiative Program" that seeks to fill some forty-five South Korean research associate positions with foreign or expatriate scientists.

Finally, *Yonhap* reports dated December 26 and 29, 1997 stated that ROK president-elect Kim Dae-jung is drafting reforms for the Agency for National Security Planning (NSP) that entail an "intensive buildup of economic information-collecting capabilities" against overseas targets. Earlier media reports of NSP involvement in economic intelligence activities emphasized foreign S&T collection in support of ROK commercial enterprise.

CANADA'S ECONOMIC SECURITY THREATENED

A Canadian study, *Economic Intelligence and National Security*, reports that competition among nations since the end of the Cold War has been waged more and more along economic rather than ideological or military lines. As a result, the cost of economic espionage activities to individual firms and the Canadian economy runs into billions of dollars annually. The report also says that Canada, as one of the world's most open and trade-dependent countries, is also one of the most vulnerable to penetration by economic spies from the intelligence services of both friends and enemies.

The study investigates the aims, existing mandates, and practical applications of economic espionage from a Canadian and comparative perspective. It concludes that if the growing damage to Canada resulting from the theft of Canadian technology is to be reversed, a number of changes will have to take place, including the following:

- The domestic legal framework covering economic espionage will have to be modified and strengthened.

- Intelligence services will have to focus more on monitoring the corrupt business practices of other nations and their firms.
- Intelligence services will have to take a more aggressive approach to countering economic espionage, including an expanded mandate to collect economic intelligence abroad.

HIDDEN IN PLAIN SIGHT—STEGANOGRAPHY

When looking through the contents of an electronic-mail (E-mail) message, it is not difficult to spot an encrypted message. It looks like a bunch of characters following some well-defined format. Sending such a message alerts anyone monitoring messages that there is, perhaps, something to hide. "Steganography" is the art and science of communicating in a way that hides the existence of the communication. In contrast to cryptography, where the enemy is allowed to detect, intercept, and modify messages without being able to violate certain security premises guaranteed by a cryptosystem, the goal of steganography is to hide messages inside other harmless messages in a way that does not allow any enemy to even detect that there is a second secret message present.

Steganography includes a vast array of methods of secret communications that conceal the existence of the message. Among these methods are invisible inks, microdots, character arrangement (other than the cryptographic methods of permutation and substitution), digital signatures, covert channels, and spread-spectrum communications. A message in ciphertext may arouse suspicion, while an invisible message will not.

This section provides a brief history of steganography followed by a discussion of modern implementation methods. There is also a brief description of known foreign steganography practices by both government and terrorist elements.

Historical Uses of Steganography

One of the first documents describing steganography is from the *Histories of Herodotus*. In ancient Greece, text was written on wax-covered tablets. In one story, Demeratus wanted to notify Sparta that Xerxes intended to invade Greece. To avoid capture, he scraped the wax off of the tablets and wrote a message on the underlying wood. He then covered the tablets with wax again. The tablets appeared to be blank and unused, so they passed inspection by sentries without question.

Another ancient method was to shave the head of a messenger and tattoo a message or image on the messenger's head. After allowing hair to grow, the message would be undetected until the head was shaved again.

During World War II, various steganographic methods, including the microdot, invisible ink, and null ciphers, became widespread.

Microdot.   The Nazis developed the microdot, which J. Edgar Hoover called "the enemy's masterpiece of espionage." A microdot was a photograph the size of a printed period that, when developed, could reproduce a standard-sized typewritten page with perfect clarity. Aside from being extremely difficult to detect, microdots permitted the transmission of large amounts of printed data, including technical drawings.

Invisible Ink.   Invisible inks were also used to great advantage by German spies. Common fluids used for invisible inks included urine, milk, vinegar, and fruit juices. With these inks, one need only heat the page on which the message is written to reveal the secret communication. More sophisticated inks required the receiver of the message to apply another chemical substance to reveal the secret. The Nazi spy George Dasch wrote messages on his handkerchief using a solution of copper sulfate, which remained invisible until it was exposed to ammonia fumes.

Null Ciphers.   With null ciphers, the real message is "camouflaged" in an innocent sounding message. Due to the "sound" of many open-coded messages, the suspect communications were detected by mail filters. However, "innocent" messages were allowed to flow through. Following is an example of an actual null message sent by a German spy in World War II:

- Apparently neutral's protest is thoroughly discounted and ignored. Isman hard hit. Blockade issue affects pretext for embargo on by-products, ejecting suets and vegetable oils.
- Taking the second letter in each word, the following message emerges:
- Pershing sails from NY June 1.

Another famous steganographic episode occurred when, in the 1960s, a photograph of several members of the crew of the U.S.S. Pueblo was released by their captors in order to demonstrate the crew's cooperation. The seemingly ordinary photograph contained a steganographic message: the hand positions of the crew members spelled the word "snowjob" in sign language.

Steganography Today

To use steganography today, a medium needs to be found that uses lots of bits. When some of these bits are changed, the overt message will then not be obviously altered.

Digital.   For example, an "8-bit" digital image, one capable of conveying 256 colors, uses 8 bits to represent one pixel, or picture element. It is not remarkable today to see an image that encodes thousands or millions of colors, where 32 bits are used to represent each pixel. Putting a message in that 32nd bit would not significantly, or even perceptibly, alter the digital image. An 8-bit digital image that measured 480 by 100 pixels, the size of many Web-page banners, theoretically can hold 5,000 letters of text. Today, that is considered a small image. A big 32-bit image could hold much more. For added security, to be steganographically applied to a digital image, the message does not have to be in plain text; it can also be encrypted. In addition, the message does not have to be a digital image; any bit-heavy transmission such as audio and video will do.

Audio and Image.   The idea of hiding messages in audio recordings is not new. There have been claims since the 1960s that when some Beatles' records were played backwards, the message "Paul is dead" could be heard. Today, there continue to be watchdog groups that find satanic messages hidden in records that are targeted at the segment of the audience that plays their records backwards.

Yet, hiding information in an audio recording can go well beyond this. Consider the following example: A person has a cassette tape of Pink Floyd's "The Wall." The plans of a top secret project (for example, device, aircraft, covert operation) are embedded, using some steganographic method, on that tape. Since the alterations of the "expected contents" cannot be detected (especially by human ears and probably not easily so by digital means), these plans can cross borders and trade hands undetected. How do you detect which recording has the message?

While this may be a trivial (and incomplete) example, it goes far beyond simply encoding an image with homogeneous regions. Part of secrecy is selecting the proper mechanisms. Consider encoding using an image. In and of itself, steganography is not a good solution to secrecy, but neither is simple substitution and short block permutation for encryption. But if these methods are combined, the result is a much stronger encryption routine.

For example, if a message is encrypted using substitution (substituting one alphabet with another), permute the message (shuffle the text) and apply a substitution again; then the encrypted ciphertext is more secure than using only substitution or only permutation. If the ciphertext is embedded in an image, video, voice, and so on, it is even more secure. If an encrypted message is intercepted, the interceptor knows the text is an encrypted message. With steganography, the interceptor may not know the object contains a message.

Modern Uses of Steganography

Germany.   According to Bavarian Interior Minister Guenter Beckstein, political extremists are increasingly using modern means of communication, including electronic mailbox systems, for their propaganda. According to the Office for the Protection of the Constitution, encoding technologies continue to complicate monitoring. In addition to the transmission of encoded data, whose decoding partly requires considerable exertion, "steganography" —the so-called hidden writing—is also sporadically used. In that case, data are "hidden" in a harmless text and the actual contents can only be recognized by "insiders."

Philippines.   The University of the Philippines is starting a graduate level course in cryptography and information security. One of the topics included in this course will be "Steganography or Message-Hiding."

Terrorists.   Probably the most controversial issue about widely available secure communications is that the same technology can be employed for legally and morally questionable purposes. It has been claimed, for example, that free application of cryptography enables drug traffickers and terrorists to communicate in secret, without law enforcement officials being able to intercept their messages. In some countries, strong encryption has been banned, or the keys have to be escrowed for government officials. With invisibility readily available to anyone with moderate programming skills, it is obvious that any such measures are ineffective. Restrictions on encryption cannot stop criminals from using it, but may hurt law-abiding businesses and individuals who could greatly benefit from mass application of cryptographic techniques.

Conclusion and Comments

Steganography has its place in security. It is not intended to replace cryptography, but to supplement it. Hiding a message using steganography methods reduces the chance of a message being detected. However, when that message is also encrypted, if discovered, it must also be cracked.

There are an infinite number of steganography applications. This article addresses only a tiny fraction of the art of steganography. It goes well beyond simply embedding text in an image. Steganography does not only pertain to digital images but also to other media (files such as voice; other text and binaries; other media such as communication channels).

Steganography relies on *security-by-obscurity*: if people do not know there is a hidden message, they will not look for it. With all the data transfers on the Internet, nobody has enough processing power to scan *every* image and data file transferred across the Internet. Yet if a person were to closely examine a file with steganographic data hidden in it, he or she might be able to locate the hidden data or at least determine there are data hidden. If the hidden data are encrypted, that is as far as it will go; however, if the data are not encrypted, he will be able to examine the actual message that someone tried to hide. Therefore, steganography should not be used as a substitute for strong encryption, but as a complement to strong encryption.

CELL PHONES—*DO* LEAVE HOME WITHOUT THEM

The U.S. Embassy in Moscow has warned business travelers against bringing unlicensed cellular phones and electronic equipment into Russia following the arrest of an American telephone technician on charges of spying.

The Embassy further advised caution in taking any wireless communication devices into Russia, even if they are only in transit and not intended to be used. This includes all emitting, transmitting, and receiving equipment, such as cellular phones, satellite phones, GPS devices, and other kinds of radio electronic equipment. Only consumer AM/FM radios are exempt, according to the Embassy.

Visitors entering the country with such equipment are required to obtain certificates in advance from Glavgossvyaznadzor, Russia's Main Inspectorate in Communications.

U.S. PHYSICIST PLEADS GUILTY

In a case apparently involving empathy instead of greed, Dr. Peter H. Lee, admitted under a plea bargain agreement on December 7, 1997, that he passed classified defense secrets to the Chinese Government in 1985 while working as a research physicist at Los Alamos National Laboratory. Lee, a naturalized U.S. citizen who was born in Taiwan, was working on classified projects relating to the use of lasers to simulate nuclear detonations. The information was declassified in the early 1990s.

Lee also admitted to making a false statement to a U.S. Government agency. This charge related to a 1997 trip Lee made to China to lecture on various topics relating to his employment as a research scientist for TRW, Inc. Following his return to the United States, Lee lied on a security form when he denied that he gave technical information to the Chinese. He was fired by TRW on the same day he pleaded guilty.

According to U.S. Government sources, Lee did receive some compensation for the information he transmitted to the Chinese in the form of travel and hotel accommodations.

RUSSIAN ESPIONAGE IN JAPAN

Japanese authorities revealed on February 3, 1998 that Russian agents had conducted industrial espionage to collect Japanese high-tech information during a seven-year period starting in 1987.

As the story unravels, the following scenario appears:

- Russian agents hire a 59-year-old Japanese man who is a freelance English translator with a technical background. He is asked to "do some translation work." A close relationship is developed.
- While translating the internal documents of high-tech companies into English, the man is able to promptly access classified high-tech information.
- Four Russian agents take turns contacting the man. They use the same fake Japanese name and meet him more than sixty times.
- The man receives about 8 million yen (about U.S. $66,000) and other valuables, including a watch.
- In May 1992, the man gives Russian agents a translated copy of a computer-related company's manual. Although it will eventually be distributed to consumers after the products are put on the market, the information is still company proprietary.
- The man translates and passes many open-source periodicals published by Japanese associations and societies. Military information is also included.
- The Russians use "flash contact" tradecraft, whereby the man passes material to his contacts as he meets them in a narrow lane in a residential area.
- A local recreational park is identified for use as an emergency contact point in case their activities are discovered by the police.
- After his arrest, the man admitted to Japanese authorities that "I knew I was collaborating with the spies, but the compensation was too attractive for me."

How many times have we heard a story like this? Like many other classic recruitments in the past, the intelligence agent starts with an apparently innocent request for some simple, innocuous documentation. Then, over time, friendships are developed, socializing occurs, tradecraft is employed, money and greed become the victim's downfall, and eventually a mistake is made or a suspicious indicator is observed. In the end, the victim, the companies, and possibly the nation, all stand to be the big losers in these situations.

The above case reinforces the belief, shared by many, that not only Russia but many other countries as well have apparently shifted their espionage target from exclusively military information to industrial information.

SOUTH KOREA ARRESTS NINETEEN FOR INDUSTRIAL ESPIONAGE

According to international wire service reporting, South Korean prosecutors have arrested nineteen people on charges of stealing top secret semiconductor technology for producing 64-megabit dynamic random access memory chips and selling it to a Taiwanese company. The investigation was initiated in January 1998, when the Samsung Electronics Company, the world's largest memory-chip maker, filed a complaint that its semiconductor secrets were being leaked, possibly by insiders.

The ringleader of the alleged group set up a firm called Korea Semiconductor Technology Company in Seoul in 1997. The company lured nineteen people from Samsung and LG Semicon, who accepted bribes and offers of big salaries in exchange for the technology. The stolen technology was then allegedly sold to Nanya Technology Corporation, a Taiwanese firm specializing in memory chips and liquid crystal displays. The company allegedly paid $100,000 a month to the South Korean company in exchange for the technology. If convicted, the engineers could face up to life in prison.

Nanya Technology Corporation officials have denied any involvement in the case, noting that the Korean firm was specifically asked not to use unauthorized materials in developing new technologies

FOREIGN VISITS: WHAT IS INAPPROPRIATE?

The Defense Investigative Service continues to receive reports from companies with U.S. Government facility clearances concerning inappropriate conduct by foreign personnel during the course of visits to facilities. Inappropriate conduct during visits is a frequently reported modus operandi (MO) associated with foreign collection activity. While visits may be more costly and slightly more risky to the foreign entity, they usually gain access to the targeted facility. For this reason, this MO is assessed to be the most damaging form of collection activity because it can result in the loss of some technology as a result of the visit. Once in a facility, good collectors can manipulate the visit to address some and perhaps all, of their collection requirements. Visiting foreign scientists or engineers can take acquired technology back to their own country and apply it directly to their needs without having to wait for it to arrive through a bureaucratic intelligence collection process.

The Techniques

While the vast majority of foreign visits take place without incident, many do result in some inappropriate or suspicious activity. Reported cases involving inappropriate conduct during a foreign visit include "wandering" visitors who become offended when confronted, hidden agendas that involve questions beyond the scope of what was approved for discussion, or the fraudulent use of data-exchange agreements. Other approaches could include arriving at the facility unannounced, taking notes and photographs, holding "commercial" discussions when the U.S. Government refuses to officially sponsor the visit, and last-minute or unannounced additions to a visiting delegation. Many of these techniques are specifically designed to produce potentially embarrassing incidents for the host in order to obtain collection objectives as a result of the host attempting to be conciliatory.

Case Studies

Many cases of inappropriate conduct during a foreign visit involve taking advantage of the escort and making the escort a vulnerability instead of a security countermeasure. This happens most frequently when there are an insufficient number of escorts to control the size of the visiting delegation. In other instances, the escort has not been properly briefed on "what to protect" and "how to respond to questions." In one case, during a visit to an aeronautics facility, a foreign delegation of ten people was provided one escort. The visiting delegation recognized the vulnerability and used an opportunity during a restroom break to split the delegation, thereby causing half the delegation to be unescorted in an area with exported controlled technology.

A frequently used technique by several foreign military attachés within the United States is to arrive at a contractor facility unannounced in a three-piece suit with a business card. The civilian business attire makes the military attaché appear less threatening to the facility personnel. However, the actual ploy is to arrive "unannounced" and rely on the courtesy of the company's management to permit the attaché access to the facility. On several occasions, and at separate facilities within the Washington, D.C. area, military attachés solicited unclassified papers and brochures and engaged in conversations to determine other venues for exploitation. What the company personnel may not have realized is that most foreign military attachés are either trained intelligence officers or acting in the capacity of intelligence officers.

Security Countermeasures

Some recommended security countermeasures to mitigate vulnerabilities associated with these collection techniques are relatively simple, inexpensive, and effective—"if implemented":

- Do not allow suspicious unannounced foreign visitors access to the facility. Simply tell them no one is available and to schedule an appointment for another date.
- Do not allow last-minute additions or substitutions to a foreign delegation to have access to the facility. Ask them to remain in the lobby while the others are permitted access. This could potentially keep an

intelligence officer out of the facility and encourage proper visitation procedures.

- Verify personal identification against the original visit request when foreign visitors arrive to ensure that they are who they say they are.
- Ensure that there are a sufficient number of escorts to control a visiting delegation if it should be split into multiple groups.
- Ensure that escorts are briefed on what is critical within the facility and that they know what requires protection from the foreign visitors.
- Ensure that facility employees are briefed on the scope of the foreign visit and that they do not discuss anything beyond what is approved.
- If a visitor becomes offended when confronted during a security incident, recognize the confrontation as a collection technique and ask the visitor to leave the facility if he or she cannot abide by the rules.
- Do not permit cameras or note taking if something in the facility is "sight sensitive."

FRONT COMPANIES: WHO IS THE END USER?

The Defense Investigative Service (DIS) receives many reports each year of suspected "front companies" that are referred to the FBI and U.S. Customs for investigation as appropriate. Front companies can present a serious problem to the U.S. Government and the defense industry because they can potentially be used to circumvent export restrictions and embargoes.

The Technique

A front company frequently operates like a consultant. It works on behalf of a customer, often with the intent of hiding the identity of the end user. Front companies may be used to locate and acquire technology legally and then export it illegally to an unauthorized recipient. Suspicious indicators may include:

- The U.S. contractor receives an unsolicited request for military-related information by fax, mail, E-mail, or phone from a "relatively unknown" company. The request itself is simple, low-cost, nonthreatening, and risk free.
- The unsolicited request is sent in "broken" English.
- The request is sent on "shoddy" business letterhead or in an unprofessional manner in contrast to standard business practices.
- The request more frequently, but not always, involves a dual-use type of technology (electronics, avionics, communications) that may or may not require a license for export, depending on the intended end use.

In addition, the front company:

- May be comprised of only a few employees. These employees may also have other incorporated businesses.
- Does not know much about the equipment being requested, which someone working with the equipment would reasonably be expected to know.
- Declines a maintenance warranty or operator training associated with the equipment.
- Conveys the impression that the equipment is for a third party and the real end-user is unknown.
- May identify itself as being in the consulting or brokering business.
- May have connections or business with a foreign embassy.
- May be financed by a foreign bank.
- May attempt to test the honesty of the U.S. contractor or its representative to determine whether an illicit deal can be arranged.
- Representative may ask if the U.S. contractor has offices in a third country to which the item can be shipped.
- Representative may offer financial incentives (bribes) to the U.S. contractor to overcome reluctance in shipping an item.
- Representative may imply that officials in the foreign country can be readily bribed to take part in an illicit deal.
- May have an office in an embargoed country.
- Wants to close the deal quickly and provides the money up front.

Case Studies

A U.S. incorporated company in California sent an unsolicited request for information to purchase jamming equipment from a U.S. defense contractor. Jamming equipment is listed under the International Traffic in Arms Regulations and requires a license if exported outside the United States. The U.S. company requesting the jamming equipment consisted of only several people and was an unknown entity to the U.S. defense contractor. The request was sent in broken English, on letterhead most likely made on a personal computer. The U.S. company requesting the jamming equipment was obviously not the end user and was more likely a front company.

In another incident, a U.S. company submitted a request for a quote (RFQ) to a U.S. defense contractor on an aircraft part for a system configuration sold only to a Southwest Asian country. The Southwest Asian country has since been placed on a U.S. embargo list. The U.S. company submitting the RFQ was a small previously unknown company in Texas. The stated end use for the part was a West European country. The request was handwritten on business letterhead most likely produced on a home computer. The contractor became suspicious when a similar request for the same aircraft part arrived from a different U.S. company in Florida. In the second request, no end user was listed, but the part number, quantity, and item numbers were exactly the same. The two U.S. companies submitting the RFQs were likely front companies either operated by or operating on behalf of the Southwest Asian country.

Some front companies can be more blatant and obvious. One company, located in Florida, sent a letter and a few weeks later telephoned a U.S. defense contractor to establish a business arrangement for the sale of a classified airborne infrared countermeasures system. The contractor could not obtain an export license for this country and therefore did not pursue the business arrangement. The company soliciting the business arrangement subsequently approached the contractor about exporting the countermeasures system through a foreign office or subsidiary in a country where an export license could be approved.

Security Countermeasures

The best security countermeasure is to know your customer. Many U.S. defense contractors conduct business with the same companies on a daily basis. When a "new company" enters the picture, requesting sensitive or classified information and technology, prudent risk management would suggest doing a little checking of the company's history. If a company fits any of the indicators mentioned above and is cause for suspicion, the company facility security officer should notify the DIS Industrial Security Representative, FBI, and U.S. Customs as appropriate.

THREE TAIWAN NATIONALS INDICTED FOR ECONOMIC ESPIONAGE

Kai-Lo Hsu, Technical Director of the Yuen Foong Paper Co. Ltd., in Taipei, and Chester S. Ho, a professor at the National Chiao Tung University, were arrested in Philadelphia on June 14, 1997 on charges relating to an alleged plan to steal trade secrets from the pharmaceutical firm Bristol-Myers Squibb Company. The two are being held in home detention under a $1 million bond secured by real estate and bank accounts. An arrest warrant was also issued for a third person, Jessica Chou, identified as a manager for business development at Yuen Foong. Her exact location was unknown.

According to the arrest warrant, and multiple open sources, Hsu and Ho conspired to illegally acquire, through an FBI undercover agent, plant cell culture technology used to make Taxol, an anticancer drug used to treat ovarian cancer. The eleven-count indictment charges that two of the three accused agreed to make a preliminary payment of $400,000 in cash, stock, and royalties to a corrupt Bristol-Myers scientist and a man they thought was a technology-information broker. The broker was an undercover FBI agent and the supposedly corrupt scientist was working with the government.

Hsu was charged with six counts of mail fraud, one count of conspiracy to steal trade secrets, one count of attempted theft of trade secrets, and other violations. Ho was charged with one count of conspiracy to steal trade secrets, one count of attempted theft of trade secrets, and other violations. Chou was charged with mail fraud, conspiracy to steal trade secrets, and other charges. Maximum penalties for the charges range up to sixty years in prison and up to a $2,500,000 fine.

It is uncertain if the attempted deal was sanctioned by high-level executives at Yuen Foong, however, Hsu allegedly made the comment that his company was diversifying its interests into the area of biotechnology and working on a government project on Taxol technology. A spokesman for Bristol-Myers noted that Taxol is a billion-dollar product around the world and that the cost of losing the technology would have been significant.

In a recent turn of events, a federal judge ordered prosecutors to turn over to the defendants and their lawyers the very documents the defendants are accused of trying to steal. The judge ruled that they needed the information to prepare their defense, and that their right to a fair trial overrides the rights of a company to protect its trade secrets. Prosecutors are appealing the ruling.

RUSSIAN SPIES: ROUND UP TIME

Russia's Federal Security Service (FSB) set up a special telephone line in June 1997 to encourage confessions from remorseful Russians working for foreign intelligence. The ultimate goal of the program was to encourage the collaborators to become double agents. There was also a pledge that any money these people earned would not be confiscated.

In less than two months, wire services are reporting that the FSB has been overwhelmed with nearly 300 phone calls, about 80 of which were taken very seriously. The Director of the FSB, Nikolai Kovalyov, was concerned that a lot of calls would be from mentally ill people, but he said that had not been the case. He added that two countries had frozen their counter-intelligence work in Russia since the telephone line was set up.

An editorial comment on this subject in the July 1997 Department of Energy (DOE)/Office of Energy Intelligence/Counter-intelligence Newsletter notes that

> One wonders what will befall any individual who takes up this offer. Will the potential double agent be welcomed with open arms or be given the typical reward that Western spies have received in the past, a one-way train ticket to the gulag or worse. Can the "KGB" leopard change its

spots? By the way, remember the whole episode will be kept confidential so no one will ever know.

In the meantime, the FSB has finished investigating the case of a Russian diplomat alleged to have spied for Great Britain, and a court will decide whether to hospitalize or imprison him. The diplomat, Platon Obukhov, a second secretary in the Foreign Ministry's prestigious Northern America Department who wrote spy thrillers on the side, has been in prison awaiting trial on espionage charges since April 1997. His lawyers claim he is mentally unstable. After Obukhov was arrested, several members of the British Embassy were expelled, followed by a similar expulsion of Russian Embassy officials in London.

The Russian press also reported that in July 1997 the Russian Supreme Court sentenced well-known Russian scientist Vadim Sintsov to ten years in prison for economic espionage. Sintsov was recruited in January 1993 while traveling in Great Britain. His dialogue with the British ended with his arrest on January 15, 1994.

TAIWAN NATIONALS INDICTED

A Taiwan businessman and his daughter have been indicted for allegedly stealing trade secrets from the Pasadena-based company Avery Dennison Corporation. Avery is one of the largest manufacturers of adhesive products, such as postage stamps and diaper tape in the United States, with more than 16,000 employees worldwide.

The twenty-one-count indictment, handed down by a grand jury in Ohio, alleges that Yang Pin-Yen and his daughter Yang Hwei-Chen plotted from 1989 to 1997 to obtain confidential and proprietary information from Avery in violation of the 1996 Economic Espionage Act. The two allegedly met in early September with Avery employee Lee Ten-Hong who, in a bargain with prosecutors, pleaded guilty to one count of wire fraud in exchange for his full cooperation in the government's case against the accused. Yang Pin-Yen is the president of Four Pillars, which makes and markets pressure-sensitive products in Taiwan, China, Malaysia, Singapore, and the United States.

CONGRESS ACTS TO PROTECT ECONOMIC INFORMATION

Three bills dealing with economic espionage were introduced in the Congress during 1995. One bill was *the Economic Espionage and Protection of Proprietary Economic Information Act of 1995.* This bill, by Senator Cohen, is designed to combat economic espionage against American companies by criminalizing foreign corporate or state-sponsored economic espionage.

Economic Espionage: The Threat from Old Friends

According to Senator Cohen,

> When France, Germany, Japan, and South Korea are included in a list of
> nations, we automatically assume that this must be a list of America's
> allies—our military and political partners since the end of the Second
> World War. Unfortunately, this is not only a list of America's trustworthy
> friends, it is a list of governments that have systematically practiced eco-
> nomic espionage against American companies in the past—and continue
> to do so to this day.

Old Game, New Target

The term "espionage" evokes images of the cloak-and-dagger side of the
United States–Soviet confrontation in the Cold War. Since the end of the
East-West struggle, however, an equally damaging and pervasive form of
spying has received increasing attention—the spying that nations undertake
against foreign-owned corporations in order to give their own firms an
advantage in the increasingly cutthroat world of international business.

To Senator Kohl, a cosponsor of the bill, the problem is not new. He
states that, with expanding technology and a growing global economy, economic espionage is entering its boom years. American companies have estimated that, in 1992, they lost $1.8 billion from the theft of their trade
secrets. And the theft of these secrets is not random and disorganized. The
press has reported that one government study of 173 nations discovered that
57 of them were trying to get advanced technologies from American companies. Senator Kohl cited the French intelligence service's admission of a
special unit devoted to obtaining confidential information from American
companies.

Congress Reacts

The 103rd Congress adopted Senator Cohen's amendment requiring the
President to submit an annual report on foreign industrial espionage targeted against U.S. industry.

The President Responds

The unclassified version of the President's first annual report, which was
prepared by the National Counterintelligence Center (NACIC), acknowledged "the post-Cold War reality that economical and technological information are as much a target of foreign intelligence collection as military and
political information." The report goes on to state:

In today's world in which a country's power and stature are often measured by its economic/industrial capability, foreign government ministries—such as those dealing with finance and trade—and major industrial sectors are increasingly looked upon to play a more prominent role in their respective country's (economic) collection efforts. While a military rival steals documents for a state-of-the-art weapon or defense system, an economic competitor steals a U.S. company's proprietary business information or government trade strategies. Just as a foreign country's defense establishment is the main recipient of U.S. defense-related information, foreign companies and commercially oriented government ministries are the main beneficiaries of U.S. economic information. The aggregate losses that can mount as a result of such efforts can reach billions of dollars per year, constituting a serious national security concern.

Growing Threat

According to Joseph Ricci of the American Society for Industrial Security, "American corporations are losing billions of dollars each year in valuable technology and proprietary information to foreign espionage." In a recent survey of Fortune 500 companies, the society notes that the number of corporations reporting that they have been victims of economic espionage has grown by 260 percent since 1985. Peter Schweizer, in his 1994 study of sponsored economic espionage, *Friendly Spies*, estimated that such espionage costs American business upwards of $100 billion annually.

Cases in Point

The Senators provided examples of actual cases to illustrate how pervasive the problem has become.

Foreign intelligence agents and corporations have been known to recruit as spies mid-level managers and scientists at American high-technology corporations. In exchange for money, these Americans have provided the foreign agents with valuable trade secrets and formulas, destroying American companies' market leadership.

The foreign offices of American corporations are often subjected to wiretaps on their phones and infiltration of their foreign national staff by agents of the host-country's intelligence service. American competitiveness, profits, and jobs are the cost.

A former employee of two major computer companies admitted to stealing vital information on the manufacture of microchips and selling it to China, Cuba, and Iran. For almost a decade, he copied manufacturing specifications—information worth millions of dollars. Armed with this information, the Chinese, Cubans, and Iranians have been able to close the gap on U.S. technology leads. Late last year, the FBI arrested this man and charged him with the interstate transportation of stolen property and mail fraud. It appears that the charges may be a bit of a stretch, because he did not actually steal tangible property. He stole ideas.

In a case of domestic theft, an engineer for an automobile air bag manufacturer in Arizona was arrested in 1993 for selling manufacturing designs, strategies, and plans. He asked the company's competition for more than half a million dollars-to be paid in small bills. And he sent potential buyers a laundry list of information they could buy: $500 for the company's capital budget plan; $1,000 for a piece of equipment; and $6,000 for planning and product documents.

Past Efforts to Counter the Problem—Too Little, Too Vague

The United States has taken some steps to counter this pervasive problem, but action has been neither strong enough nor smart enough to make a real dent in foreign corporate and state-sponsored economic espionage in the United States and against Americans abroad. Admiral Studeman testified in January, "the private sector's concerns about increasing signs of 'economic espionage' . . . are well founded. Despite the continuing necessity to protect sensitive sources and methods, more can and must be done against state-sponsored economic espionage." As an NACIC report delicately puts it: "efforts across the government to investigate and counter economic and industrial intelligence collection activities were fragmented and uncoordinated . . . resulting in many partially informed decisions and diverging collection and analytical efforts."

Civil Remedies Inadequate.   Senator Kohl asserts that current civil remedies are inadequate to deal with the problems of theft of American proprietary information. "Although many companies can privately sue those who have stolen from them, these private remedies," says Senator Kohl, "are too little, too late." A private lawsuit against a foreign company or government often just goes nowhere, and the company continues to use the stolen information without pause.

"Similarly," says Senator Kohl, "our current laws are not specifically targeted at protection of proprietary economic information." Most Federal statues deal with tangible property and not intellectual property. According to Professor James P. Chandler, President of the National Intellectual Property Law Institute in Washington, D.C., "the United States is the world's leader in the production of intellectual property." Professor Chandler points out that a company cannot manufacture anything it does not have a legal right to. It has to own the intellectual property before it can market a good. "Intellectual property is as important to business as blood is to a human being. Without it, we die. And without it, a business dies."

The New Legislation: Clarified Issues

Economic espionage by foreign governments targeting U.S. industry and innovation is an issue the Senate Select Committee on Intelligence has been examining for some time, said Senator Specter. The Committee has held a number of hearings that addressed this issue and has met extensively with the intelligence and law enforcement communities. Senator Specter cites then-Director of Central Intelligence Robert M. Gates who, in 1992, informed the Committee:

> We know that some foreign intelligence services have turned from politics to economics and that the United States is their prime target. We have cases of moles being planted in U.S. high-tech companies. We have cases of U.S. businessmen abroad being subjected to bugging, to room searches, and the like . . . We are giving a high priority to fighting it.

It is a crime to engage in foreign corporate or state-sponsored economic espionage.

GAO WARNS OF ALLIED THREAT TO U.S. DEFENSE CONTRACTORS

In 1996, the General Accounting Office (GAO)—Congress' investigative arm—released a report entitled *Defense Industrial Security: Weaknesses in DOD Security Arrangements at Foreign Owned Companies* that highlights the extent of industrial espionage being conducted by selected Allied nations against U.S. defense contractors.

Internationalization of Defense Contracting

This report notes that, since the mid-1980s, development, production, and marketing of weapon systems have been increasingly internationalized through government-sponsored cooperative development programs and various kinds of industrial linkages, including international subcontracting and teaming arrangements, joint ventures, and cross-border mergers and acquisitions. Foreign companies have acquired many U.S. defense companies and have legitimate business interests in them. The U.S. Government allows such foreign investment as long as it is consistent with U.S. national security interests. Some foreign-owned U.S. companies are working on highly classified defense contracts, such as the B-2, the F-117, the F-22, and military satellite programs.

Some Examples.   The following are examples of some sensitive contract work being performed by fourteen foreign-owned U.S. companies that the GAO sampled:

- Development of computer software for planning target selection and aircraft routes in the event of a nuclear war.
- Maintenance of DoD's Worldwide Military Command and Control System. Production of signal-intelligence-gathering radio receivers for the U.S. Navy.
- Production of command destruct receivers for military missiles and National Aeronautics and Space Administration rockets.
- Production of carbon/carbon composite for the heat shields of the Trident D-5 missiles.
- Production of the flight controls for the B-2, the F-117, and the F-22.

Culprits Identified—Almost.   The document also identifies five Allied countries that are engaged in industrial espionage. Designating them as countries "A through E," the report illustrates the threat posed by each individual nation and cites its information-collection efforts.

IRAQ OVERTLY TARGETS WESTERN TECHNOLOGIES

Seemingly Innocent Requests

The Iraqis seek Western technologies, possibly using as their opening gambit apparently innocent requests for information and samples. Between September 1994 and March 1995, a Western manufacturer of electronic transceivers and display software received twelve unsolicited letters from eleven different companies and individuals in Iraq. Although the contents of the letters varied, the general theme for each letter was a request for information on the firm and a request for demonstration discs or samples of the firm's software. Only one letter cited a specific product of the firm. Many of the letters included a sentence of appreciation for the firm's "good work" and/or a wish of "good relations" between Iraq and the firm.

Concerted Campaign?

Similarities in the letters suggest a common source. Most of the air mailed letters requested information on the Western firm and its products. Eleven of the letters originated from Mosul, and the twelfth came from Baghdad. Eleven of the letters were handwritten and displayed a P.O. box return address, and all of them were short, consisting of one paragraph. The majority of the letters identified the author's own company. Although it appears different authors wrote the letters, each letter asked for demonstration discs or samples of the Western firm's products without identifying a specific product of interest. Most authors made the same English usage mistakes with one exception. On the basis of the above similarities, the authors probably copied their letters from a common manuscript.

Open requests for company brochures and sample products are not uncommon. In this case, however, twelve letters from the same country requesting information and samples from one Western company indicate a determined effort by Iraq to obtain information on radar and imaging transceivers and display software technologies. The requests may also be a precursor for a more concerted campaign to acquire these capabilities through technology transfer operations. Each of the letters stated that the requester "wanted good cooperation between firms and 'information disk illustrations' of the firm's products."

Be On Guard

On the surface, these types of requests are not alarming—until the Western company is asked to send the materials to the country. It is imperative that U.S. companies continually review requests for their brochures and samples of their products in order to determine if it is legal to export this information to the requesting nation.

ROOM SEARCHES IN A EUROPEAN CAPITAL

The manager of an information security program in a U.S. company reported that, in 1992, his room was being used to secure briefcases and other paperwork brought to the hotel by the visiting company's representatives. Shortly after a bus transporting the company's representatives departed the hotel for a tour of the city, three men used a key to enter the source's room unannounced. After being challenged by the source, one man with a key—dressed in hotel work attire—left the area immediately. When queried, the other two said they were looking for air conditioning wires because there had been a complaint from the adjacent ballroom. The two men declined an invitation to continue their search and exited the room.

The source followed the two men and observed their activity. They entered the ballroom, looked around quickly, and walked to the next room. It was evident they were not looking for wires, as they had no tools with them and they merely glanced at the walls. The individual with the key had disappeared.

The source filed a complaint at the hotel's reception desk, and he insisted that the two men be challenged to determine their actions. About the same time, the two men entered the lobby. When approached by the reception clerk, they said that they were from a company that did business with the hotel and that the head engineer called them to check on the air conditioning. The reception clerk called the hotel engineer, who verified that they do business with the company in question. The clerk, however, never asked if there had been a request for the company to be present in the hotel that day. The two men left, and the hotel denied a request to speak with the head engineer.

The following day, the source reported the incident to a point of contact for the corporation, asked for additional information on the two men, and requested to speak with the hotel engineer. Later that day, the hotel informed the source that the two men in question were from a company doing business with the hotel for some time, but that they should not have entered the source's room without knocking. He also learned the man with the key was a hotel employee. Upon his insistence to speak with the head engineer, the source was told he was gone for the day and would be out of town for the remainder of the week. The man identified as the hotel employee was never seen again during the remainder of the week.

Note: That was 1992 and now it's 1998, and this type of information-gathering is still continuing on a daily basis.

BURGLARIES IN EUROPE

A European office of a U.S. company was burglarized in late January 1996. The office, located on the sixth floor of a twelve-story office building, was entered from the outside ledge by breaking a window. Once inside the office, the professional thieves ignored the company's expensive computers and other valuable items and went directly to their target—the company's marketing and business data, client and business contact lists, and banking information. Since the thieves ignored other more lucrative commercial offices in the building and took only business information that has no value, except to competitors of the company, this was obviously a case of industrial espionage.

TRAVELING WITH LAPTOPS

Laptop computers have become a prime target for theft throughout Europe, according to a recently received travel advisory. International travelers who anticipate carrying such items should be particularly wary while transiting airports and report any losses to the appropriate authorities immediately. Two recent incidents at separate airports demonstrate the modus operandi of thieves operating in pairs that target laptop computers.

Airport security at Brussels International Airport reported a theft centering on the use of security X-ray machines. The first thief preceded the traveler through the security checkpoint and then loitered around the area where security examines carry-on luggage. When the traveler placed his laptop computer onto the conveyer belt of the X-ray machine, the second thief stepped in front of the traveler and set off the metal detector. With the traveler now delayed, the first thief removed the traveler's laptop from the conveyer belt just after it passed through the X-ray machine and quickly disappeared.

While walking around the Frankfurt International Airport in Germany, a traveler carrying a laptop computer in his roll bag did not notice a thief position himself to walk in front of him. The thief stopped abruptly as the traveler bypassed a crowd of people, causing the traveler also to stop. A second thief, who was following close behind, quickly removed the traveler's laptop computer from his roll bag and disappeared into the crowd.

All travelers, both international and domestic, should be alert to any sudden diversions when traveling, especially when transiting transportation terminals. If victimized, travelers should report the thefts immediately to the authorities and be able to provide the makes, model information, and serial numbers of their laptop computers, or any items of value.

YELTSIN ADMITS RUSSIANS ENGAGE IN ECONOMIC ESPIONAGE

According to media sources, Russian President Boris Yeltsin confirmed in Moscow on February 7, 1996 that Russia is involved in industrial espionage, but that the data being collected by Russian intelligence agencies are not being used effectively. Speaking before a meeting of his Security Council—which included Mikhail Barsukov, Director of the State Security Service (FSB), and Vyacheslav Trubnikov, Head of the Foreign Intelligence Service (SVR)—Yeltsin noted that foreign intelligence service activity in Russia is causing the technology gap with the West to grow. He then ordered top state officials to close the gap by more efficiently using industrial intelligence. He also expressed concern over the emigration of talented Russian technicians and said that less than 25 percent of the information collected by Russian spies abroad is used in Russia, even though he claimed information was derived directly from foreign blueprints and manuals.

LONG-TERM FOREIGN VISITS THREATEN SECURITY

The Threat

According to a recent article provided by the Defense Investigative Service, long-term foreign visits to cleared U.S. companie—as well as non-DoD companies in the private sector—can pose a serious threat to security without appropriate countermeasures to mitigate the vulnerabilities associated with the foreign presence.

Given access to scientific, technical, and other proprietary information, foreign experts can glean significant information to clarify and confirm reports obtained through intelligence channels to aid in their own research and development. The vast numbers of foreign scientists visiting the U.S. make it difficult to assess the full extent of their collection effort. Often the difference between the technology used in unclassified research and a classified weapons program is nothing more than the "application" of the technology.

Some Real-Life Cases

In one instance involving a cleared U.S. company, the company security officer reported the company's desire to employ the son of a prominent foreign scientist from a European country. A name check of the scientist revealed he had previously cooperated with a foreign intelligence service. The company specializes in providing training, engineering, and other technical services.

In another example, prominent foreign scientists take long-term employment with U.S. companies and immediately begin sending acquired information via fax transmissions back to their former associates in their native language. In yet another case, a foreign student attempted to gain employment with a cleared U.S. company (a company under contract with the U.S. Government to perform classified work) for "free" in lieu of military service in his home country. This modus operandi had been used previously by the same foreign country and is still being used today.

Countering the Threat

U.S. industry reporting of security countermeasures concerns continues to indicate that, without sustained security and counterintelligence (CI) awareness training programs, assimilation of foreign personnel into the work environment usually results in a relaxation of security awareness among U.S. employees. In this type of environment, a security compromise frequently occurs. Here are some security countermeasures to consider in such instances.

Local Area Network (LAN) Restrictions. In anticipation of gaining access to an LAN, some foreign employees are trained in hacking techniques. Good risk management means reducing vulnerabilities to the technologies or information you are trying to protect. It may mean providing long-term visitors with a "stand-alone" computer instead of access to a LAN.

Fax Machine Restrictions. Unless a company has a trusted employee who is able to read and review the documents, a foreign visitor should not be given access to company fax machines. Foreign employees' uncontrolled access to fax machines reduces the risk of detection to them by eliminating the need to remove documents from the facility.

A Technology Control Plan (TCP) or Similar Document. A TCP will educate all employees on what needs to be protected and what their responsibilities are to prevent the loss of classified, intellectual property, or proprietary information. It will also help educate facility employees on CI awareness issues. Facility employees should be pre-briefed prior to the arrival of a foreign national on the potential foreign collection techniques that could be used, particularly elicitation. Facility employees should also be aware of the reporting procedures for potential economic espionage indicators.

Periodic Liaison. Periodic liaison with the local supporting CI office should be conducted on the issue.

Periodic Interviews. To spot potential espionage indicators, facility employees should be periodically interviewed if they are in contact with foreign employees.

INTERNET SECURITY: UNRAVELING THE GORDIAN KNOT

(Prepared by Dr. James Kasprzak, Information Resource Management College, National Defense University, and Charles Crowl, Defense Information Systems Agency.)

Internet Security Issues

The Internet has shown a wide range of vulnerabilities to hackers, viruses, and unintentional breakdowns. Since its original design emphasized easy accessibility rather than security, control, and integrity of data, it will be difficult and expensive to retrofit these qualities into the system. Because of these weaknesses, governments and others are reluctant to put critical national security functions on the Internet. By "critical functions," we refer not only to classified data, command and control, and emergency operations but also to police functions, finance and banking, transportation, and other key civil support activities. This is not to say that all critical functions will not, or should not, be on the Internet. Worldwide experience with the Internet in times of disaster, oppression, and civil unrest has shown the critically pivotal role of Internet-style access to information. After earthquakes in Japan and California, typhoons in Hawaii, and hurricanes in Florida, national and local governments and individuals used the Internet to find relatives, distribute emergency supplies, and coordinate disaster relief. In Bosnia, China, and Mexico, it has been used for public information (and disinformation) in times of political and military conflict. Thus, far more activities will inevitably move to the Internet, and some of these will be essential functions. Future concerns with potentially serious effects include the increasing interconnectivity of the Internet and the public switched network. About 90 percent of government telecommunications use the public network, and, if this infrastructure is attacked, government operations could be degraded significantly.

The business community has also been reluctant to commit its most essential and sensitive functions to the Internet. Surveys reveal that many companies have experienced security intrusions through the Internet, and that users and security personnel have perceived a rise in attempted break-ins of their systems. The notoriety surrounding the arrest of a hacker who stole 20,000 credit card numbers highlights and reinforces the widely held view that financial transactions may not be safe in cyberspace. In 1996, commercial enterprises transacted about $500 million worth on the Internet—an insignificant amount when compared with the U.S. retail marketplace. To date, many of these transactions seem to be in a small number of industries—such as entertainment and computer equipment—and only involve a small number of buyers. The Internet is not secure, and many businesses and government organizations know this fact and conduct their activities in this medium accordingly. While the Internet will become an important vehicle of commerce, many risks must be overcome in the next few years of transition.

Threats to Internet Security

The Internet has no special vulnerability to natural disasters because it is so geographically dispersed. Fires, earthquakes, and floods can only affect very limited segments of the Net at any one time. However, the great number and diversity of its machines, software applications, and networks render the Internet vulnerable to other kinds of problems. For example, computers on the Internet have the same susceptibility to software viruses as their non-networked cousins, but they arguably have greater exposure. Because the many aspects of computer, communications, and information security are too extensive to be covered here, only some peculiar vulnerabilities of the Internet will be surveyed.

Malicious Software.   A variety of software threatens systems attached to the Internet or the Internet itself. A *Trojan horse program sabotages unknowing users with unforeseen built-in problems. A virus program spreads by making copies of itself in one way or another. Self-sufficient, a worm program spreads by spawning copies of itself on other hosts on the network. A back door, a "hole" in the software, permits access without going through normal procedures. It can be inserted into a system by a programmer or hacker in order to circumvent normal security procedures.*

While all of these programs can infect machines not connected to a network, the Internet's public and undisciplined nature permits faster and more widespread infection. For example, the worm spread by a student in 1988 infected thousands of computers and, within a day, effectively shut down the Net. Virus creators, however, continue to make rapid advances in the state of their art. A few years ago, virus infection could be avoided by just not running certain kinds of programs (.exe files and .com files, for example). Today, a much greater range of viruses exists, infecting a wider range of files. For example, "macro" viruses, programs attached to compressed files, "automatically decompress the file" (and infect your machine) and other ruses. New languages and "scripts" such as Java and CGI scripts download small programs (applets) and run them on remote computers. Some believe that applets may provide significantly higher levels of risk to those browsing the Internet. Finally, some of the search engines send out software agents (called "spiders," "ants," and other insect names) to search through data files and index or fetch information. The difference between these "good" software programs and "worms" or "viruses" is a matter of debate. If somebody else's machine seeks to download large amounts of data just for indexing, and ties up access ports on another's machine, the victim might well conceive of this as an antisocial act—a partial denial of service.

Unauthorized Intrusion. "Hacking" into computer systems has become more popular than ever, and a new generation of hackers appears to be motivated by more sinister motives: greed, ideological vengeance, and deliberately malicious behaviors. For example, one hacker assaulted emergency 911 systems, denying services for potentially life-threatening calls, while another changed the path of a hurricane on an Internet weather map, misleading viewers on the locations threatened by the storm. In addition, evidence indicates that a number of nations have taken a military interest in the Internet. For terrorist states, organized hacking offers the advantages of low cost, low risk, and potentially a high gain against the most highly developed nations. This threat may be the most serious of all Internet vulnerabilities. Organized, well-planned, and appropriately timed attacks are potentially far more dangerous than the erratic sniping of amateurs—even brilliant amateurs.

Break-ins occur at an alarming rate because the Internet provides an especially comfortable and interesting place for hackers. For one thing, the Internet—a large, intricate network—has limited security and many software flaws. For another, it is easy to remain anonymous on the Net. An expert can weave a trail through a dozen systems, making it almost impossible to track him. Finally, the international, multi-organizational, multidimensional, and highly decentralized Internet makes it difficult to get attention and cooperation across such boundaries, even under the best of circumstances.

In the latest development in hacking, hackers use sophisticated tools, including complex software programs, to exploit holes in the security of computer systems. Experts create and pass on to others these automated tools—war dialers, password crackers, "Satan," sniffers, and others. Because many are stored on the Internet, relative newcomers can download and use them, raising the level of sophistication of hackers of all types.

Security Solutions

The United States now spends considerably more than $100 million a year to resolve the security problems of the Internet. Some avenues likely to bring success may depend on advances in technology. As computers increase in power and speed, some real-time enhancements become possible. These approaches look hopeful:

- Changes to TCP/IP (Transmission Control Protocol/Internet Protocol) that bring greater security.
- Cheap, very fast encryption that is highly secure.
- Smart cards containing complex passwords and perhaps biometric data.
- Low-cost "firewalls," continuously maintained, sealing off computers, including switches, from unauthorized access.
- Identification of Internet users by digital signatures.

GERMAN COMPANIES WARNED OF RISING INDUSTRIAL ESPIONAGE

In late 1996, several German factions spoke out to warn companies and the government that they must tighten security precautions in the face of industrial espionage from Russia and Eastern Europe, which is costing them billions of dollars a year.

In November, Germany's Federal Prosecutor warned that, although the end of the Cold War had reduced military and political tension between East and West, foreign intelligence services were more active than ever in trying to steal secrets from German companies. Citing damage to German industry by espionage at about 8 billion marks ($5.31 billion) a year, he said that many foreign intelligence services concentrated on industrial espionage in order to justify their continued existence, and he warned all sectors that it was not just the industrial giants who were being targeted by foreign spies.

Russia and Eastern Europe were identified as the biggest threat, but the rapidly growing economies of southeast Asia and Communist countries such as North Korea and China were also acknowledged as seeking German know-how. Modus operandi included placing agents in international organizations, setting up joint-ventures with German companies, and setting up bogus companies. The report also warned business leaders to be particularly wary of former diplomats or people who used to work for foreign secret services, because they often had the language skills and knowledge of Germany that made them excellent agents.

Another source claimed that trade thefts cost German companies as much as 20 billion marks ($13 billion) in 1996, and a third source added that most thefts involved German companies spying on their German competitors. A growing number, however, involved intelligence services from Eastern European countries. It was also alleged that about a 1,000 cases of espionage against German firms go unnoticed or unreported each year, primarily due to the ensuing negative publicity the cases would generate.

AUSTRALIA ACTS TO REDUCE ECONOMIC ESPIONAGE

According to its annual report to the Federal Parliament, the Australian Security Intelligence Organization (ASIO) claims that foreign governments send agents into Australia with "shopping lists" of requirements for information and technology. In its preamble, the domestic intelligence agency noted the global trend toward concentration on economic, scientific, and technological espionage, as well as the traditional staples of political and military espionage.

The agency started an investigation in early 1996 by contacting industry groups, research centers, and manufacturing firms, and soliciting information about suspected espionage attempts against them. The responses helped assess the level of economic espionage activity and the identity of government sponsors. Underlining the continuing interest of foreign intelligence agencies in Australia, ASIO said that it rejected sixteen people who sought temporary or permanent entry to Australia in 1995 and 1996. Of the sixteen individuals, it rejected eleven because of their potential to commit espionage, and it suspected another one of seeking to procure technology for weapons of mass destruction.

INDIAN BUSINESSMAN PLEADS NO CONTEST TO SPYING

According to recent press reporting, an Indian businessman, Aluru J. Prasad, was sentenced on December 9, 1996 to fifteen months in prison for spying for the former Soviet Union during the 1980s. The suspected spy pleaded no contest to trying to gather secrets about the U.S. "Star Wars" anti-missile defense system, the stealth bomber, and other classified defense projects.

At the plea hearing, Prasad admitted to working with Subrahmanyam Kota of Northboro, Massachusetts—an Indian-born software engineer—to steal high-tech information from the Mitre Corporation, including the formulas for the paint used to cloak the stealth bomber from radar detection. Earlier in the year, Kota had testified against Prasad and pleaded guilty to wire fraud, three counts of tax evasion, and a charge relating to biotech theft. He is due to be sentenced in March.

Another of Kota's contacts, Vemuri B. Reddy—a research scientist at a Framingham company with access to genetically altered cells used to produce blood pressure medicine—is scheduled to go on trial on February 3, 1997.

CHINA: U.S. TRAVELERS BEWARE

(The following was developed by the Naval Criminal Investigative Service, with a contribution from the NACIC, the National Counterintelligence Center.)

A continuing analysis of open-source newspaper reporting over the past few years indicates a continuous interest by the Government of the People's Republic of China (PRC) to uncover spies and punish official corruption. Official corruption reported in open-press sources included embezzlement, profiteering, nepotism, and involvement in alien smuggling. The PRC press and high-ranking Communist Party officials constantly replay the theme of a "foreign connection" to dissident or antigovernment movements.

In the PRC, virtually any government document or official statistic falls under the definition of a "state secret." The PRC intelligence services have linked a perceived increase in foreign intelligence activities to the PRC policy of opening to the outside world. The leadership particularly fears a peaceful evolution, an alleged U.S. and Western conspiracy aimed at toppling Communism through social, cultural, and political contacts. Beijing regards even relatively mundane information—if not officially published—as "neibu," or internal, and not for distribution to ordinary citizens and foreigners. This practice spans the gamut from the number of sheep in the country to missile production figures.

In July 1993, the government adopted the Detailed Regulations on the Implementation of the State Security Law of the PRC: "The 28 articles . . . give state security organs sweeping powers to detain individuals believed to be a threat . . . including hostile organizations." The regulations clearly stipulate that "foreigners may not meet without authorization with Chinese citizens or groups deemed to be a threat to national security, nor may they give them support or financial help." The regulations further allow the Ministry for State Security to ban foreigners "regarded as likely to carry out activities endangering the security of the PRC once they have entered the country," and to "check the belongings of personnel whose identity is unknown and who are suspected of endangering state security." The two articles raise particular concern because they stipulate jurisdiction over "electronic telecommunications equipment or facilities incompatible with the needs for safeguarding state security" and "specialized espionage equipment."

For the Communist Chinese leadership, the enemy is everywhere. Foreign elements constantly attempt to infiltrate Chinese society to promote the destruction of the Communist revolution and further imperialism through the process of "peaceful evolution." In the minds of security officials, political stability and the protection of state secrets are vital to national security, the survival of the PRC, and its economic modernization. According to a recent article from the Chinese press, the emphasis of spy warfare since the end of the Cold War has shifted from the political and military sphere to the economic sphere. Economic secrets are viewed as equally important as military secrets. Secret document number 7, leaked during the 14th Party Congress (October 1993), emphasized the importance of security work in the economic sector and against foreign targets. The PRC perceives an increase in the threat to "social stability and economic development," accusing "hostile forces . . . of stepping up efforts to infiltrate the country."

Given China's preoccupation with foreign espionage threats, the following precautions for American officials and private citizens who travel to China are offered:

- Much of what Americans consider open information may still be considered sensitive information by the Chinese.
- Assume that all residences and offices are bugged. Do not engage in conversations or activities that may be seen as suspicious or compromising.
- If you become aware of surveillance or any monitoring devices, do not let those watching you know that you are aware of them.
- Be prepared to have your possessions in the hotel room searched.
- Because of some restrictions on photography, check with the tour guide or a policeman if in doubt before taking a picture.
- Do not engage in any black-market activity. Do not sell or trade any of your possessions. Do not purchase Chinese currency from unofficial sources.
- Expect mail censorship. The PRC intelligence services particularly seek information useful in identifying potential recruits or any indications of wrongdoing that could be used for blackmail.
- Remember, people who consume too much liquor or engage the services of a prostitute are vulnerable to coercion.
- Personal computers are vulnerable to being tapped.

- Anticipate heightened security at international airports. For example, immigration officials carefully screen ethnic Chinese carrying American passports. After producing their passports, recent arrivals, both male and female, were asked to provide their names in Chinese characters. These names were then either entered into a computer or checked against names already in a computer. This may be an attempt to keep out human-rights activists.
- Keep control over your official U.S. passport and other official travel documents. These are in great demand by the highly efficient—and illegal—organizations that deal in Chinese alien smuggling. The corruption of airline personnel, airport authorities, and government officials is a key factor that makes this business so successful. The PRC Government's attempts to crack down on alien smuggling rings have been sporadic and ineffective. The Chinese pay $25,000 to $35,000 each to be smuggled to the United States. The United Nations estimates that the Chinese gangs running this business earn about $3.5 billion a year.

If you get into trouble with the Chinese authorities or suspect that the PRC intelligence services are unusually interested in your activities, report this information to the U.S. Embassy or Consulates in person.

ENVIRONMENTAL ENGINEERING: THREAT TO SECURITY

According to a Defense Investigative Service report, foreign intelligence services and foreign companies working in the United States could, under the pretext of conducting environmental studies of a facility and the surrounding environment, acquire sensitive defense or proprietary information.

For example, a cleared defense contractor became suspicious and reported two environmental engineering specialists who turned out to be foreign nationals working in the United States. Intelligence Community and foreign entities are becoming increasingly interested in environmental engineering technologies. Environmental engineering organizations are very active in nuclear waste disposal problems, particularly in the former Soviet Union.

More important, environmental scientists are experts in technical capabilities related to an intelligence discipline known as measurement and signature intelligence (MASINT). MASINT can provide clues to a facility's activity through sophisticated analysis of its air, water, residue, and trash. If the mission of the facility is unclassified or not sensitive, the MASINT threat would not be an issue. If, however, there is something classified or materially sensitive in the facility, the potential for MASINT collection should be a factor in any risk management decisions about the security of the facility.

Other governments and foreign companies may use this method of operation to acquire sensitive or classified information. Foreign environmental engineers do not have to be spies. They could simply be questioned by their country's intelligence services upon returning to their home country.

Is this a problem? What are you trying to protect? U.S. contractors and their facility security officers can reduce the risk of losing classified or proprietary information by remaining current on their facilities' sensitive information and vulnerabilities as well as periodically reevaluating security countermeasures.

CANADA: THWARTING FOREIGN ECONOMIC ESPIONAGE

(The verbatim excerpt below on economic security appeared in the 1995 Public Report and Program Outlook of the Canadian Security Intelligence Service, or CSIS.)

Economic Security

The era when traditional global security relations overshadowed economic concerns and regional conflict has passed. Accelerating economic interdependence and international competition have emerged as major sources of tension and conflict among world powers. In this uncertain environment, developed countries eager to maintain their standards of living, and developing countries equally determined to improve their own, are under pressure to use whatever means they have to improve their productivity and ensure their economic security. One such means is economic espionage, which can be described as illegal, clandestine, or coercive activity by a foreign government to gain unauthorized access to economic intelligence, such as proprietary information or technology, for economic advantage.

The Canadian Government has transformed its national requirements for security intelligence to reflect this modified threat environment. Currently, the government has identified economic security as one of its priorities. CSIS has responded to these changing dynamics and to their impact on Canadian defense, foreign policy, and economic interests.

The Service's economic espionage mandate is to investigate clandestine activities by or on behalf of foreign governments that are detrimental to Canada's economic and commercial interests. CSIS seeks to forewarn government when the otherwise level playing field of free market competition is deliberately tilted against Canadian interests.

CSIS does not investigate commercial industrial espionage—the practice of one private-sector company spying on another. If these activities are of a criminal nature, they may be investigated by law enforcement agencies.

Canada has world-class skills in many technology-intensive fields. Aerospace, biotechnology, chemical, communications, information technology, mining and metallurgy, nuclear, oil and gas, and environmental technology are key industrial sectors in the Canadian economy. Canadian enterprises maintain and develop information and technology of economic significance, the protection of which is essential to their economic viability and, by extension, the economic well-being of Canada.

A number of Canadian companies operating in these sectors have been targeted by foreign governments to obtain economic or commercial advantage. The damage to Canadian interests takes the form of lost contracts, jobs, and markets, and, overall, a diminished competitive advantage. Information and technology that have been the target of economic espionage include trade and pricing information, investment strategy, contract details, supplier lists, planning documents, research and development data, technical drawings, and computer data bases. Two incidents among many serve as examples:

- A Canadian company's technology was compromised when the company, hoping to secure a lucrative contract from a foreign government, allowed a national of that country to work on a sensitive, leading-edge technology project. The foreign government then proceeded to duplicate the technology based on the information obtained through the direct access their representative agent had to this project.
- A foreign government is believed to have tasked its intelligence service to gather specific information. The intelligence service in turn contracted with computer hackers to help meet the objective, in the course of which the hackers penetrated databases of two Canadian companies. These activities resulted in the compromise of the companies' numerous computer systems, passwords, personnel, and research files.

The Service established a national Liaison and Awareness Program to deal with economic espionage and proliferation issues in January 1992. The program seeks to develop an ongoing dialogue with public and private organizations concerning the threat posed to Canadian interests by foreign government involvement in economic and defense-related espionage, including the proliferation of weapons of mass destruction. The program enables CSIS to collect and assess information that will assist in its investigation of economic espionage activities against Canada, and in the subsequent provision of advice to government.

The CSIS program now consists of more than 1,600 contacts within Canadian industry and government. Thirty percent have expressed a security concern, 76 percent of which related to economic security.

MASKED CUSTOMERS STEAL SECRETS

In a recent issue of *Defense News*, an article described a new consortium—a West European group planning to do 80 percent of its U.S. business with the U.S. defense industry-appearing to function as a facilitator for linking U.S. defense companies with its mother country's companies. This operating pattern is very similar to other programs that attempt to link U.S. experts with institutes and companies in other countries.

This and other foreign consultants have made numerous unsolicited requests for information on behalf of their clients—unknown foreign institutes and companies. Sometimes, the consultants generalize and state they are working on behalf of their country's armed forces. In any case, the final recipient often remains unknown. In some cases, the foreign consultant was identified as working on behalf of a foreign company that was the primary competitor for the U.S. defense contractor.

Information on foreign consortiums or consultants—specifically "unsolicited" contacts with defense contractors—should be viewed as suspicious and reported to the local supporting counterintelligence activity. The purpose of reporting "unsolicited" contacts is to develop a database for this information about possible foreign technology or intelligence collection requirements. This information can then be used to support future analysis or investigations. It can also be consolidated and returned to other U.S. companies as "threat appropriate" information for the application of cost-effective and rational security countermeasures for the protection of their classified or proprietary information.

RUSSIA'S ECONOMIC AND INTELLIGENCE PURSUITS

According to press reporting, Alexander Lebed, Boris Yeltsin's national security chief, recently outlined his thinking on defense expenditures and intelligence goals. Given his dominant Kremlin position on military and security matters, his wishes probably will receive strong backing.

Among his financial and economic pursuits, Lebed hopes to:

- Ensure constant monitoring of the international world markets of armaments, aviation, and space equipment and to search for information on existing or developed technologies in the design of new armaments.
- Search for new designs in commercial technologies, both by state-run and private enterprises.
- Search for critical information on the plans and activities of the leading international financial institutions, major transnational corporations, banks, and investment companies of all countries of the world.

- Organize information campaigns in foreign countries to attract more investment in the Russian economy.

Lebed will also seek to allow the Russian intelligence services to cooperate with major domestic production and financial enterprises, citing the experiences of France, Germany, Japan, and China, all of which have proved the efficiency of such cooperation for raising the competitiveness and technology potential of the domestic economy.

COMPETITIVE BIDDING TO GAIN PROPRIETARY INFORMATION

According to a report from the Defense Investigative Service, officials of a U.S. defense contractor reported an incident in which their company was invited to prepare a proposal for an electronic control system and bid on a defense contract for a West European government. The company prepared what it believed was the best, most detailed proposal of all other bidders for the foreign government contact, and also the lowest bidder. Despite this, after all the bids were in, the foreign government decided to build the control system itself.

The U.S. company believed in retrospect that the foreign government never had any intention of awarding the contract to a U.S. company, but rather it was only interested in obtaining technical information. Later, while attending an international trade show, the U.S. contractor saw a foreign-built control system from the same country that rejected its bid, and the foreign country's control system looked identical to the U.S. company's own system.

The U.S. company was probably deliberately deceived in order to gather sensitive technical information. By deceiving the company, the foreign government acquired preliminary concepts and designs from proven systems and saved money and time in the R&D process. While the U.S. firm may have anticipated some risk in providing technical proprietary information to the foreign government, it also expected an honest competitive process.

Other government and foreign companies may use this method of operation to acquire sensitive technical information. Sometimes, foreign entities demand that U.S. companies divulge large amounts of information about their processes and products, at times much more than is justified by the project being negotiated. U.S. contractors can reduce the risk of losing such information by conducting research on their prospective foreign partners and by factoring the potential for being the victim of industrial espionage into their cost-benefit analysis. If a particular country or foreign government has a documented history of economic or industrial espionage, companies may decide that it is not in their best interest to conduct business with that country or foreign company. At a minimum, companies may elect to provide the absolutely minimum amount of information necessary to compete for the contract.

CANADA: A GLIMPSE INTO THE WORLD OF SPIES

Newly released court documents show that Canada's spy-catchers believe a Toronto man and woman recently deported from Canada are members of the Russian Foreign Intelligence Service (SVR). The pair gained "access to persons and information of interest to the SVR" by assuming false identities, the Canadian Security Intelligence Service (CSIS) said in a court submission made public.

The documents claim the man known as Ian McKenzie Lambert is actually Dmitriy Vladimirovich Olshanskiy, while the woman claiming to be Laurie Catherine Mary Lambert is Yelena Borisovna Olshanskaya. The CSIS document states that "over the course of our investigation of this couple, the service has confirmed their operational methodology, tradecraft, and clandestine intelligence techniques." According to the CSIS, the SVR—which replaced the Soviet KGB in 1991—sends intelligence officers to Canada and other countries to collect political, economic, technological, and military information. According to Canada's spy agency, these two Russians are highly trained "illegals," professional spies who take up residency in a foreign country and spend years building up a false identity before embarking on tasks ranging from recruitment to military and economic espionage.

Experts contend that Canadians as well as Americans are learning that, when the Cold War ended, Russian spies simply shifted their focus from stealing the West's military and diplomatic secrets to stealing its business secrets to gain an economic advantage.

SOUTH KOREA: INDIRECT TECHNOLOGY TRANSFERS

(The information in this article was derived exclusively from South Korean press reports. South Korea's efforts to obtain foreign proprietary technology are well-documented in substantial South Korean open-source information.)

Government and Private-Sector Efforts to Steal U.S. Tech Secrets

South Korean media reporting over the past two years reveals that the Republic of Korea (ROK) Government and South Korean companies are engaging in systematic efforts to obtain foreign proprietary technology through indirect methods. Faced with a decline in the competitiveness of its products, the high cost of buying foreign technology, and the difficulty of developing new technology through its own resources, South Korea reportedly has contrived a host of oblique means to access the technological secrets of advanced countries.

According to ROK press reports, these techniques range from the use of academic exchange programs to the use of the country's intelligence service for industrial espionage. Several of these technical acquisition programs reportedly target U.S. citizens through databases and through recruitment programs focused on expatriate Koreans. Many such initiatives reportedly are designed and managed by the ROK government itself.

This article highlights the indirect processes used by South Korea to obtain foreign technology, particularly from U.S. companies, as described in the South Korean press. Of note, ROK firms are losing interest in Japan, traditionally South Korea's main technology source, because the Japanese demand high royalties for technology transfers.

The Most Wanted Technologies

South Korean companies and government research institutes seek U.S. technologies such as aerospace, automobiles, bioengineering, computers, communications, electronics, environmental, machinery and metals, medical equipment, nuclear power, and semiconductors. Within these areas, the South Koreans frequently target electronics, data communications and processing, and semiconductor technology—South Korea's major high-tech export fields. These data were based on reported cases of attempted technology transfer and press reports of the targeted fields. Within the frequently targeted group, the highest priorities include high-speed CD-ROM, ultrahigh-resolution monitor design, traffic-control systems, flash memory, digital signal processors, application-specific integrated circuits of all types, cable television converters, digital communications, image-data processing, asynchronous transmission mode technology, fiber optics, and audio-video compression technology.

Techniques of Indirect Technology Transfer

South Korea's eagerness to assimilate foreign technology without paying royalties is reflected in the variety of indirect transfer techniques outlined below.

Academic Cooperation

Centers of Excellence.   Setting up "centers" staffed by leading foreign institutes provides ROK researchers with opportunities to "come into contact" with high-level scientists and advanced equipment.

Academic Exchanges.   Under this strategy, the South Korean Government sends ROK researchers abroad in order to acquire advanced technology through their studies. (Korea Herald, January 14, 1995)

Technical Links to Foreign Universities.   Large South Korean manufacturers form "international industrial-academic cooperative associations" with foreign universities to do "joint research" in advanced technology.

International Cooperation

International Research Projects.   Because the initial focus of this research is noncommercial, foreign companies reportedly are more willing to share their technology than they would through conventional channels.

International Forums and Foundations.   The South Korean Government has sanctioned the establishment of "S&T forums" to act as a corridor between the ROK's commercial S&T establishment or state-subsidized "foundations" and U.S. high-tech companies in order to facilitate the transfer of U.S. technology.

Cooperation between South Korea and Foreign Companies

Strategic Cooperation.   This process involves identifying gaps in indigenous technology, finding a foreign company that has the technology, and engaging the latter in some kind of cooperative relationship that results in the transfer of the technology to South Korea.

Joint "Research" and Development.   When South Korean technicians obtain foreign technology through the development process as part of a transfer agreement, the transfer is described by the South Korean press as "joint development."

Obtaining Foreign Patents

Bargain Basement Patents.   A large number of ROK firms and research institutes have been obtaining needed technology through cheap patents acquired in Russia.

Buyouts of Foreign Firms.   ROK press reports reveal that buyouts of high-tech foreign companies are another popular way to obtain patented technology.

Employing Foreign Talent

Hiring Overseas Specialists. Hiring foreign experts is another favored, low-cost means used by South Korea to transfer technology indirectly; it is recommended by government experts, facilitated by official and semiofficial ROK organizations, and widely practiced in ROK industries.

"Brain Pools." South Korea's Government and industry also operate systems to identify potential recruits who are in a position to transfer high-level technology and, because of their ethnicity, are predisposed to accept offers to "contribute" their knowledge to South Korea.

Direct Overseas Involvement

Overseas Technical Training. On-site training at overseas companies allows South Korea to obtain technology at a fraction of its market cost.

Establishing Overseas Subsidiaries. Judging by press reports, South Korean firms have also discovered that overseas branches provide another shortcut to technology transfer.

Overseas "Research Centers." In addition to obtaining technology through overseas subsidiaries, South Korean companies acquire foreign technology by establishing "research" facilities abroad and staffing them with host-country scientists who transfer knowledge of technological processes to their employers, according to ROK press reports.

Collection Networks

International Trade Organizations. The Korea Trade Promotion Corporation—an ROK Government-run organization that is officially chartered to facilitate the export of South Korean products and that has eighty-one overseas trade offices—also promotes technology transfer.

Employees as Intelligence Collectors. ROK firms also have discovered that ordinary employees can yield a wealth of information on competitors' technologies and plans. Although this does not necessarily lead to technology transfer, it does allow corporations to get a pulse on worldwide R&D activities and to use this information in its own policies.

Ethnic and Personal Relationships. Substantial media documentation exists on South Korea's interest in exploiting the ethnicity of overseas Koreans to obtain commercial and technological information.

Foreign Databases. ROK Government institutes have also helped facilitate the transfer of technology by providing South Korean companies access to foreign databases with industrial, scientific, and technological data from foreign and domestic sources.

Commercial Espionage

National Intelligence Service.   South Korea's Agency for National Security Planning, the country's national intelligence agency, is also involved in the indirect transfer of foreign technology.

Corporate Spying.   In addition to government-sanctioned efforts to collect technological information, Seoul media report widespread industrial espionage by South Korean companies against each other to obtain a competitor's proprietary technology.

WARNING SIGNS OF POTENTIALLY VIOLENT INDIVIDUALS

According to a research project by the Defense Personnel Security Research Center (PERSEREC) and entitled *Combating Workplace Violence,* there is no exact method to predict when a person will become violent. One or more of these warning signs, however, may be displayed before a person becomes violent but does not necessarily indicate that an individual will become violent. A display of these signs should trigger concern because they are usually exhibited by people experiencing problems. The signs are:

- Irrational beliefs and ideas.
- Verbal, nonverbal, or written threats or intimidation.
- Fascination with weaponry and/or acts of violence.
- Expressions of a plan to hurt himself or others.
- Externalizing blame.
- Unreciprocated romantic obsession.
- Taking up much of supervisor's time with behavior or performance problems.
- Fear reaction among coworkers/clients.
- Drastic change in belief systems.
- Displays of unwarranted anger.
- New or increased source of stress at home or work.
- Inability to take criticism.
- Feelings of being victimized.
- Intoxication from alcohol or other substances.
- Expressions of hopelessness or heightened anxiety.
- Productivity and/or attendance problems.
- Violence towards inanimate objects.
- Steals or sabotages projects or equipment.
- Lack of concern for the safety of others.

RUSSIA: ECOLOGISTS AND FOREIGNERS FACE STRONGER FSB

Background

During the Soviet period, the KGB—through counterintelligence (CI) operations within the USSR and active measures abroad—tried to hide ecological catastrophes or shift the blame to foreign governments. For example, the KGB tried to suppress all information about leaks of biological warfare agents near Sverdlovsk in 1979 that killed more than fifty people. Some of President Yeltsin's supporters, who were critical of the KGB's monopoly on such information, helped draft the present Russian Constitution, which includes the right of citizens to conduct research on ecological issues. Articles 62 and 66 of the Constitution state that the rights of citizens to be informed about environmental and health questions supersede other legal considerations.

Environmentalists as a Security Threat

Over the past year, however, the Russian security service—now known as the Federal Security Service (FSB)—has again targeted environmental researchers. The Russian press indicates that Russian citizens interested in military or military-industrial polluters have become a target of the FSB:

> Authorities arrested Vladimir Petrenko, a former military officer in Saratov Oblast, in mid-1995 following his research into the danger posed by military chemical warfare stockpiles. He has been in pretrial confinement for seven months on what Amnesty International and Russian human rights observers believe is a trumped-up charge of assault.

Nikolay Shchur, chairman of the Snezhinskiy Ecological Fund, has been in pretrial confinement for six months following his survey of military pollution near Chelyabinsk.

The FSB Given Broader Power to Protect State Secrets

During the Soviet period, the KGB was the arbiter of state secrets, a power it abused regularly and lost in the aftermath of the fall of the Communist regime. Since last summer, however, the FSB, one of the successors of the KGB, has regained considerable operational and legal authority for controlling state secrets:

> The July 1995 Law on the Federal Security Service gave the FSB greater authority to conduct physical and technical surveillance, recruit informers, conduct searches, and hold suspects in pretrial detention.

Moreover, in September 1995, FSB Chief General Barsukov was named deputy chairman of a new State Committee to Control State Secrets and given authority to define state secrets and to protect them using newly countenanced CI operations.

Russian Government Pushes for Stronger FSB

A spate of recent articles in the national and provincial press by spokesmen for the FSB trumpets the service's role in protecting the state from foreign subversion. For example, in a series of press articles in January and February 1996, FSB officers noted that the service has the responsibility to monitor foreign astronauts at "Star City" and to prevent the emigration of Russian scientists.

The FSB has also recently bragged about the arrest of Israeli, Turkish, and North Korean spies as well as the expulsion of a British businessman and an Israeli diplomat.

Outlook

Government moves against the ecologists indicate a resurgence of FSB internal power. The nation's leadership appears to be increasing its political support for the FSB. This may enable it to reestablish its bureaucratic authority over security and CI. In addition, the expulsion of a British businessman and the recent press articles highlighting the need for a stronger FSB suggest that the FSB will also take a harder line against Western commercial or academic research in Russia.

LAPTOP VANISHES IN EAST ASIAN HOTEL

A major U.S. consumer products company suffered a possible loss of proprietary information as a result of a theft in East Asia. A laptop computer containing sales data, market estimates, and strategic business plans for one of its business units was stolen from a hotel conference room during a lunch break. Hotel staff—under the supervision of a company employee who was preparing remarks for the next presentation—cleaned the room for the afternoon session. The employee did not continuously guard the computer and discovered the loss shortly before the session reconvened.

WIRETAP EPIDEMIC POSSIBLE SANCTIONED BY PARIS

According to a March 28, 1996 Reuters report, about 100,000 French telephone lines are illegally tapped each year, and state agencies may be behind much of the eavesdropping. Citing information from an annual report by the independent National Commission for the Control for Security Interceptions, the press article states that the wiretapping restrictions imposed on government officials may be prompting them to hire private firms to do their illegal bugging.

According to the press article, magistrates can only approve legal wiretaps in criminal cases or to protect national security, prevent terrorist threats, or safeguard essential scientific or economic information. The article stated that the magistrates okayed about 3,000 legal phone taps in France in 1995, mainly for national security or antiterrorism purposes. They also authorized an additional 11,300 wiretaps in support of criminal cases.

SWISS EXPEL RUSSIAN DIPLOMAT FOR ESPIONAGE

According to an April 9, 1996 Reuters report, Switzerland ordered a Russian diplomat to leave the country for spying. A Justice and Police Ministry statement said the first secretary from the Russian Embassy in Berne was caught in the act of espionage by federal officials and police in Zurich. No further details were provided.

TECHNOLOGY COLLECTION TRENDS IN THE U.S. DEFENSE INDUSTRY

(The Counterintelligence Office of the Defense Investigative Service prepared the following based solely on reporting from the defense industrial security community)

On the basis of U.S. defense industry reporting of suspicious activity, the Defense Investigative Service (DIS) continues to observe trends of low-level collection interest and activity by foreign companies and governments. These foreign collection methods of operation (MO) exhibit subtle changes to adapt to rapidly changing international political and economic environments.

The MOs and Targets

The Targets.   Foreign collection continues to focus on economic as well as scientific and technology (S&T) information and products. Collection sponsored by both foreign governments and foreign companies consistently targets programs associated with dual-use technologies. Although traditional foreign threats continue their collection activities, DIS continues to observe the expansion of nontraditional foreign threat collection in industry, where entities now rely on both covert and illegal—as well as overt and legal—activities as part of their collection MOs. While foreign intelligence services (FISs) continue their clandestine efforts, they also significantly rely on the use of overt and legal collection methods. Areas of foreign collection activity and interest—as identified from U.S. defense industry reporting—include the following areas from the Military Critical Technology List (MCTL):

Aeronautics systems.	Armaments and energetic materials.
Chemical and biological systems.	Directed and kinetic energy systems.
Electronics.	Guidance, navigation, and vehicle
Information systems.	control.
Manufacturing and fabrication.	Information warfare.
Materials.	Marine systems.
Sensors and lasers.	Nuclear systems.
Space systems.	Signature control.
	Weapons effects and countermeasures.

In addition, defense industry reporting continues to reflect increasing trends of foreign collection against proprietary strategic management information, including bid proposals, price structuring, and marketing plans.

The MOs.   While U.S. defense industry and foreign interests often interact in benign and advantageous ways, the various threats—reported collection Mos—against defense industry security countermeasures (SCMs) include:

- Unsolicited requests for S&T information.
- Inappropriate conduct by foreign nationals visiting at U.S. Government contractors.
- Exploitation of joint ventures and joint research.
- Outright acquisitions of technology and companies.
- Using the Internet to identify and target information for collection.
- Targeting cultural commonalities.
- Targeting at international exhibits, seminars, and conventions as well as solicitation and marketing of services.
- "Marketing survey" ploys for competitive intelligence.
- Communications with foreign employees.
- Targeting of former U.S. contractor employees.

Unsolicited Requests

Foreign collectors use unsolicited requests—the most frequently reported MO—in their effort to obtain U.S. defense industry S&T program information. These requests generally reflect a wide range of interests and often represent an information-management problem for the U.S. defense industry. A growing number of incidents involve faxing, mailing, E-mailing, or phoning such requests to individual U.S. persons rather than corporate marketing departments. Usually associated with alleged employment opportunities, these foreign collectors increasingly use headhunters to solicit information from employees.

Foreign Visits

According to U.S. defense industry reporting of suspicious activity, foreign visits to U.S. industry represent a significant security risk absent threat-appropriate and sound risk management practices. With few exceptions, security compromises reported from foreign visit incidents could have been prevented if U.S. personnel had been properly pre-briefed as part of the risk management process. Potential exploitation methods include:

- Hidden agendas beyond the stated purpose of the visit.
- Last minute and unannounced persons added to the visiting party.
- "Wandering" visitors who become offended when confronted.
- Conversations with escorts beyond the approved scope of the visit.

To obtain collection objectives, collectors use many of these techniques and seek specifically to produce potentially embarrassing incidents for the host who is thrown off balance and consequently becomes conciliatory toward the collector. In addition, foreign companies and governments sponsor workshops, tours, and the like as a potential ploy to circumvent a disapproved visit request. These foreign entities attempt to exploit the different visit procedures for U.S. Government-sponsored, nonsponsored, and commercial visits—playing each against the other and in the confusion hoping to gain access to excluded and protected information. Finally, many foreign collectors manipulate the potential for misinterpretation of a U.S. Government-sponsored foreign visit to a U.S. contractor by presenting the attitude that any inquiry or activity by the foreign party "must be OK."

Joint Ventures, Joint Research, Co-Production, and Various Exchange

Agreements. These targets potentially offer significant collection opportunities for foreign interests. As with frequent foreign visits and other international programs, joint efforts place foreign personnel in close proximity to U.S. personnel and afford potential access to S&T programs and information. Access can be intentional or unintentional and, for both, legal or illegal. According to U.S. defense industry reporting, SCM professionals remain concerned about the assimilation of foreign personnel into the work environment without security sustainment training programs. Without these programs, U.S. employees relax their security awareness that often results in security compromises.

Foreign Acquisition of Technology and Companies

This acquisition in the U.S. defense industry continues to generate significant concern among SCM professionals because of the foreign access to U.S. markets or sensitive and proprietary information. Once a foreign entity gains ownership, control, or influence over a U.S. company with classified contracts, that ownership, control, or influence must be mitigated through an insulating instrument approved by the Defense Department. Without an approved insulating legal instrument, the U.S. company and the foreign investor face the possibility of contract cancellations and loss of future classified contracts.

The Internet

A significant increase in U.S. defense industry reports of SCM incidents associated with computer-based collection attempts reflects the growing popularity and expansion of the Internet. Foreign governments or companies use the Internet to gain a direct method of communication for their collection efforts-gaining access to a company's bulletin board, home page, and employees. This opens many avenues for foreign collectors to broaden their collection efforts.

International Exhibits, Conventions, and Seminars

Foreign collectors find these activities provide rich collection targeting opportunities. These functions directly link programs and technologies with knowledgeable personnel. Consequently, U.S. defense industry reporting shows rampant collection activity at these events. Good risk management processes—which accurately identify the exposed information, including what, where, when, and to whom—are essential for implementing threat-appropriate, cost-effective, and rational security countermeasures to balance marketing requirements.

Reports of foreign individuals with technical backgrounds offering their services to research facilities, academic institutions, and even cleared defense contractors—at little or no apparent cost—increased during the past year. In addition, foreign entities request that U.S. technical experts visit their countries and share their technical expertise. According to U.S. defense industry reporting, while many requests are routine and benign, SCM professionals view some with suspicion as representing significant SCM threats.

Marketing Surveys

Foreign "consulting" companies fax or mail various kinds of these surveys to U.S. companies, often exceeding generally accepted terms for marketing information. Often, there are strong suspicions that the "surveyor" is employed by a competing foreign company. Surveys may solicit proprietary information concerning corporate affiliations, market projections, pricing policies, program or technology directors' names, purchasing practices, and dollar amounts of U.S. Government contracts. Foreign governments or companies also survey customer and supplier bases for a particular company to garner more information about it.

Co-Opting Former or Foreign Employees

Incidents involving the co-opting of former employees who had access to sensitive proprietary or classified S&T or program information remain a potential counterintelligence concern. Frequently, foreign collectors target cultural commonalities to establish rapport in a collection attempt. As a result, quite often, foreign governments or companies specifically target foreign employees working for U.S. companies. Defense contractor employees working overseas may be particularly vulnerable to foreign offers of employment as their contracts expire. Foreign entities view former employees as excellent prospects for collection operations because they consider them less likely to feel obligated to comply with U.S. Government or corporate security requirements.

Meeting the Challenge

In a changing and maturing international political and economic environment, U.S. defense industry strategic management processes will be increasingly challenged to balance international marketing and partnerships with sound security countermeasures. *Good risk management practices will ensure the proper training of cleared employees empowered to recognize and report suspicious activity.*

INTERNET: THE FASTEST GROWING MODUS OPERANDI FOR UNSOLICITED COLLECTION

On the basis of reports of suspicious foreign contacts reported to the Defense Investigative Service, use of the Internet is the fastest growing modus operandi of unsolicited correspondence using computer elicitation between foreign entities and cleared U.S. companies and their employees. Reports continue to arrive at DIS about foreign entities using the Internet to

contact a wide variety of knowledgeable persons, potentially to collect various pieces of information from different experts that enables these entities
to put together an amazingly clear, detailed mosaic not available from any
one individual.

Collection Advantages

Use of the Internet offers a variety of advantages to a foreign collector. It is
simple, low-cost, nonthreatening, and relatively "risk free" for the foreign
entity attempting to collect classified, proprietary, or sensitive information.
These foreign entities can remain safe within their borders while sending
hundreds of pleas and requests for assistance to targeted U.S. companies
and their employees. The unsolicited request for information, to include
using the Internet, is the most frequently used modus operandi by "closed
countries" and often may be worded to appeal to cultural commonalities.

Some Case Studies

Through the Internet recently, one foreign entity blatantly requested from
cleared U.S. contractors references to military projects that use software
tools for networked real-time operating systems (airborne, space, missile,
tactical, intelligence, and so forth). In the request, the foreign entity
acknowledged that much of the information would probably be classified.
Because the requester also acknowledged that his foreign "military customer" was too classified to to send the request over the Internet, he agreed
to perform the request as a service to the foreign government.

In another report of suspicious activity involving the Internet, a
cleared U.S. company received a request to market a software program with
intelligence applications to intelligence and security organizations in an
East European country. The software program enables the quick integration
of multiple data sources and millions of documents with incredible speed
and can be used as an investigative tool to search various Websites. At a
minimum, the software program can be used by foreign companies to
acquire competitive business intelligence off the Internet.

In many foreign countries, access to the Internet is potentially through
a government host. Any foreign contact with these countries via the Internet
is subject to intelligence and security service vetting and monitoring to prevent the loss of technical secrets and is, therefore, also subject to their
potential collection and exploitation of western technology. Access to Internet search software will undoubtedly assist foreign intelligence and security
services in searching and monitoring the Internet for both intelligence and
counterintelligence purposes. In one East European country during the past
two years, the number of Internet hosts has grown exponentially, making it
more difficult to isolate intelligence officers attempting to use the Internet to

break into U.S. computer systems. Foreign intelligence services are known to use computers to conduct rudimentary on-line searches for information, including visits to governments and defense contractors' on-line bulletin boards or Websites on the Internet. Access to Internet advanced search software programs could possibly assist them in meeting their collection requirements.

Lessons Learned

While the use of advanced software tools by foreign intelligence services is inevitable, security lessons can be learned from these reported incidents, and we can implement security countermeasures to mitigate demonstrated vulnerability. We know foreign entities use the Internet because it provides an easy, low-cost, and risk-free means to solicit information. We also know foreign intelligence and security services monitor the Internet and have the advanced software tools to make their searches and investigations much easier.

All requests for information received via the Internet should be viewed with suspicion. Only respond to people who are personally known and only after verifying their identity and address. Verification is important because foreign entities can present themselves as impostors. If a request were received from an unknown source or were significantly different in character from a regular or known source, a copy of the request should be provided to the security officer, and the request should not be responded to in any way. The following is a list of suspicious indicators of foreign collection efforts via computer elicitation:

- The address is in a foreign country.
- The recipient has never met the sender.
- The sender identifies his/her status as a student or consultant.
- The sender identifies his/her employer as a foreign government or that the work is being done for a foreign government or program.
- The sender asks about a technology related to a defense-related program, project, or contract.
- The sender asks questions about defense-related programs using acronyms specific to the program.
- The sender insinuates that the third party he/she works for is "classified" or otherwise sensitive.
- The sender admits he/she could not get the information elsewhere because it was classified or controlled.
- The sender advises the recipient to disregard the request if it causes a security problem or if it is for information the recipient cannot provide due to security classification, export controls, and so forth.
- The sender advises the recipient not to worry about security concerns.

- The sender assures the recipient that export licenses are not required or not a problem.

FOREIGN VIDEO CREWS: A MULTIDISCIPLINE THREAT

During the past year, the Defense Investigative Service (DIS) has received numerous reports of suspicious requests for foreign video crews to visit cleared U.S. companies. Following a similar pattern in most cases, a foreign television news crew requests to do a documentary on a U.S. company's advanced or critical (dual-use) technology of known collection interest to the foreign country.

The Technique

As a modus operandi (MO), the use of a video film crew proves a highly effective method for collecting technical information, falling under the more general MO known as a "foreign visit." According to cleared U.S. industry reporting to DIS of security countermeasures concerns, the foreign visit continues to be the second most frequently used MO to collect information after the "unsolicited request for information." While the foreign visit puts the collector at greater risk, it also positions them to possibly do great damage to cleared U.S. companies.

A foreign entity, which gains access to a cleared facility, usually fills some collection requirements. More specifically, a foreign film crew can provide a historical audio and video record that can be reviewed numerous times. This record becomes the "ground truth" to calibrate other imagery or measurement and signature intelligence collection systems: it can capture biographic data; it catches audio "slip-ups" and background noises; and it provides excellent background cover for human intelligence (HUMINT) operators to ask questions. This MO is one of the best for intelligence collection because a trained human collector, in conjunction with a video camera, combines HUMINT, imagery intelligence (IMINT), and signals intelligence (SIGINT) disciplines into one collection package resulting in a "multidiscipline" collection effort. Depending on the type of film used (infrared), a video camera can also record differences in temperature, thereby adding measurement and signature intelligence (MASINT) to the collection equation.

While some of these foreign visit requests are legitimate, two requests were identified as economic espionage attempts. In these incidents, probably either foreign companies attempted to dominate a particular technology area or a foreign government attempted to acquire technology to avoid the costs and time associated with lengthy R&D. Often, these foreign companies lead the world in one aspect of a technology such as hardware but lag in other aspects such as software, making them less efficient and not competitive with industry leaders. In one request, the foreign individual repeatedly inquired about the location of "classified research."

In another instance, the foreign video crew hired a U.S. consultant to act as a potentially unwitting "researcher" for identifying and locating U.S. targets of interest. This also fits a known MO on the part of many nontraditional threat countries of hiring consultants and researchers to identify and locate technology for exploitation.

Lesson Learned

Oddly enough, while cleared facilities often prohibit U.S. employees from bringing cameras onto the grounds, these same facilities all too frequently allow foreign video film crews onto their same grounds. Who is the greater threat? The best security countermeasure prohibits access of any foreign video film crew into a cleared facility. Often, a video presentation can be prepared by the company public affairs or marketing office, under controlled conditions, for public release.

AN ESPIONAGE EXAMPLE

The most useful CI incidents are those that reflect specific methods, circumstances, and general geographic areas or types of organizations. An understanding of how espionage can happen when an organization is not fully aware of what a visitor really wants can go a long way in identifying weaknesses within that organization's security education and awareness program.

In late July 1996, a South African company representative contacted an employee of a U.S. defense contractor in northern Virginia by phone and E-mail. The representative sought to arrange a visit by three company representatives to the U.S. contractor's site and observe a demonstration of various electronic systems. Before sending the E-mail requesting specific information on digital interception and recorders, the South African indicated he had studied the company's Website, which contained information on its products and services. A meeting was arranged for August 6, 1996. The two other individuals who accompanied the representative were actually members of the South African Intelligence Service.

After their arrival on August 6, the head of the delegation openly expressed an interest in seeing the U.S. company's classified projects. When told this was only possible through official government-to-government channels, he retreated by expressing that his interest was facetious. He then indicated more interest in the things the company might be selling to the

U.S. Customs Service or the Drug Enforcement Agency. After viewing the demonstrations, the South African party left the company.

This incident reinforces the technology collection trends reported by the Defense Investigative Service earlier in this edition and emphasizes the importance of carefully screening information posted on company home pages of the Internet. Also, any time a foreign intelligence officer is identified as part of a delegation, the FBI or the appropriate DSS office should be notified in advance.

ECONOMIC AND INDUSTRIAL ESPIONAGE: SOUP TO NUTS

- According to an August 5, 1996 article in the Australian Business News, corporate crime in Australia involves more than unscrupulous employees stealing the company's property, it also includes corporate espionage. In this regard, the article states that corporate crime costs the economy about $18 billion a year.
- Two men who allegedly installed a hidden camera at a Volkswagen test track in Germany were recently arrested on industrial espionage charges. The two are accused of selling photos of new Volkswagen models to automobile magazines. The camera was found in March 1995 at a track near Volkswagen Headquarters in Wolfsburg.
- Industrial espionage by foreign companies is on the rise in Finland, according to Security Police Chief Seppo Nevala. He notes, however, that Finnish police are on top of the situation.
- In San Francisco, a restaurant owner has taken special precautions to prevent the theft of prized recipes by preparing her signature dishes in an area sealed off from the main kitchen. Waiters pick up her "culinary treats" from a slot in the smaller kitchen's wall, thereby precluding imitation or pilfering of the cooking ingredients and processes.

The above incidents reaffirm that economic and industrial espionage is an international concern and not necessarily limited to high-tech companies involved in critical technologies. Regardless if it is a major company protecting sophisticated manufacturing technologies, or an entity trying to survive in a smaller competitive market, protecting trade secrets and proprietary information should be a daily preoccupation.

KODAK: TWO CASES

A retired Eastman Kodak Company manager has pleaded guilty to stealing formulas, drawings and blueprints from Kodak. Harold C. Worden, 56, spent his last five years at Kodak as a project manager for the 401 Machine, designed to inexpensively produce the clear plastic base used in consumer film. The base is lined with emulsions using a secret formula that determines the quality of the photographs. Worden set up a consulting business in South Carolina after ending a tweny-eight-year career with Kodak in 1992, after which he is accused of profiting from his inside knowledge of Kodak's photography technology and by buying confidential data from his successor and dozens of Kodak retirees.

On November 13 1997, Worden was sentenced to a year in prison and fined $30,000. He will start serving his prison sentence in February and has agreed to cooperate with investigators in the meantime. One week later, Eastman Kodak accused another retired employee of leaking trade secrets. Kodak said that Melvin Sterman, 67, of Rochester, N.Y., provided unspecified data to what was then 3M's photographic film division in Ferrania, Italy.

For the second time in two years, Kodak had another major incident with great potential damage to the company.

Chung-Yuh Soong, a software engineer who worked for Kodak for a year before resigning on April 17, 1997, was accused of transmitting several large data files listed as "highly confidential" to a Xerox computer in California, just days before she left Kodak. According to court documents, the alleged theft was discovered because the data being transmitted was so large that it crashed a Kodak server and alerted the company's computer-security system.

Soong, 37, was charged in federal court with wire fraud related to interstate transfer of Kodak's software and has also been sued by Kodak in civil court for misappropriation of trade secrets. She pleaded innocent to the fraud charge and her case was adjourned until September 11, 1998. Kodak said it did not know who the files were intended for and where precisely they ended up. Soong's lawyer maintains she was sending them for safekeeping to her sister, who works for Xerox, and had no intention of passing them on to the copier company or anyone else.

SPY SUSPECT NABBED

Huang Dao Pei, a Chinese-born naturalized U.S. citizen living in Piscataway, New Jersey, was arrested by the FBI in July 1998 on charges that he tried to steal trade secrets for a hepatitis C monitoring kit he hoped to sell in China. Huang, a former scientist who worked at Roche Diagnostics from 1992 to 1995, allegedly tried to buy information from a scientist who worked for Roche. The scientist was cooperating with the FBI.

Huang told the Roche scientist he needed the information so his firm, LCC Enterprises, could develop a similar kit and sell it in China. As reported in the open press, the FBI declined to say whether Huang was working for the Chinese, but it was noted that China is among the most aggressive countries going after U.S. trade secrets.

A Roche representative stated that if a competitor were to obtain the information sought by Huang, it could avoid spending the millions of dollars a year that Roche spent developing the product.

MORE ON FRENCH SPYING

The French magazine *Le Point* reported in mid-June that France systematically listens in on the telephone conversations and cable traffic of many businesses based in the United States and other nations. The article also reports the French Government uses a network of listening stations to eavesdrop and pass on commercial secrets to French businesses competing in the global economy.

The article goes on to state that the French secret service, DGSE, has established listening posts in the Dordogne (Southern France) and also in its overseas territories, including French Guiana and New Caledonia. The article attributes to an unnamed "senior official within this branch of the French secret service" the claim, "This is the game of the secret war," adding that U.S. listening posts do the same. The magazine report says Germans who bought into the French Helios 1A spy satellite system are being given access to political and economic secrets as part of a Franco-German agreement to compete with a commercial information agreement between the United States and Britain.

MEXICAN HACKERS MOUNT ATTACK

According to an August 1998 Reuters report, a small group of computer hackers have declared electronic war on the Mexican state. They have plastered the face of revolutionary hero Emiliano Zapata on the Finance Ministry's Website and claim to have monitored visits by Mexican Senators to X-rated Internet sites. They also have vowed to attack official databases for incriminating numbers and publicize government bank accounts, cellular phone conversations, and E-mail addresses. So far the cyber-pirates, who say they are a trio of Mexicans, appear to be more a nuisance than a serious threat, but they are serving as a wake-up call for computer security in Mexico, experts said. One of the hackers stated during an on-line interview with Reuters that "We protest with the weapons we have, and those weapons are computers." The hackers surfaced in February when visitors to the Finance Ministry's official Website were surprised to find Zapata staring back at them.

According to Mexican authorities, the hackers appear more interested in propaganda than sabotage or espionage, but they do represent a potential threat to government and corporate computer systems, industry executives said. The chief concern is that they can hack into systems and acquire very important data and erase it or put it to their own use, according to a spokesman for a California-based maker of antivirus and computer network security products. He also noted that with relatively few hackers in Mexico, the most common threat comes from in-house. Few companies there have adopted internal computer network security measures common in the United States to limit access to sensitive databases and files. This has made the potential for corporate espionage relatively easy, although few companies have publicly acknowledged security breaches. The article concluded by saying that "Espionage is very, very large in Mexico."

RUSSIA COMBATS FOREIGN ESPIONAGE

According to June 1998 Reuters reporting, President Boris Yeltsin has taken action to step up the counterintelligence service's efforts to protect Russia's economic, constitutional, and computer security. The Kremlin said earlier this year it was concerned about growing foreign espionage, including via computer networks. It said foreign secret services were massively intruding "with the aim of influencing state structures, banks, industrial enterprises, scientific organizations and mass media." At that time, Yeltsin had discussed the issue with Nikolai Kovalyov, head of the Federal Security Service (FSB), which is the main successor body to the Soviet-era KGB secret police.

For reasons not totally clear, and perhaps as a result of his handling of several recent incidents, including the spy dispute with South Korea, Kovalyov was fired, replaced by Vladimir Putin, a former KGB spy. Putin's appointment was the latest by Yelstin to return the intelligence agency's clout by tapping into the KGB's experience of imposing control and gathering information.

Some senior officials have expressed concern about the spread of the Internet in Russia. They say computer hacking and other computer-related crimes are on the rise in Russia, posing a threat to national security. But Russia's government communications security service has stated that its lines are impregnable to hacking due to high-tech, antibugging devices and top-secret data encryption, and is now marketing some of its voice and data encryption technologies for common use.

INTERNET SITES OF INTEREST

To directly access individual sites, use the addresses listed below.

Central Intelligence Agency
http://www.odci.gov/cia/

This site contains a wealth of resource information, including CIA maps and publications, a suggested reading list of intelligence literature, and access to the CIA's 560-page *World Fact Book*.

Federal Bureau of Investigation
http://www.fbi.gov
The Federal Bureau of Investigation (FBI) is the principal investigative arm of the U.S. Department of Justice. This site provides an overview of the FBI, information on current investigations (like the Unabomber Case and the Oklahoma City Bombing Case), and statements from the FBI's Office of Public and Congressional Affairs.

Defense Intelligence Agency
http://www.odci.gov/ic/usic/dia.html

U.S. Army
http://www.army.mil/

U.S. Navy Online
http://www.ncts.navy.mil/

U.S. Air Force
http://www.afin.af.mil/

National Security Agency
http://www.nsa.gov:8080
This site contains the unclassified, public releases of the previously "TOP SECRET" VENONA material. During the early 1940s, the KGB and GRU sent thousands of encrypted cables from the KGB Residencies in the United States to Moscow; approximately 2,200 cables were decrypted by the NSA and have been recently declassified and made available to the public. The first release was a compilation of 49 VENONA translations that related Soviet espionage efforts against U.S. atomic bomb research, including messages about the Rosenbergs and the Manhatten Project. The second release and subsequent releases of the remaining 2,151 VENONA translations will be scanned-in images that will be arranged chronologically by communications link to Moscow.

National Military Intelligence Association (NMIA)
http://www.cais.com/NMIA
The NMIA was formed in 1974 as an organization to network intelligence professionals in the military services, the intelligence agencies, and offices of the U.S. Government and Congress, within which they can share and exchange ideas for their individual professional enhancement and the good of the entire Intelligence Community.

U.S. State Department Travel Advisories
http://www.stolaf.edu/network/travel-advisories.html

This site contains a wealth of information on more than 160 countries, including entry requirements, travel conditions, maps, areas of instability, travel warnings, and Consular Information Sheets.

IntelWeb: The WWW Site of Intelligence Watch Report
http://www.awpi.com/IntelWeb/
This privately maintained Website reports on public and private intelligence agencies and organizations from around the world. According to its home page, users will have access to text and image files and in the near future will have access to audio and video files too. Its stated purpose is to assist in the serious study of intelligence agencies.

North American Center for Emergency Communications (NACEC)
http://www.nacec.org/
NACEC offers an Internet service to help keep military families in communication with each other. This free-of-charge service is available worldwide to all U.S. active-duty military personnel and their families in all branches of the miliary.

Government Printing Office
http://www.gao.gov

Commission on the Roles and Capabilities of the United States Intelligence Community
http://www.access.gpo.gov/int
On March 1, 1996, the Commission on the Roles and Capabilities of the United States Intelligence Community—generally known as the Aspin-Brown Commission—released its final report entitled *Preparing for the 21st Century: An Appraisal of U.S. Intelligence*. This Commission was chartered by Congress in October 1994 to conduct a comprehensive review of American intelligence. The entire 200-page Brown Commission Report is available free of charge on the Internet through the Government Printing Office (GPO). For answers to questions about GPS's Internet service, call (202) 512-1530.

Search Engines

To explore other home pages or articles on the World Wide Web, individuals should try searching the word "counterintelligence" in the following search engines or directories:

http://www.yahoo.com

http://www.lycos.com

http://www.webcrawler.com

http://www.altavista.digital.com/

Note: The search engine ALTAVISTA is very powerful; it also prioritizes the hits it retrieves on a particular search, so you are more likely to find and be able to review first those articles that are most relative to your particular search. If the word counterintelligence is searched, it will produce approximately 3,200+ hits.

Security Internet Sites

Internet addresses that may be of interest to security professionals are listed below.

Guide to EO I2958 DIS Bulletin Board
http://nish.jcte.jcs.mil

National Security Bulletin Board
Telnet IP Address: 140.229.1.7
Modem Phone Number: 301/826-3736
communications parameters: 8 bits, 1 stop bit.
Login: isb
Password: nisbl

Federation of Atomic Scientists (FAS)
http:www.fas.org
    The FAS site holds an abundance of information relating to security, intelligence, and counterintelligence, in addition to numerous links to other sites of interest to security personnel and risk managers.

World Wide Web Travel Advisories

These are available through:

Gopher Address
gopher.stolaf.edu
http://www.stolaf.edu

DISCO E-Mail
    For matters relating to facility clearance processing, changed conditions, and key management personnel, use address: discofac@dislink.jcte.jcs.mil

NRO Home Page
http://www.nro.odci.gov

White Paper on Information Assurance
http://www.fas.org/put/gen/fas/sgp/
    (prepared by Security Policy Board)

Department of Energy
http://www.doe.gov (via Opennet)

Preparing for the 21st Century: An Appraisal of U.S. Intelligence
    Prepared by the Commission on the Roles and Capabilities of the United States Intelligence Community and available at: http://www.access.gpo.gov/int

Making Intelligence Smarter: The Future of U.S. Intelligence
    Published with permission of the Council on Foreign Relations and available at: http://www.fas.org/pub/gen/fas/irp/crf.html

IC21: The Intelligence Community in the 21st Century
    This report on intelligence reform was offered by House Intelligence Committee Chairman Larry Combest and is available at: http://www.fas.org/pub/gen/fas/irp/offdocs.htm#ic21

Computer Emergency Response Team (CERT)
    It is on the Internet at FTP site: info.cert.org

Index